C000097610

Melanie Allen was born in 1963 in
where she now lives with her family.
degree and hopes one day to become a health visitor.

the trouble with Alex

A Child Too Damaged to Love

MELANIE ALLEN

POCKET
BOOKS

LONDON • SYDNEY • NEW YORK • TORONTO

First published in Great Britain by Simon & Schuster UK Ltd, 2008
This edition first published by Pocket Books, 2009
An imprint of Simon & Schuster UK Ltd
A CBS COMPANY

Copyright © 2008 by Melanie Allen

This book is copyright under the Berne convention.
No reproduction without permission.
All rights reserved.

The right of Melanie Allen to be identified as the author of this work
has been asserted by her in accordance with sections 77 and 78
of the Copyright, Designs and Patents Act, 1988.

This is a work of non-fiction. The names of some people and some
details have been changed to protect the privacy of others. The author has
warranted that, except in such minor respects not affecting the substantial detail
of events, the contents of this book are accurate.

1 3 5 7 9 10 8 6 4 2

Simon & Schuster UK Ltd
1st Floor
222 Gray's Inn Road
London
WC1X 8HB

www.simonsays.co.uk

Simon & Schuster Australia
Sydney

A CIP catalogue record for this book is available
from the British Library.

ISBN: 978-1-84739-011-0
Printed by CPI Cox & Wyman, Reading, Berkshire RG1 8EX

For Alex, who deserved so much more

Acknowledgements

First and foremost I'd like to thank Rob and Daniel who made it possible for me to tell this story. Your encouragement, support and patience have never wavered. And Daniel, thanks for your little mantra. You have always been a ray of light.

I'd also like to thank my agent Jane Graham Maw at Graham Maw Christie for taking on the book; for her support and invaluable advice throughout. Kerri Sharp at Simon & Schuster for sticking with the book. I will be forever grateful! Clair, who was there from the beginning. She gave so much more than editorial advice. Michael, who helped us to understand. Those involved with the care of children like Alex could learn a great deal from him. Thank you also to those authors, worldwide web contributors, and attachment specialists from whom we learned so much. Also, thanks to Tim Tiley Ltd, for permission to reproduce the poem *Heaven's Very Special Child* by Edna Massionilla.

And lastly, a huge, heartfelt thanks to family and friends for their love, friendship and support when we needed it. They helped pick up the pieces and put us back together again. And thanks also to everyone in the office – for their stability, their voice of reason and the laughs.

About My Story

You are about to read the true account of how a normal middle-class family in an ordinary town in the UK was torn apart. That family is mine. The little girl we adopted . . . she wasn't responsible for what happened.

Every life is priceless. As communities die out and the extended family becomes a thing of the past, no organisation has a greater duty to remember this than our Social Services.

I don't know if this story will make a difference or whether it'll merely join the long line of Social Services casualties, to be filed away and forgotten. I suspect the latter. What must not be forgotten, and what can no longer be ignored, however, is that the number of people with mental health problems is at its highest ever and growing. This situation affects every one of us and, unless it is addressed now and with the urgency it deserves, we could soon see a *really* troubled society.

For further details on mental health see the SANE website: www.sane.org.uk

Melanie Allen, January 2008

Chapter One

'*H*urry up, Daniel, we're going to be late!'
'Wait! I just need to finish this,' said my eight-year-old son, adding a border of smiley faces to the front cover of the joke-book he'd hand-made for Alex.

'OK, but be quick,' I said, and hurried back into the hallway.

I called upstairs to my husband. 'Rob? Are you ready?'

'Two minutes. Mum's on the phone.'

He was going to have to switch his mobile off; Jean was our fifth well-wisher this morning.

Pumped up by the nervous excitement rolling round my stomach, I paced the hallway. Had we remembered everything? I ran a mental check. Yes, enough clean underwear in the case and the case in the boot; raincoats and umbrellas by the front door. I'd got my bag, the directions, my keys . . . but wait! I pounded up the stairs, two at a time, and into the second bedroom. Prising open the flimsy wardrobe door, I pulled out a Tesco carrier-bag. Inside lay a Beanie Baby: Dotty the Dalmatian.

Just the sight of it brought on another hot burst of trepidation. I pulled Dotty out of the bag and scrutinised the toy. Would she like it?

'She'll love it,' Rob said gently. I spun round, my face creased with anxiety. 'If not,' he continued undeterred, 'we'll get her something she does love.'

I smiled and stuffed Dotty back in the bag, then crossed over to Rob and curled myself into his arms. 'God, I'm nervous.'

'Me too,' he said, pulling away, 'so, let's get this over and done with.'

Rob fired up the car engine and our *Grease* CD exploded into life. Rob hit the mute button, I switched it off.

The first few miles took us along a cliff-top coastal road towards the city. The warmth enveloping us from the heater of our beloved but aging Volvo Estate did little to compensate for the blanket grey sky and the choppy waters of the West Coast sea below. I pulled down the visor and glanced at Daniel's reflection in the mirror. He was gazing out of the window.

I swivelled round. 'How're you doing?' I asked, stretching awkwardly to touch his knee.

'OK,' he grunted.

'Are you excited?'

He nodded.

'Are you nervous?'

He nodded again and turned his gaze back to the window. That was fine – I didn't feel much like talking either. For the umpteenth time that day, I wondered how Alex would be feeling right now. She was surely terrified.

'Far from it Mrs Allen,' Karen, her social worker, had said this morning. 'She can't wait to meet you all.' But it was no doubt a stock phrase they reserved for all their prospective adopters.

I bent into the foot-well and pulled out a pristine yellow folder. Stuck to the front was a printed label which read: Alex – Placement Week. Inside were various clear plastic sleeves containing copies of our correspondence with Social Services, contact numbers, places to visit, maps and, finally, an all but empty sleeve labelled 'Alex'. I reached into the bottom of it and pulled out the only picture we had of her – the print of a passport-size black and white photo, standard for all children 'advertised' in adoption magazines. I studied the photo, exploring every line and nuance of her face for some clue as to the person she might be. Would she be this beautiful in real life? Everyone who'd met her seemed to think so. Beneath the photo, and above the forty-word summary of her life, was her name.

A-l-e-x . . . I sounded the name inside my head, savouring it. Until we'd been given the official go-ahead to meet her today, I'd hardly dared use it, just as I'd avoided unnecessarily revisiting her photo. I'd not wanted to jinx this placement: in the past year we'd been linked with two other children, but they'd both fallen through. Each time we'd been devastated, convinced that we'd never find a more perfect match. Then Alex's details had dropped through our letterbox, as perfect as the other two, only this time the link had been successful.

I slid the photo back into its sleeve and glanced across at Rob. He was sitting right back in the driver's seat, arms outstretched, hands on the steering wheel, deep in thought.

'How much further?' I asked.

'A couple of miles.'

'Is that all?' I said excitedly, snaking my hair round my fingers.

A few minutes later, we turned into Alex's road.

I pulled down the visor again, checked for any stray lipstick, took a deep breath and said, 'Right. Are we all ready for this?'

'Yup!' Rob said.

I turned round to Daniel and raised my thumb at him. He did the same back.

'Good!'

The large semi-detached house was perched on a steep, grassy bank. It was set back from the road by a lawn which led to a flight of treacherous-looking steps that fell unevenly to the pavement. I could just make out the small, lone figure of a five-year-old girl looking down at us from the top of the steps. Cursing myself for not wearing my glasses, I began the precarious climb towards her. It wasn't until I'd reached halfway that her face came into focus: Alex. She was unmistakable as the girl in the photo.

My heart began to pound and a jumble of messages whirled around my brain. I forced myself to breathe calmly. She was so beautiful – and she was smiling. Rob gave me a little nudge from behind and my legs moved again. I climbed the steps slowly, not wanting to frighten Alex away, but even as my concern registered, something about the way she was standing told me she wasn't going anywhere.

Her eyes seemed to have a magnetic pull, and as each step drew me closer, they grew larger. The photo had done those eyes no justice at all, nor had it captured the striking gloss of her silken fair hair which hung to her waist. I was in love already! I dragged a shaky leg over the final step.

'Hello Alex,' I said, bending down and offering her my hand, but she didn't take it. Her eyes were fixed on mine and my gesture had gone unnoticed, so I tried again. This time she took it, momentarily lowering her eyes. Her own hand was warm and soft.

"Lo,' she said quietly. The corners of her delicate mouth were twitching in a nervous smile. Our arms, locked at the hand, started moving up and down like a piston. A voice from behind us broke the spell.

'Do you know who these nice people are?'

I recognised the voice as Ken's. He was standing with his wife and two of the other foster children under the porch of their front door. Reluctantly I let go of Alex's hand, but before I could open my mouth to greet them, Alex answered, 'It's my new mummy and daddy.'

The answer brought a lump to my throat. She'd spoken the words so quietly that I had to replay them in my head to make sure I'd heard them right. With a thrill I realised I had. I had a sudden and strong impulse to pick her up, hold her close and thank her, but I didn't want to scare her and spoil the moment. Instead, I knelt down again, looked her deep in the eye and smiled.

'That's right,' I said, 'we're your new mummy and daddy.'

Her eyes brimmed with a pleasure that mirrored my own. I wondered what was running through Rob's mind and then realised, shamefully, I'd not yet given him or Daniel a look in. I moved aside and Rob stepped forward.

'Hello Alex,' he said, and offered his hand.

"Lo,' Alex said again, smiling, and then turned her attention back to me.

'And this is Daniel,' I said, pulling him in front of me and resting my hands on his shoulders.

Daniel raised his head bashfully. 'Hello.'

"Lo,' she said once more, though her eyes kept darting back to mine.

'Why don't you give her the book?' I suggested to Daniel.

He reached into his rucksack, pulled out the book and held it out to Alex. When she didn't take it, he shuffled closer. She took it then, but gave it only a cursory glance before dropping her arm and letting it hang down by her side. I felt Daniel's disappointment.

'It's OK,' I jumped in, 'she'll look at it later, I'm sure.'

Ken's wife, Pat, who'd noticed this exchange, came striding from the porch followed by Ken.

'Oh Alex, wasn't that lovely of Daniel to make you a book?' Pat gushed. 'What do you say?'

'Um . . . fanks.'

Pat lifted the book from Alex's fingers, and put on the spectacles that hung round her neck. Then she opened the book, made a great show of laughing at the first few jokes, and enthused over the cartoons.

'You are a clever lad,' she said finally. Daniel smiled and flashed me a look of pride.

'Thank you,' I mouthed at Pat, but she brushed aside my gratitude.

She was a short, round lady in her early sixties, with smiling eyes. Ken towered above his wife, as lean a man as I'd ever seen. He was supporting himself with a walking stick but he wore a wide grin on his face.

'Ghosts!' Alex shrieked suddenly. 'Play ghosts. Come quick!' Her eyes were dancing eagerly at Rob and me as she pointed towards the house, and I found myself laughing. It was as though someone had flicked a switch. I glanced at Rob, who looked as surprised as I felt.

'OK, OK!' I said. 'Give us a minute just to—'

'But ghost coming! Quick!' Alex said, tugging first at my coat and then at Rob's.

Her face alive with excitement and twinkling with mischief, she looked even more adorable. I raised my arms in a what-can-we-do gesture to the Radfords and apologised. Pat rolled her eyes. 'We'll have that cup of tea later, then,' she said.

I grabbed Daniel's hand and the four of us ran off into the house, exchanging rushed greetings with the children loitering shyly in the porch.

Slithering backwards, I reversed under Alex's bed, managing to squeeze my bottom into the gap. I curled into a foetal position, rested my cheek on the thick pile carpet and grinned at Alex, who was similarly curled up next to me. We lay face to face, no more than a few inches apart, panting excitedly.

'Seventeen, eighteen, nineteen, twenty – coming, ready or not!' Daniel yelled from the bottom of the Radfords' stairs.

Alex squealed and then giggled at having made the sound.

'Sshh!' I said, pressing my finger to my lips. She giggled again, and so did I. I'd only known her for forty minutes and already I was laughing with her as if I'd known her for years. In the semi-darkness of our hidey-hole, my eyes danced across her face, taking in every contour, every detail. Her skin was soft but not pale. She had wide, almond-shaped eyes with lashes long enough to curl. Her nose was small and slightly upturned, and her mouth asked to be kissed.

Daniel's ghost impersonations grew louder and I braced myself for the bedlam of excitement which would explode when he inevitably found us: Alex had repeatedly chosen the same hiding place since the game had begun twenty minutes earlier.

'Whooo, whooo,' Daniel sounded purposefully into her room and walked out again.

Alex tried unsuccessfully to stifle another giggle, so I reached out my arm and placed my hand gently over her mouth. The air from her muffled laughter filled my hand, which she pushed away but then she let her hand linger on mine, and my heart missed a couple of beats. It lingered some more, and only when she finally pulled it away did my heart start beating again.

We lay in our den, eyes locked and sniggering, until we saw Daniel's upside-down face peering at us from beneath the mattress.

'Ah, save me! I need a cup of tea,' I cried, and fled downstairs.

'Have a seat, love,' Pat said, gesturing to a plump green sofa.

'Thanks,' I puffed. It was verging on dark outside and the room was lit with several floor lamps. An open fire crackled cheerfully in one corner.

'Are the others still playing?' Pat asked.

'Yes, I ran out of steam,' I replied.

'You'll need plenty of energy with Alex. Now, how do you like your tea?'

'Milk with two, please,' I said, settling back into the sofa and looking around the cluttered but cheerful room. My eyes stopped at the wall to my left. Covering almost its full height and width were at least fifty framed photographs of children, from infants through to teenagers, of assorted shapes, sizes and looks: curly-haired, straight-haired, bespectacled, freckled, pimpled, thin, chubby. All of them were smiling.

'Are all of these foster children?' I asked, my eyes wide.

'Yes, every last one of them.' She looked up and gazed at the pictures with an air of affection and pride. 'We still keep in touch with most of them.'

'How long have you been fostering?'

'Too long,' she said. 'Since the last of our three sons left home. Ken was at work all day and the house was too quiet. I was working as a volunteer at a local refuge for runaway children and one of them needed a home. The rest, as they say, is history.'

She handed me a mug of steaming Earl Grey and continued. 'Ken keeps moaning that we ought to be retiring to a nice bungalow overlooking the sea, but it's all huff and puff. He'd be lost without the children.'

I laughed. A nice image of Rob and me with similar pictures on our wall drifted across my mind. Then I scanned the wall for a picture of Alex.

'That was taken at our sailing club,' she said when I'd found it. 'She loves it there, especially the band nights when she can entertain everyone with her dancing.'

My heart swelled. If she loved music, my family would adore her.

'Shortbread?' She passed the plate.

I gratefully accepted a biscuit and asked, 'Where's Ken?'

'He's taken the other two to pick up some bread. He'll be back soon.'

I bit into the warm, sweet buttery biscuit, trying not to make a crumbly mess.

Pat sat down in the chair opposite. 'So, what do you think of our Alex, then?'

I grinned. 'Just lovely and so happy — nothing like the shy and withdrawn picture the magazine painted of her.'

'That was written some time ago,' Pat said. 'She's changed a lot since then. You wouldn't recognise her as the same child who'd turned up on our doorstep a year ago.'

'Oh?'

'Yes. When Alex arrived here she was in a terrible state. In fact, for the first few weeks she never spoke. She would sit where we put her and rock, back and forth, back and forth – almost in a trance. The world around her barely existed. Then, just when we thought she might never recover, she smiled – at one of Ken's stupid jokes, I think – and she's not looked back since. From the child who couldn't say two words, we now have a child who chatters all day long.'

'Wow.'

While the floorboards thundered above us, I extracted from Pat all I could about our future daughter. Not just her history – we'd read her file – but about how she was now: her likes and dislikes, her fears, and so on. And, of course, about the problems we were bound to encounter.

'She's prone to acting up if she doesn't get her way,' Pat told me, but when I made some glib remark about all children being prone to acting up, something in Pat's expression triggered an alarm. I silenced it. Acting up I could deal with, whatever the grade, I believed.

'Anything else we should know?' I asked nonchalantly. Nothing so far had given me any real cause for concern, quite the reverse. It seemed to me that she just needed a lot of attention and had learning difficulties.

'Do you work?' she asked.

'I resigned last week.'

Pat seemed relieved. 'Don't underestimate the time you'll need to give Alex. She can be exhausting. Not because she's naughty, she's not,' she added quickly, 'but she needs a lot of time. She's way behind the other children in things like dressing herself or catching a ball. We don't know if that's because she may have some brain damage from the alcohol her mum drank during pregnancy* or whether it's

---

* Foetal Alcohol Spectrum Disorder (FASD) describes a syndrome of permanent birth defects caused by maternal consumption of alcohol during pregnancy. Maternal alcohol crosses the placental barrier and can stunt foetal growth or weight, create distinctive facial stigmata, damage neurons and brain structures and/or cause other physical anomalies. Foetal alcohol exposure is regarded by researchers as the leading known cause of mental retardation in the Western world. Source: wikipedia

because of her earlier neglect. Either way, I think it's just fair to warn you.'

'Thanks,' I said, but I wondered, what did she mean, warn us? I was poised to ask her when our ears were suddenly filled with the clatter of feet charging down the stairs. I experienced a moment of mild panic. I needed to know why she'd spoken so gravely about something we knew already. It made no sense.

Just then, Alex appeared at the door and my panic subsided. It wasn't as if I'd been told that she was vicious or destructive, so I settled for the fact that Pat was getting on in age and no longer had the energy she once had.

'Good game?' I asked Rob, taking in his red and perspiring face.

'Excellent,' he puffed. 'I was *definitely* the scariest ghost.'

'No, I was!' Alex and Daniel yelled simultaneously.

While Pat poured out another round of tea, I made room for Daniel on the sofa. Rob sat down at the other end of the sofa, leaving room for Alex if she wanted it. She did, and as she snuggled in between Rob and me, my heart soared.

Time was getting on, and we needed to find the cottage that was to be our temporary accommodation during our visit to get to know Alex.

'What are your plans for the week?' Pat asked.

'We thought we'd ask Alex what she wanted to do,' Rob replied, turning to face her.

Alex's eyes flew to Pat, who slowly repeated what Rob had said. Alex was considering her response with an 'Mmm' and an 'Um' when, with what I felt was an undue flicker of impatience, Pat suggested the bowling park.

At the mention of bowling, Daniel's eyes lit up. We turned to Alex. Her smile was back and she nodded eagerly.

'Tomorrow?' Rob suggested.

'Yeah!' the two children chorused.

We made arrangements to pick Alex up at ten o'clock the following morning.

Five minutes later, we stood huddled in the porch with our bags and coats. I knelt down to Alex and we locked eyes.

'It's been really, really nice meeting you,' I said, reaching for her hand. 'Thank you for a lovely afternoon.'

She smiled coyly and I wanted badly to kiss her. Would that please her, or would she feel intimidated? Alex resolved my dilemma by leaning into me and kissing my cheek. The warm spot she left with her soft little child's lips radiated across my face and deep inside me. I folded her in my arms and kissed first her cheek and then the silky crown of her head.

'I'll see you tomorrow,' I said, pulling away.

'See 'morrow,' she said.

I was still aglow with the warmth of Alex's affection when I turned to Pat. 'Thanks for preparing her so well,' I whispered as we hugged.

'I wish that were true. Alex did most of that herself,' she replied. 'Anyway, I think she's very lucky to have found you three.'

Compliments have always embarrassed me. 'I hope so,' I mumbled.

I threw an arm round Daniel's shoulders as we walked back to the car and gave silent thanks to whomsoever one was supposed to thank for the joy that Alex had already brought in a couple of short hours.

''Night, Daniel,' Rob said. 'See you for bowling in the morning.'

''Night, Dad.'

I folded Daniel's trousers and hung them over the back of a chair. Although the heating had been left on all day, the temperature in the room felt more like a November evening than a late August one, and Daniel was watching me from beneath several mismatched blankets. I perched myself on the side of the bed and ran a hand through my son's mop of blond hair.

'Did you have a good day?' I asked.

'Yeah. Can we play ghosts again?'

I smiled. 'I'm sure Alex would love that. She's nice, isn't she?'

'She's funny.'

I chuckled. 'She certainly is.'

'Can she be on my team when we go bowling?' he asked. 'I can help her with the ramp.'

'Of course she can,' I said, smiling down at him and thinking how much I loved him.

'Are we going to adopt Alex?' he asked, breaking the tranquil silence.

'I hope so.'

He took a moment to digest this and I stayed until he fell asleep.

Rob handed me a glass of red wine and, shaking my hair out of its band, I sat back into the small upright sofa. Rob placed a bare sinewy arm round my shoulders and I joined him in resting my slipper-socked feet on the coffee table. For a while we stared silently into the fire. We'd already replayed the events of the day over a spaghetti bolognaise and I could feel my mind winding down to peaceful contentment.

'How was your mum?' I asked.

'Fine, although her arthritis is still playing up. I don't think it'll be long before she moves in with Russell and Diana.'

Talk of Rob's family in Australia always brought poignancy to the air. It was the price he'd paid for falling in love with me the night we met in a Fulham pub. Had he served the customer next to me instead, he'd be back in his native land, settled with a wife and two kids and close to his mother and brother in Brisbane. He'd be the one caring for his mum in her arthritic state.

We'd mentally cancelled this year's annual visit to Australia, but having now met Alex and seen how easy she was, Rob asked, 'Do you think Social Services will allow us to take her to visit Mum in the summer?'

I smiled. 'It would be nice, wouldn't it?'

Rob pulled me into his arms. 'These last four years have been worth it, haven't they?'

'Oh yes,' I said, suddenly aware that the interminable forms, the endless interviews, and then the long wait for that 'special' child was finally over.

'Here's to us,' he said.

'To the four of us.'

Chapter Two

A midst the hubbub of tumbling pins, clattering balls, and general high spirits, I sat on the white plastic bench like a puffed-up mother hen surveying her brood. This was one very happy-looking outfit and I wanted everyone to notice.

'Dad,' Daniel pleaded, breaking through my reverie, 'tell Alex she's got to push the ball harder.'

Alex wasn't taking her bowling as seriously as Daniel would have liked, but then who could blame her? I'd never been too enamoured with the game either. Nevertheless, like a small thorn pricking through my veil of contentment, I felt his disappointment. For the past half an hour he'd stood patiently by her side, his expression set with helpful intent, shouting out instructions while straining to keep the guide ramp pinned to the wooden floor. So far to no avail.

With a renewed burst of vigour, Alex punched the second of her two balls off the ramp. Rob, hovering a few feet behind them, threw me a wry look over his shoulder. With a painful thud, the ball bounced onto the floor and straight into the gully. If that wasn't bad enough, she'd managed to knock the ramp out of Daniel's grip and over the red line, causing an alarm to sound out a foul. Daniel looked spent.

'Yeah!' Alex rejoiced, holding a palm up to Daniel for a high-five (she had yet to grasp this was a celebratory gesture to be earned), and he slapped her palm miserably.

Alex skipped back to the bench and slapped my hand. 'Hi fi,' she said with feverish joy.

'High five, you clever girl,' I lied, and patted the bench beside me. She began skating up and down the length of the bench squealing in delight. Eventually she careered into my side, laughing, and I grabbed her.

'You're a monkey!' I said affectionately, and ruffled her hair. She nestled there until it was my turn to bowl.

'Why can't she do it properly, Mum?' Daniel asked a little while later. Rob had taken over and was now helping Alex with the ramp.

I put a consoling arm round him. 'You did a great job teaching her. She will learn, but maybe not today,' I said. 'There's far too much going on for her to concentrate. Her head is probably so full with strange and nervous feelings, there's no room to think about anything else.'

Daniel looked bemused.

'Sometimes when you're nervous,' I elaborated, 'you want to hide it, don't you?'

'Yes.'

'Well, I imagine that's what Alex's doing at the moment,' I said.

'She doesn't look nervous,' he said, with a tinge of petulance in his voice.

'She is,' I said. 'Think of it like having ants in your pants that make you wriggle and giggle.' I did an 'ants-in-your-pants' impression and he smiled. 'Well, Alex has got nervous feelings inside her that are making her wriggle and giggle.'

Daniel's eyes grew thoughtful and he nodded.

'Next time, she'll find it much easier,' I reassured him.

Half an hour later, I sat on the floor by Alex's feet and unlaced her tiny bowling shoes. I looked up and met her smile with one of my own. Not in my most fanciful daydream could I have expected a more wonderful start, and I felt my heart swell with unbridled admiration for her. Aside from a few subdued minutes in the car, she'd been upbeat and perky all morning. I'd not known resilience or bravery like it. No one deserved a lifetime of happiness more than she did and, as we made our way to the cafeteria, I resolved that we were going to make sure she got it.

'Do you want me to cut that up for you?' I asked Alex, as she attempted to slide the whole dinosaur bite into her mouth sideways.

'Yes,' she replied. I leant across the cafeteria table, which was strewn with styrofoam cups, straws and sauce bottles, to slice the limp breaded mass into bite-size chunks.

'What other things do you like eating?' Rob asked, making conversation.

She frowned.

'What food do you like best in the world?' I encouraged.

'Mmmm . . .' She paused.

'How about spaghetti? Do you like that?'

'I like 'ghetti,' she said, her expression melting into a broad smile.

'What about sausages?'

'Mmmm,' she said. 'I like shosage.'

'My best is pizza,' Daniel piped up. 'We have pizza every Friday, don't we Mum?'

'I like pizza,' Alex said.

'Is there anything you *don't* like?' Rob asked.

'I like sweets,' she said.

Rob and I smiled. Alex grabbed her Styrofoam cup of Coke and sucked greedily on the straw.

'And you like Coca-Cola I take it?'

She nodded, draining the cup of its contents in one go.

'Whoa! Careful,' I said, 'or you might go pop.'

'Or do a gigantic burp,' Daniel said, doing a fine impression of a noisy belch.

'Yes, thank you Daniel,' I said, throwing him a stiff smile.

Suddenly, Alex burped — a deep, richly vibrating and highly unladylike burp. My hand flew to my mouth as I looked around us; thankfully there was no one close by. My instinct was to scold her, but by now she'd dissolved into a laughter that was not only infectious, but also appropriately edged with guilt. Daniel stifled a giggle and Rob's attempt at a scowl did nothing to stem her amusement.

'Alex!' I exclaimed, but then I also erupted into laughter and the four of us laughed until our jaws ached. I made several half-hearted attempts to bring order back to the table, but each one met with even more mirth.

'Sorry,' Alex said, when the laughter eventually died out. Her tone was apologetic, but there was a glint of laughter still in her eyes.

'You're forgiven,' I said, 'but maybe a bit quieter next time, yes?'

She nodded dutifully, and began forking baked beans into her mouth one at a time.

'Do you want a spoon?' I asked.

'Yes,' she said, and I handed her a plastic teaspoon.

Rob, Daniel and I finished our meal, but Alex had barely made a dent in her food.

'Aren't you hungry?' I asked.

She shook her head.

'OK,' I said, despite my aversion to wasted food. Now was not the time or place. 'Just leave it.'

Daniel began gesturing at the nearby jumble of arcade machines. 'Can we have a go now?' he asked.

Rob and I looked at our watches. Alex was due back in a quarter of an hour.

'Two goes each,' Rob said.

The two children went off to the machines with Rob. I settled the bill and found them a few minutes later, trying to extract Laa-Laa the Teletubby out of a large glass-fronted machine. Predictably, Laa-Laa slipped from the three-pronged claw and back into the reservoir of unclaimed soft toys.

At their collective groan, I announced it was time to go.

'Oh please, Mum, just one more go,' Daniel pleaded.

'Nope, that's it now,' Rob said firmly.

Ignoring Daniel's down-turned mouth, we turned to go. However, Alex remained rooted to the spot.

'Come on, Alex,' I said, holding out a hand but dropping it immediately. Her eyes had fixed on mine, and though I couldn't put my finger on it – couldn't have described it – there was something about the look that unsettled me.

'Are you all right?' I asked, and like a receding cloud, the look vanished. She nodded, found my hand, and clasped it all the way to the car.

The following evening, the antiquated phone in the lounge rang yet again. I shouted up to the children, 'Ten more minutes, then it's time for bed,' and grabbed the receiver. 'Hello?'

'Only me!' my best friend, Sophie, trilled down the phone.

With a satisfied smile, I curled up on the sofa.

'I'm in love already,' I said, and told her everything. 'And the best bit is that she seems to like us too. We've only known her two days and she's already asked to stay the night. She's here now.'

Sophie had grown uncharacteristically emotional. 'God Mel, I'm so pleased.'

'Yeah, me too.'

'How's Daniel taking it?'

'Listen for yourself,' I said, and held the phone in the direction of the stairs, where Daniel's and Alex's excited laughter could be heard.

'What *are* they doing?'

'Jumping on the beds,' I admitted, but I had no intention of stopping them. The inevitable fallout after Alex's arrival in Daniel's life had begun earlier today when we'd been shopping for a new suitcase for Alex. He had been much quieter than usual, complaining of a stomach ache, and Alex's exuberance hadn't helped. So to hear him laughing now was music to my ears.

I gushed some more before Sophie broached the subject of Alex's learning difficulties. She'd been one of many whose delight for us had clouded on hearing about it. Twirling the phone flex round my finger, I contemplated my response.

'To begin with, we thought we'd been given the wrong girl. There's nothing obviously slow about her, if you know what I mean, and socially, she seems as quick as they come,' I told her. 'But, yeah, she does have some problems. Her speech is affected and she doesn't always understand what you're saying.' I paused. 'No great shakes though. You'll see what I mean when you meet her.'

'Can I be the first?' she teased eagerly.

I laughed. 'You might have to fight my family for that!'

'Second then.'

I smiled. 'We'll see.'

'Can't wait. I'll have the Chardonnay on ice,' she said.

I hung up and went to see the children into bed.

'Night, night love,' I said, leaning down and kissing Alex gently on her forehead, and said again, 'You know where we are if you want anything?'

She nodded, her sweet eyes anchored to mine.

'And I mean anything,' I stressed. 'It doesn't matter if you're worried, or you're thirsty, or you just want a cuddle. You promise me you'll wake us?'

'I p'omise,' she said.

Dotty had been neatly tucked under the duvet at the far edge of her bed. I instinctively pushed the cuddly toy closer to her and then lingered for a moment by the bed, unwilling to break the gaze that Alex held. Eventually, her eyelids began to flicker sleepily.

'It's really nice having you here,' I said, smiling. She smiled back, and I switched off the light and left the room.

When we crept in half an hour later, Dotty had been neatly put back in her original place. Alex was fast asleep.

I emerged from a dreamless sleep to a soft, persistent pecking sensation on my cheek. I wrenched open my eyes to find Alex, illuminated by the landing light, hovering over me. The finger-tapping stopped.

Heaving myself into a sitting position, I asked if she was all right.

'I dirty nappy,' she said, her voice booming across the night's silence. The digits on our travel alarm said it was four forty-three a.m. I grimaced. Maybe it *was* morning for Alex – Pat had warned us she was an early riser.

'Oh, OK,' I croaked. 'We don't want that, do we?' I said quietly. Rob stirred.

'Morning.' I leaned across and planted a kiss on his cheek.

'Mmm,' he murmured, attempting a smile.

'I've got to see to Alex's nappy,' I said, and got out of bed to see Daniel standing in the doorway, rubbing his eyes.

'Alex told me it was time to wake up,' he said, weaving sleepily into our room.

'Well, good morning to you, too.' My outward cheer masked a silent groan. I'd have to have a word with Alex about not waking him next time.

Alex was now shuffling from side to side, her legs splayed in an attempt to make the dirty nappy more comfortable.

'Let's get that nappy off you,' I said and led her into the bathroom.

I placed a towel on the floor and, without prompting, Alex laid herself flat on her back, fixing her eyes on my face.

As I knelt on the icy tiles and straddled her legs, I was aware my smile was strained. It wasn't that the nappy offended me in any way; I'd spent a lifetime changing nappies. It wasn't even that I considered a five-year-old too old to wear nappies – there were thousands of children of her age still in nappies. It was the motionless way she lay beneath me, her inscrutable eyes never leaving my face. There was nothing exactly untoward about the stare, yet ... Berating myself, I shook off the sense of unease. How else was the poor child supposed to behave?

'I can't wait to see your nursery today,' I said, and began a course of bright chatter.

A smile formed, melting the impassivity from her face, and my shoulders dropped.

Once I'd cleaned her up, I searched for any signs that Alex had picked up on my earlier falter. She looked happy enough, but that moment of unease had been a stark reminder that, as confident as I'd been about taking on a special needs child – I'd cared for many as a voluntary worker in a residential home for disabled children – I was by no means experienced enough to be complacent about it.

I smiled at the child, held out my hand, and led her downstairs where she 'helped' me make a pot of tea.

Five hours later, with the children waiting in the car while Rob and I gathered up the last bits and pieces, the phone rang. We exchanged an exasperated smile. We were beginning to regret ever giving the number to our families.

'Hello, you're through to House of Madness,' I said. 'How can I help you?'

'Mrs Allen?'

I winced. It was Karen Whittle, Alex's social worker.

'Oh yeah, hi! I mean sorry, it's chaos here.' I mouthed her name to Rob, who came and pressed his ear as close as he could to catch the conversation.

Karen chuckled in her neat little way. 'Have you got a moment?'

'Of course,' I said, growing suddenly apprehensive. 'Have you got a moment?' usually equated to 'sit down and brace yourself'. I sat down. Were we going to fail at the first hurdle?

'I spoke to Ken and Pat Radford yesterday,' Karen said, cutting through my rising apprehension. 'They say things are going well, so how would you feel about taking Alex home with you earlier than arranged?'

I shot a stunned look at Rob. *How would we feel about taking her home earlier than arranged? How would we feel about . . .* I could feel the grin spread to the tips of my ears. 'We'd love to!'

'There's no pressure, of course. We just thought that, with things going so well, there's no point dragging this out for the sake of it.'

'We'd need to speak to Alex first,' I said.

'Of course,' she said.

'And to Daniel.' As the words drifted from my mouth, the reality of the situation began to sink in. Rob had clocked it and was grinning too.

'The Radfords have requested one last night with her, though,' Karen said.

'Of course,' I said, then suddenly realised it was important that the three of us should have a final night alone, too.

'Let me know what you decide. The paperwork's ready our end.'

'I suppose we'd better call the children in from the car,' I said to Rob, prising myself out of his embrace.

It occurred to us that we ought to speak to Alex about it first, before telling Daniel. So Rob took Daniel to the village shop to buy some sweets.

'Sit down, love,' I said, patting a space on the sofa beside me, 'there's something we want to ask you.'

She shuffled to the back of the seat and our eyes locked.

I took a deep breath and, fixing her with a gentle smile, I asked, 'How would you like to come home with us? Soon?'

A coy smile and an affirmative nod.

I exhaled. 'Sure?'

She nodded again.

'Because, we can wait as long as you—'

'I want to,' she cut in, her voice concrete and clear.

I studied her expression, my gaze flickering over her eyes, measuring each blink, noting her unwavering stare, and I knew she spoke the truth. I leaned forward and clapped my hands over her knees.

'Oh Alex, I'm so pleased. I can't wait to show you everything.' I began to list the attractions for her; her new house, her new bedroom, her new toys; then, with an effort, I reined myself in. I thought she looked happy enough, but there was a mechanical air about her furious nodding that suggested she needed longer to digest the news before being bombarded with details.

'And Cooter,' she added, when I'd stopped. My eyes shot wide open. Scooter was our cat.

'You remember!' I exclaimed. Scooter featured in the folder of our life that Social Services had been asked to make for her.

'He bring 'limy frogs,' she said.

I grinned.

We got away from the damp of falling rain and found a table deep inside McDonald's. We'd spent the morning in the hands of Alex's adoring nursery school teachers before dropping her off at the Radfords with her new suitcase.

'So what are *we* going to do today?' Rob asked, unwrapping his Big Mac.

We looked to Daniel, who seemed pale and uninterested.

'I dunno.'

'Are you feeling all right?' I asked, stooping to meet his gaze.

'My stomach hurts.'

'Still?'

'It keeps hurting,' he said, looking miserably at his burger.

Rob and I exchanged frowns. We'd never known Daniel to abandon a burger. The reality of Alex coming home with us tomorrow, and the implications this brought with it, had clearly hit home.

'What say we finish up here and go and have a *proper* game of bowling?' Rob suggested.

An hour later, Daniel had scored his first strike, his stomach pains seemingly forgotten.

*

The following day, 29 August 1997, we stood on the Radfords' front lawn, our car packed up and ready to go.

'Come here, my girl,' Ken said, lifting Alex into his arms. Alex giggled and planted a kiss on her foster carer's ruddy cheek.

'Bye Kenny,' she said sweetly, but was nevertheless wriggling to get down. Ken held firm.

'You look after yourself and be good for your new mummy and daddy.' Alex nodded, still wriggling, so with a roll of the eyes and a final kiss, Ken lowered Alex back down.

I watched the exchange with a mixture of awe and sadness. She clearly loathed goodbyes and I hoped she'd never have to endure this wrench again.

Ken moved aside to make way for Pat, who bent down and hugged Alex, mumbling a few things close to her ear and punctuating each one with a kiss. With a final squeeze she released her.

'Please let us know how she's getting along,' Pat implored as we took our leave, 'and remember, if there's anything you need to know give us a ring.'

'Thank you.' I was confident we'd covered the essentials over the past few days and, of course, there would be many things I'd forgotten to ask, but short of sounding conceited, I was sure we could take over from here.

We descended the steps for the last time and settled the children into the Volvo. As I was stepping into the car, I glanced up at the Radfords for a final wave and my smile stiffened to a small frown: the Radfords were unmistakably exchanging a look of some significance. Although I couldn't grasp the meaning of that look, the faint sound of a distant warning bell sounded in my head, but then Ken and Pat were furiously waving back, their smiles bright. Like a droplet of icy cold water falling onto a sun-baked stone, my droplet of apprehension dried up. Clearly, I must have imagined things.

I pulled the car door shut behind me, and with a final flurry of horn-tooting, we set off for home.

After a stop for lunch, I took over the driving. Our hunger satisfied, a calm quiet finally descended over the car. I glanced at the two children through my rear-view mirror. Daniel was gazing through the windscreen. Alex, sitting behind Rob, was flicking vaguely through the pages of our road atlas. Suddenly, she closed the book, reached across the seat and took Daniel's hand in her own.

A flicker of bemusement crossed Daniel's face as he glanced at her. With half an eye on the road, I watched nervously, sensing that Daniel wanted to retract his hand. Then Alex smiled at him – a smile as gentle and genuine as it was warm and contented. He gave a small smile in return and, though still embarrassed by the gesture of affection, resumed gazing out of the windscreen leaving his hand still tucked inside hers.

With a joyous pounding in my chest, I tried surreptitiously to catch Rob's attention. His head was planted firmly back on the head-rest and his eyes were closed. I couldn't wait to tell him. Neither could I wait to recount the moment to those who'd doubted our decision to adopt.

Chapter Three

*O*ur home was a four-bedroom, Sixties-style semi in a cul-de-sac of forty-eight houses. Ours was number twenty-two, the last one on the left-hand side before the road branched out to feed a semicircle of houses and two large green areas where the children played.

Our house had two tiny gardens, one at the front and one at the back. To the rear of the house lay a large double garage with a pit, housing the third love of Rob's life – his Triumph Spitfire. Renovating it was a never-ending job, but as long as I didn't have to don any greasy overalls, I didn't care.

Inside, the house was bright and airy, with four bedrooms upstairs sitting two and two on either side of a narrow passage, with a toilet at the end. Downstairs, the hallway led to three further rooms: a kitchen with breakfast area at the back, a huge bathroom, and a thirty-foot-long room with dining area at one end and sitting area at the other. Patio doors opened onto a small paved area and the back garden.

We'd fallen in love with the house as soon as we saw it, and had mortgaged ourselves to the hilt to buy it. That had been five years ago.

Now, after a week holed up in a tiny cottage in the middle of nowhere, the sight of our home filled me with familiar warmth.

'Here it is,' I beamed at Alex.

She gave the house a cursory glance before swinging her face back to mine.

'Do you want to see your room?' Daniel asked eagerly, for we'd spent the previous fortnight decorating it.

'Yes,' she replied and smiled.

Leaving everything in the car, we went inside. Alex took a

moment to examine her surroundings before following Daniel upstairs.

'This is yours,' he said, pointing to the big, bold nameplate he'd made a week earlier. 'Look, your room is next to mine,' he said, gesturing, but Alex wasn't listening. She opened her bedroom door and peered inside. When she didn't move, I put a hand on her shoulder and led her inside. Smiling with anticipation, we watched her face.

Her eyes swept the room: A new bed with a Disney duvet set, a bookshelf stacked with books, a wardrobe and set of drawers, a bright yellow and red desk, a bean bag and a purple toy-box.

'Do you like it?' Rob asked.

Her face broke into a grin. 'I like it.'

Daniel moved past her to the toy-box. 'Look,' he said, lifting the lid to a stack of boxed games, jigsaws, dolls' paraphernalia, and other bits and pieces. 'Some of these are mine, but you can have them.'

But he was talking to Alex's back; she'd seen enough of her room for now.

'Don't worry,' I mouthed at him, 'she needs a moment to settle in.'

The tour moved swiftly after that. When we reached the final room – the sitting room – Alex barely looked at it before turning her big eyes onto mine and asking if we could play Ghosts. I shook my head. 'We need to unpack the car first,' I said, and turned to Daniel. 'Why don't you show Alex the climbing frame and the swing?'

Alex stalled just a fraction before following Daniel out through the patio doors. As Rob and I walked back down the hallway, we heard him yell 'Don't wobble it, we'll fall off!' Then they both giggled.

However, we'd managed just one run into the house with the luggage when Alex was back inside and hovering by the front door.

Daniel had followed her inside. 'She wants to play ghosts,' he explained.

Rob and I rolled our eyes heavenwards and smiled resignedly. The unpacking would have to wait.

A couple of minutes later, the house was filled with laughter. It was a nice sound.

The following day, Daniel stood in the doorway of the kitchen, Alex hovering behind him. 'She doesn't want to play any games,' he said wearily.

I put down the washing basket. 'OK love, thanks. Alex can stay with me.'

'Can I play with Bradley and the others now?' he asked, eager to catch up with his best friend and the gang of neighbourhood children.

'Tomorrow.'

Daniel looked poised to argue but resisted. He knew the score: Alex needed a day or so to settle in before being overwhelmed by other children. He turned around and went back upstairs.

I looked at the mountain of washing on the floor. 'Would you like to watch some TV?' I suggested to Alex. After a small hesitation, she nodded. I settled her in front of some cartoons with a drink and a biscuit and returned to the dirty linen. I was tired. Since Alex had woken us at four-thirty that morning, I'd read with her, did colouring-in with her and, relieving Rob, played ghosts for an hour. I opened the washing machine door and began piling in the clothes, but was arrested by a flicker of movement. I looked up to see Alex at the door. She smiled shyly.

'Don't you want to watch TV?'

'No.'

I suppressed a sigh. The washing would have to wait until Rob came home with the groceries.

'Come on then,' I said, standing up and beckoning her into my open arms. 'We'll read another story, but then I *must* get on, OK?'

Her beautiful face lit up and we left the kitchen.

After we'd finished reading, I asked her how she was feeling. Although she appeared upbeat, she'd been restless and unable to settle into anything much this morning.

'Um, fine,' she said, though from the change in her expression I could tell she wasn't.

'Are you missing Patty and Kenny?' I broached.

She paused, unsure what to say.

'It's OK,' I said.

'Um . . . yes,' she admitted finally, in a whisper.

I pulled her into my arms. 'I thought you might be,' I said.

For the next few minutes, I soothed her with words of reassurance, promising her things would get easier with time and that we'd take good care of her. And I emphasised that whenever she felt sad or lonely she shouldn't be afraid to tell us.

Scooter, our cat, emerged from his hiding place of the past twenty-four hours and pounced onto the sofa. Alex recoiled a fraction, as though she was afraid, but then she reached out a tentative hand and patted him on his back.

'Where are the dogs?' Alex asked suddenly.

I frowned. 'You mean the dogs in the folder? Oh, they don't live here, they live with Grandpa. Would you like to meet them?'

'Yes,' she said eagerly, astounding me with her ability to bounce back. She reached for the red folder lying on the coffee table and for a third time in twenty-four hours, I talked her through the pages of photos.

'That's Nanny, Dad's mum. She lives in Australia. And that's Grandpa, my dad, and . . .'

'Who that?' Alex asked, before I could turn the page. She was pointing to the woman standing some distance behind my father.

'That's my mum but she's up in heaven now. Her name was Georgina, you would have loved her.' My voice was soft and wistful for the beautiful mother I'd lost when I was eighteen years old. 'I know she would have loved you,' I added, ruffling her hair.

Alex smiled shyly and we resumed our ramble through the folder until we'd turned the final page. 'And that's Grandpa's house – can you see? – right next to the sea.'

'Can I go there?'

'Of course.'

She nodded. 'I want to.'

An hour later I heard Rob's car. 'I'll be back in a minute,' I said to Alex, who was helping me finally get the washing into the machine. I intercepted my husband at the front gate.

'How would you feel about having my family round tomorrow?' I asked. 'I know we said we'd wait a week or so, but Alex is ready.'

Rob agreed. By five o'clock the phone calls had been made, the house was presentable and the clothes had been washed, dried and put away. We were in bed by nine.

I poured out a fresh round of tea and coffee and settled comfortably into the rocking chair at the back of the dining area. I closed my eyes contentedly and began to rock. It had been a good day so far. No – better than good. It had been a brilliant day.

My sister Tess had been the first to arrive, at two o'clock. She'd thrown her arms around me with her usual intensity, but only briefly because she was busy scanning the hall. 'Where is she?' she asked, with a sense of urgency. Alex had answered her question by peering coyly from behind one of the doors.

Tess melted. Their introduction had needed no mediation from me. Drawn together like magnets, they'd met in the middle, shaken hands and, as though powerless to resist, Tess had embraced Alex. I'd watched with pride, smiling and unsurprised. My sister had been looking forward to this moment more than anyone in my family. She not only loved children, but was training to be a child-therapist. No doubt, she had her relationship with her future niece mapped out already. Alex had wanted to show Tess her new room, and without a backward glance, Tess had followed like a lap dog.

The next to arrive had been my dad, followed shortly afterwards by my brother Matt. Both had approached Alex more tentatively but had quickly relaxed. They'd barely taken off their coats before she had them playing a frenzied game of ghosts.

Then my brother Tim, who'd made the last-minute drive from Exeter University, turned up. I smiled to myself now, as I recalled the moment Alex had said to him, 'You've got nice hair.' Tim, only twenty-one, owned a head of cropped, bleached hair and a pierced ear. 'Yours is pretty cool, too,' he'd laughed, swishing her freshly washed hair.

I was dragged from my reverie by a fresh clamour of joyful excitement rushing past my chair. Matt, a big bear of a man, ran through to the hallway with Alex bouncing precariously on his shoulders. They were being pursued by Dad. I smiled at Tess across the room. She came over and perched herself on the sideboard next to me. 'You look like the Cheshire cat that's got the cream,' she said.

'Actually, I feel like the Cheshire cat who's got her kittens.'

'When can you adopt her?'

'If all goes well they reckon we can go to court in about eighteen months' time.'

Tess's jaw dropped. 'That long?'

'Yeah, they need to be certain we're all happy with each other.'

'Her mum can't ask for her back, can she?' she asked.

'No. That's one thing we don't have to worry about. In fact, apart from birthday and Christmas cards, she's allowed no contact with her until she's at least eighteen.'

'Thank God for that. She should never have been allowed to have her in the first place,' she said, before embarking on a tirade against unfit mothers.

I didn't agree. 'She had a boyfriend who promised to stand by her and the baby and said he'd help her get off the alcohol and the drugs.'

'So what happened?'

'He did a runner two days after Alex was born.'

'What about her family? Couldn't they look after Alex?'

'What family? She grew up in care herself.'

Tess shook her head, appalled by an existence so alien to our own. 'And Social Services? Why didn't they step in sooner?'

'It was eighteen months before they even knew about Alex and when they did step in Michelle managed to get herself clean. But then she got this awful boyfriend who moved in with them, and before long she was back on the drink and drugs again. Alex was taken into care for good, when she almost burned down the house trying to fry fish-fingers when her mum was out cold on the floor.'

There was a pause as we both reflected. Tess spoke first, breaking the sombre mood. 'Fortunately, it doesn't seem to have affected her too much,' she said. 'I've had umpteen hugs already.'

I smiled at her gooey-eyed expression. My sister had recently found 'the one' – a man she'd met on a training course five months ago and with whom marriage and babies seemed imminent.

We spoke for a few more minutes, but all this talk of Alex was reminding me of Daniel and I excused myself. I found him in the kitchen with Tim, playing dominoes.

'I might have known!' I said to my youngest brother, but I was grateful, and made a mental note to thank him later.

Shortly afterwards, Dad got up to leave. As he placed his cap on his trademark thicket of grey, permanently windswept hair, he said, 'She's a lovely girl, Mel. A *really* lovely girl.' Dad had been chuffed to bits that Alex had asked to see the dogs.

'Thanks,' I beamed.

'It's just a shame Mum couldn't be here to meet her,' he said, tingeing the air with the sweet sadness that lingered in our lives even after all these years.

'I know,' was all I could say.

We hugged and made arrangements for Alex to come and visit.

Matt left next, but not before saying, 'Lilly's going to adore her.' I smiled. Lilly was Matt's long-standing Spanish girlfriend. 'When *are* you two going to get married?' I asked. He rolled his eyes and I snuggled up to him. 'You know you want to.'

He threw his hands up in despair. 'Sisters!'

An hour later, Tess was the only visitor remaining and she had to prise Alex off her arm.

'If it's OK with you, I've asked Alex if she wants to come swimming with me one day next week.'

I flashed Alex a doubtful look. Could she swim? Was it too soon to leave her with someone else? Wasn't it my job to take her swimming for the first time?

But Alex was looking on hopefully and Tess was about to tell me to relax, that she'd look after her, so I agreed. Besides, Alex and I had the next few months alone together before she joined pre-school in January. We'd have plenty of opportunity to go swimming. And to do all the other exciting things I had planned for her.

The primary concern for Mary and her team when we'd turned up at their offices, champing at the bit to adopt, had been for

Daniel. He'd been a much loved only child for almost seven years. Could he cope? Could he adapt? However, Daniel wanted a brother or sister. Everyone his age on the street had one, and so, after months of preparation, he'd convinced the team that his desire was genuine, that he understood the implications, and that, yes, he could cope.

So why was I feeling so anxious for him now, when he'd been prepared for the arrival of a child with far worse special needs than Alex was displaying?

As the rest of the house slept off the exhaustion of a successful day, I tossed and turned, uncomfortably aware that Daniel hadn't been prepared for the sweetness and charm of Alex. I was not quite sure how to handle his stomach ache: a knot of confusion and disquiet.

So, when I heard him in his bedroom an hour later, whimpering with stomach ache, I folded him in my arms and told him no one was expecting him to love Alex. That if he never wanted to love her, that was OK too. The words had come from nowhere and taken both of us by surprise. I knew they'd done the trick though, as I watched the colour return to his cheeks.

'Do I have to kiss her?' he asked sullenly.

I smiled. 'Yes, she needs lots of kisses at the moment.'

'But they're slimy,' he complained.

'Daniel!' I admonished. But I knew what he meant.

For the next few minutes, I talked to Daniel about the impact Alex had had on all our lives, explaining how things would eventually settle down. Then slowly his eyelids began to droop.

'How would you like one more day off school to let your stomach get completely better?'

He smiled happily. A second later he was asleep.

I drew the curtains closed, switched off the light, settled into the sofa between Daniel and Alex and hit 'play' on the remote control.

'This is nice,' I said, putting an arm round each of their shoulders. My head dropped contentedly onto the back rest. Although it had been a wrench to see Rob leave for work, the morning had been good. It had started at five a.m. with a clean nappy, the first clean one since she'd arrived, and I'd been feeling very pleased with myself ever since. It was a good sign, I thought. Although I'd not made too big a fuss of it, Alex knew I'd been proud of her achievement. She'd been her happy, loving and excitable self all day.

Adding to my contentment was seeing Daniel back to his chirpy self. In fact, he'd been almost as exuberant as Alex this morning.

The three of us had gambolled cheerily to the corner shop, bought some popcorn and rented a copy of *Toy Story*.

Now, a couple of minutes into the film, Alex asked, 'Where Cooter?'

'He's probably asleep upstairs,' I whispered.

'In your bed?'

'I think so.'

'Or in Daniel bed?'

'I don't know. Come on, let's watch the film,' I urged her. She looked instantly humble and fell silent. I pulled her closer to me.

A few moments later she began flicking at the underside of the duvet we'd draped over us. It grew more and more distracting as the duvet jumped higher and higher. When Daniel leaned across to see what was causing it, I asked her to stop. She stopped.

We'd just settled back into the story when Scooter pushed open the door and sauntered in. Alex began urging our cat onto the sofa by tapping furiously on the duvet and hissing his name. Scooter, still overwhelmed by Alex's high spirits, turned round and walked out. Alex began kicking at the duvet again.

I paused the video. 'Alex, please. Don't you want to watch the video?' I asked.

'Er . . . Um . . .'

'Come on, then,' I conceded, 'let's find you something else to do.' As I heaved myself off the sofa, I asked Daniel to save my seat and said I'd be straight back. I had no intention of abandoning him now, not after last night.

I found Alex some pens and paper and laid them out on the coffee table. She sat down on the bean bag and began drawing feverishly. I snuggled next to Daniel and hit 'play' again. It wasn't long though before Alex began to chatter to herself and, as the minutes ticked on, the chatter grew steadily more animated. I sighed. The video had been a dumb idea.

I turned the volume up loud, hoping the Taylors next door – both retired – were not having a nap.

Later that day, we were midway through a game of Lotto.

Alex, bubbling with excitement, turned over another upturned card from the pile on the carpet.

'Shoes!' she shrieked and began frantically scanning the four boards for the matching picture. A few seconds later, unable to locate it, she turned to me, perplexed.

'Take your time,' I urged her, 'it is there.'

She scanned the boards a second time, but couldn't find it.

'Look at the red board,' Daniel said with a conspiratorial look to me.

Her eyes lit up. 'Shoes!' she said triumphantly, before haphazardly slapping the card on the board, half concealing the butterfly picture next to it.

I squared it up. 'Well done!'

Daniel and I took our turns in equally animated style – Alex's enthusiasm, at least, was infectious.

Then it was Alex's turn again. She turned over a picture of a rainbow and stared at it, unable to name it.

'That's a rainbow,' I said, suddenly conscious that she'd probably never seen one before.

With our help, she located the matching picture. 'Rai'bow!' she said, placing the card on the board – upside down. Daniel righted it.

Shortly afterwards, Alex lost interest in the game. While Daniel and I finished it, Alex spun excitable circles on her toes, making herself pitch with dizziness until she fell over. We couldn't help but laugh.

'It's my turn to play snakes and ladders now,' Daniel said eagerly.

'Yeah!' I said, affecting an enthusiasm that I didn't feel.

My misgivings were confirmed five minutes into the game – it was proving too complex for Alex to play.

'Mum!' Daniel pleaded. Unable to sit still, Alex had accidentally knocked the board for the third time, sending our pieces flying out of position.

'OK! OK!' I said, waving my arms in surrender. 'Daniel, you and I can play this later.' I glanced at the mantel clock. It was only three-thirty – another two hours before Rob came home. We decided to run off Alex's energy at the playground instead.

A morning in early December and the phone started to ring.

Not now, I pleaded silently. 'Alex! Can you get your shoes and coat? Tess will be here any minute,' I called out and ran down the stairs to take the call.

Alex had been with us for three months, and it was Mary, ringing to confirm the date for our review meeting. She commented that I sounded harassed.

'Harassed but happy,' I replied.

As I replaced the receiver the doorbell rang. 'Alex!' I shouted cheerfully. But she was there already, opening the door to Tess, who scooped the child up into her arms. Alex giggled.

'Are we ready to go?' Tess asked, putting her down.

Alex nodded vigorously and Tess offered her an outstretched hand.

'Hang on a minute, Tess,' I said, noting Alex's attire. I took off her coat, and put it on the right way round. 'Are you sure you want to wear your wellies?' I asked. Her choice of shoes and clothing was often inappropriate. It had a certain cute appeal, but I was beginning to feel a little exasperated by it.

'Yes.'

I kept the roll of my eyes affectionate. She leant on me as I replaced the wellies on the correct feet. Then I reached into my handbag for the wet-wipes and wiped the crusty breakfast off her face.

'All beautiful!' I said, before grabbing the buggy and setting off for our walk into town.

'So! How are you feeling?' Tess asked, as soon as Alex had run ahead.

'Great. Happy. Fulfilled.' We both laughed. Reluctant to spoil the moment, I kept the exhausted bit to myself.

'She's one very special little girl.'

'I know,' I said.

Alex turned around and waved, not for the last time, I was sure. We waved back.

'Didn't I say it would work out?' my sister teased with a good-natured air of smugness.

'You did,' I agreed. And Alex waved again. And again. And again. And then, suddenly, 'It's a donkey!' she shrieked. My stomach clenched in what I silently had to admit was desperation: we passed this field four times a day and each time I reminded her that the animals were horses. I didn't know where to put this feeling.

'It's called a horse,' Tess laughed. I swallowed my irritation. And Alex waved again.

We stopped off at the playground and I was happy to let Tess take over. I found a corner bench, gave myself a stern ticking-off for my earlier lapse of tolerance, and then sat back to watch with pride as Tess and Alex laughed and played their way around each apparatus.

As we left the park, Alex's skipping and waving slowed down and grew sluggish. I offered her still relatively weak legs the buggy. Two minutes later, she'd fallen asleep.

While Alex slept, Tess and I ate jacket potatoes and Danish pastries in our favourite café, basking in the subject of my future daughter. Alex only woke up at the sound of our chairs being pushed back from the table as we rose to leave. Her eyes snapped open. We grinned at her and, beaming back, she hopped out of the buggy. However, she was still disorientated and stumbled over the leg of a chair, landing with a painful thud on her knees at Tess's feet and bursting into tears. I dashed around the table, but before I got to her, Tess had picked her up.

Instinctively, I held out my arms to take her but dropped them immediately. Alex was clinging to Tess, her face sobbing deep into her chest, which was why Tess didn't see Alex lift her head, fix me with a piercing stare and then nuzzle back into Tess's chest.

I stood rooted to the floor in humiliation and confusion while Tess continued to stroke Alex's back and make soothing sounds into her ear. The seconds ticked by painfully until I forced myself to think logically. She'd only been with us for a short while – how could I expect to be 'Mummy' so soon? Feeling marginally reassured, I knelt down and commenced a big show of kissing Alex's knees better, holding my smile even as Tess carried her out of the café.

Chapter Four

With an audible sigh of frustration, I put the dishcloth down for the third time. 'Alex, please, please can you go and play now, I've *got* to tidy the house.' For a moment she didn't move, then quietly turned and left the kitchen.

Almost Christmas, and all week I'd been attempting to tidy up what now looked like the fallout from a minor earthquake, for the review meeting. Alex, never more than two minutes from my side, had remained resolutely disinclined to follow any of my suggestions for amusing herself. I had just two hours to rescue the mess before 1) collecting Daniel from school, 2) brewing a delicious-smelling pot of percolated coffee, and 3) throwing on some decent clothes and brushing my hair.

I ran a cloth round the hob and sink and surveyed the kitchen. It would have to do. Then I resurrected the Hoover and moved to the lounge. I found Alex sitting on the sofa with a piece of skipping elastic and a long face. My resolve began to weaken. Then she looked up and threw me a frail smile and my resolve crumbled completely.

'All right then,' I relented with a smile, 'you can be my helper.' So what if the house was a mess? Alex's needs were paramount at the moment. Social Services would understand that.

For the next couple of hours, through a stream of happy chatter, Alex beavered away. She managed to vacuum one corner of our carpet to within an inch of its life, knock over a vase of dried flowers, and put a mouldy coffee cup in the bathroom sink instead of the kitchen sink. She also rearranged the throws on our sofa to leave three gaping holes and an ugly display of worn and torn red velour sofa beneath it. But it didn't matter.

'You've done a grand job,' I said, stroking her hair. She may not have been the most adept of helpers, but she was definitely the chirpiest and most willing.

At three o'clock, I looked around the house one last time. It was passable. Besides, a house that was too tidy always sent big alarm bells ringing, didn't it? I shrugged. After all these years, Rob and I still had no answer to the tidy/messy house issue.

Not only had Karen Whittle turned up for the review, but so had her boss, Simon Davies – an angular-faced man in his mid-fifties with a fair moustache, long clean fingernails and a cardigan. He sat with a straight back, holding a blue file, and was flanked on either side by the two social workers – Mary and Karen. He was here to oversee the meeting, he explained.

Like interviewees, we sat before them on the sofa, Alex tucked under my arm and Daniel under Rob's. Simon did most of the talking. He spoke softly and with an air of studied earnestness. The questions he asked were tactfully worded for the benefit of the children:

How are things? Chaotic I bet! We all laughed. *Not too tired I hope?* Another laugh. *Do you like your new home Alex?* Yes. *And how about your new cat? Scooter is he called? He's enormous.* We tittered. *And what are you going to ask for from Father Christmas?* Alex had forgotten. A new bicycle, Rob prompted her. *And you, Daniel, what would you like?* Daniel gave him a list.

And so the questions rolled on.

When the informal interrogation was over, my jaws ached with the effort of smiling. It was a relief to get onto more practical matters. Karen took down the details of Alex's pre-school for her file, and details of our doctor so they could forward on her medical records.

Alex was moving closer and closer to becoming ours.

The date for the next review meeting was agreed, and before the trio left, everyone congratulated themselves on the success of the placement. Mary, the social worker we'd grown to love over the past few years, had never had any doubt, she said. Then, after a hail of happy farewells, they were gone.

We'd passed the first phase with flying colours. We were one of the success stories.

*

Sophie stood on my doorstep, a bottle of wine in her hand and an excited flush on her face: in less than twenty-four hours she and Oliver would be on a plane to Thailand.

'You look tired, girl,' she said an hour later, when Daniel and Alex had finally gone to bed. 'Everything all right?'

'I'm still getting used to the early mornings.'

'Nothing else?'

'Nope!'

Sophie cocked an eyebrow, narrowing the other eye to a slit. 'Sure?'

'Sure!'

She still looked dubious. My enthusiasm had been unconvincing in our last two phone calls, and we could read each other like a book.

'What?' I protested too weakly and took a large gulp of the cold Chardonnay. 'Listen, stop worrying will you?'

Silence.

My shoulders slumped and I dropped my gaze, my conviction that everything was 'just fine' dribbling away. Everything wasn't just fine and I was being forced to admit that fact for the first time, even to myself. Though what was wrong – correction, *why* it was wrong – I didn't really know. The problem was with me, surely.

'I guess I underestimated the amount of my time Alex would need,' I began, 'and it's taking me a while to readjust. Not just to my routine, but mentally I suppose. Stupid, huh? They warned us it would be hard, but did I listen?'

Sophie smiled kindly.

'When we're alone during the day, all she wants is me. And I'm not exaggerating,' I stressed. 'She's not interested in her toys, she doesn't watch TV, and even when we're out and about she's at my side the whole time. I took her to the aquarium last week. It took us an hour to get there and less than twenty minutes to do the tour of the tanks. No interest at all, just a fleeting glance and then onto the next tank. It was the same at the farm and the steam fair, and even at the playground we go to.'

'Maybe she's overwhelmed by it all.'

'Maybe, though you wouldn't know it to see her. I've never seen so much energy. She's as chirpy as they come.'

'I'll second that. Does she always make so much noise?' she asked, referring to Alex's earlier constant chatter, interspersed with frequent bouts of loud hilarity as she chased Daniel around the house in a one-sided game of kiss-chase.

'Yes. But at least we know she's happy. Every time I feel like hiding out in the garage, I remind myself of the sort of child we could have ended up with.'

For a moment we wordlessly contemplated my life with a withdrawn or aggressive child.

'How's it going with her learning?' Sophie ventured, 'making any progress?'

I winced inwardly. If I were honest, it wasn't the amount of attention Alex needed that was fraying my edges; it was her seeming inability to learn anything at all. I knew as I sat there, ashamed of this admission, that this was not an understatement. All the reading and preparation in the world could not have prepared me for Alex's learning difficulties. She was incapable of retaining anything she'd been told. She needed help with everything, from dressing herself to choosing her breakfast to switching on the TV, or understanding what day of the week it was and remembering the names of her extended family. Her difficulties spanned every corner of her development. The hours upon hours I'd invested, since her keen desire to learn was achingly apparent, had so far yielded little, if any, progress.

'Not yet,' was all I could say.

Silence hung in the air for a moment.

'Give her time,' Sophie said eventually, repeating what she'd said a month ago.

Later, when it was time for Sophie to go, I tried to stand up. I glanced at the wine bottle which stood empty.

'God, are you going to be all right to drive?' I exclaimed.

'I've only had one glass.'

'Whoa!' I said, trying to steady myself, 'why didn't you stop me?'

'You looked like you needed it.' Her smile was kind.

And I had needed it, I thought, falling into bed. It had been good to offload. Well, almost offload – there was one small, grey, prickly thing I'd not been able to share with Sophie. Something I found hard to address even to myself. An image of Alex's impassive, unnerving stare fixed on my face swam into my brain; so at odds with her excitable and animated little self. I pushed the image away but it swam back. It was a while before I fell asleep.

Christmas Eve, and the children were tucked up in bed.

I passed Rob on the stairs. 'Is she excited?' I mouthed. He nodded and I carried on up the stairs and into Alex's room.

'I want no peeking if you're awake when Father Christmas comes down the chimney,' I joked.

She locked her eyes onto mine and giggled. I perched on the side of her bed. 'What do you think he might bring you?'

It took a while for her to remember. 'Um . . . a bicycle,' she said grinning.

'Only if you've been good, though!' I teased. Then I reined in my enthusiasm. Alex's smile was looking overcooked, and I felt a stab of self-reproach – so far we'd given no consideration to the array of mixed-up emotions she might be feeling at a time like this.

'Shall we ring Patty and Kenny tomorrow and wish them Happy Christmas?' I suggested.

Something flitted across her smile as she nodded. I began gently stroking her forehead as we gazed into each other's eyes. The silence of the room felt suddenly very tranquil, but then the gaze lingered too long and I bent down to kiss her. ''Night my love,' I said, and she curled her arms tightly round my neck. I waited a few seconds and then gently prised her arms away.

'Happy Night-Before-Christmas.' I smiled and switched off her light.

'Happy Christmas!' Rob and I called out, as we stumbled bleary-eyed into the sitting room.

Alex's new Polly Pocket lay, unwrapped but still in its box, next to her unopened art box. Her new bicycle stood proudly by the fireplace. She was hanging over the sofa chatting excitedly to Daniel.

'Look what I got!' Daniel enthused, springing up from the floor and gliding over to us on his new roller-blades. Then he gestured eagerly at his invisible ink pen and a box of magic tricks, the contents of which lay strewn across the carpet.

We made some enthusiastic noises back. 'And what about you?' Rob asked Alex.

With a big smile, she pointed at the contents of her three presents.

'Wow! Do you like your new bike?'

She nodded eagerly. Rob said no more – we'd agreed last night not to make too big a fuss of things. After Scooter had torn open his new pouch of catnip, we made for the tree, with a mountain of presents beneath it. The children were squealing with anticipation.

'Can I go first?' Daniel asked.

I deliberated a moment and then suggested we all open a parcel at the same time, after which we'd take it in turns.

However, it quickly became apparent that Alex either couldn't grasp the concept or her patience didn't stretch that far.

'I open this one!' she cried.

It was the fourth time she'd interrupted Daniel's turn and I could feel my sadness and frustration growing.

I picked up the box of Operation she'd just unwrapped and handed it to her, suggesting that she have a look at it until it was her turn again. From the corner of my eye, I watched her pull out the game's contents and give them the briefest of glances before sliding them back in the box. I stretched my neck and ordered myself to stay calm. But then, with a flick of her eyes at Daniel, Alex picked up a CD case lying next to her and began clicking it open and closed. Realisation dawned.

'That's enough!' I said sharply.

There was a stunned silence. Alex's smile gave way to an expression of abject fright, her eyes paralysed to mine. Rob and Daniel looked both alarmed and bemused. It took me a moment to know what to do next.

In the end I patted my knee, gesturing Alex to sit on it which she did, her mouth twitching and on the edge of tears.

'It's OK Alex. I'm not angry, but interrupting and making those noises wasn't fair to Daniel,' I said. 'Just like it wouldn't be fair if Daniel kept interrupting your turn. Yeah?'

Like a frightened rabbit caught in the glare of headlights, she nodded. I resolved to explain her feelings to her as soon as possible, but not now. Today was Christmas and Alex had not been acting maliciously.

'Listen: how about, just for this year, we forget about taking turns? We can all look at each other's presents afterwards.'

'Good idea,' Rob agreed.

There was a flicker of disappointment on Daniel's face but it didn't linger long. There was still a stack of presents lying tantalisingly unopened.

Alex's recovery was also quick and her screech of excitement the loudest when we all dived in, but I barely registered my own gifts as I unwrapped them. My mind was too busy slotting things into place. Alex wasn't a 'perfect child' after all and her exhausting and constant presence by my side suddenly made more sense. It seemed that she was no more immune to a bit of jealousy and attention-seeking than the rest of us. The relief I felt was huge.

With the last present opened, the floor was a sea of wrapping paper, boxes and gifts. Rob began scrunching the sheets of paper into small balls and putting them in a bin-liner. However, Alex, restored to her high-spirited self, had other ideas and began throwing them at Daniel. Daniel responded, and soon the two of them were tearing round the house firing paper missiles at each other. When, a few hours later, we were all dancing round the room to Slade's 'Merry Christmas', I was one very happy lady. Added to which, Dad was cooking Christmas lunch this year, which meant lots of people for Alex. I could put my feet up and do some quiet thinking.

A week later, while all around us people were singing 'Auld Lang Syne', Rob and I stood together looking intently into each other's exhausted but contented eyes.

My husband raised his glass: 'Here's to a new year and to a new life.'

As I drank to the toast, I felt all warm and gooey inside.

Chapter Five

'Alex, sit down a minute, there's something important we want to say to you.'

Alex perched herself on the sofa between Rob and me.

'First of all, we want you to know how much we love you,' I began. She twitched me a smile. 'And how lucky we feel to be your new mum and dad. Super lucky.'

Her smile became coy.

'And when you love someone that much, it's impossible to forget them,' I continued. 'No matter how busy or how tired we are, we'll always love you.'

Rob took over. 'We might be watching the TV, reading a book, or talking on the phone,' he said, 'and still you won't be forgotten. You'll be here, in our heads,' he said, tapping a finger at the side of his temple. Alex twitched her mouth self-consciously.

'I want you to know something else,' I said. 'Just because Daniel came from my tummy, doesn't mean we love him more than we love you. We wanted to adopt you just as much as we wanted Daniel, I can promise you that,' I stated honestly. 'Mums and dads love their children equally. It doesn't matter that one of their children might be better at drawing or that the other might be better at dancing. Everyone is good at different things.'

She nodded and I elucidated by comparing my strengths and weaknesses with those of Tess, Matt and Tim, and vice versa. 'No one can be good at everything,' I went on. 'You're the bravest little girl I know. You're funny and loving, and we love you for that. You're special, just like Daniel's special, and that will never change.'

I rubbed her knee reassuringly and she looked to have grasped my words. That she might not yet believe them was understandable. That would come in time.

I initiated a final hug, before having to prise her tiny arms from my neck.

A week had passed since Rob and I had attempted our reassuring heart-to-heart with Alex. Now, as I buried myself in the colossal backlog of paperwork I was trying to do, Alex was fiddling with a picture that hung on the kitchen wall.

'Alex, leave the picture frame alone or you'll knock it off the wall,' I said, wearily. 'Now, off you go.'

She fixed her eyes on me, lingered for an uneasy moment, and then walked softly from the kitchen. I picked up a letter from the pile and began reading, but halfway down the page I realised I hadn't absorbed a word of it. I put it down and stared despondently out at the garden. I couldn't go on like this. I simply couldn't keep entertaining her from the moment she came home from pre-school until Rob came home from work. There was Daniel to look after, dinner to cook and a house to run. The memory of Pat Radford asking me whether or not I'd be working came to mind. How I'd underestimated the significance of her words! And how little effect our affirmations of love and acceptance were having on Alex. Her pursuit of attention was so relentless that part of me wanted to scream. My more rational side knew she needed more time, but if only she knew how to amuse herself occasionally!

Suddenly an almighty crash sounded and I rushed into the sitting room. On the floor lay the shattered remains of a glass vase and its now scattered contents of dried flowers. A skipping rope hung guiltily across the armchair a few feet from the mess, and Alex stood rooted to the spot wearing a look of abject terror.

Were it not for her fright, I would have ordered her upstairs for an hour, at least. God knows, I could have done with the peace. However, I dismissed the idea as, judging from her expression, it had been an accident.

I picked up the skipping rope, looked her sternly in the eye and said, 'I've told you several times not to play with that inside. If I see it inside again, we'll take it away until you're old enough to play with it properly. Do you understand?'

She nodded, mortified.

'Now, will you go and find something else to do,' I pleaded, as I opened the patio doors and put the rope back into the garden.

She hadn't moved when I turned back round. 'Alex!' I snapped, dangerously close to exploding. She jumped, but before she could scurry out, I had her by the hand and was leading her upstairs to her bedroom.

Once there, I began opening the cupboard doors. 'Here are your puzzles; these are your games; here are your books, and here is all your colouring stuff. These,' I said, lifting the lid of her toy-box, 'are all your toys – most of which you've never played with. Now what do you want to bring downstairs?' I asked.

'Er . . . the Barbie,' she said, her eyes still anchored timidly to mine. I leant into one of the cupboards and pulled out the pink plastic Barbie box. She followed me dutifully downstairs and back into the sitting room.

'Here you go,' I said, plonking the box on the floor. 'We've got an hour before we have to collect Daniel, so please don't interrupt me any more.'

Twenty minutes later, intrigued by the unexpected silence, I re-entered the room. Alex was fast asleep on the couch, her Barbie stuff untouched.

I crawled into bed, limb by limb. I felt pale and sapped. Somewhere at the edge of my senses I could hear Rob chattering about some exciting refurbishments to the football team's club house.

'Do you know?' I cut in zombie-like, 'Alex only leaves my side to use the bathroom.'

It was spoken as a revelation. And Rob didn't know what to say.

However, the next day, Rob took the afternoon off work, met Alex from nursery and the two of them went to the park.

January rain was bucketing down and Rob's Sunday-league football match had been cancelled, along with thoughts of any other outdoor pursuits. While Rob lit the fire, I switched on the lights and drew the curtains. 'Who wants to listen to records?' I asked cheerily.

Daniel peered grudgingly over the top of his Game Boy.

'I'll do my robot dance for you,' Rob teased.

Daniel grunted, unimpressed, and returned to the game.

'What about you Alex?' I asked.

'Yeah!'

I ran upstairs, retrieved our box of old singles from under the study table and lugged it downstairs.

'Bags go first,' I said, picking out a Bananarama single. I placed it on our ancient turntable, balanced a two-pence piece on top of the needle, and pressed play. I began to dance.

Suddenly Alex, who until now had been knee-jumping on the bean bags, sprung to her feet and began gyrating her own hips. She was good. Really good.

I stopped dancing, causing a moment of self-consciousness to cross Alex's face. Rob looked up and we began to clap her on. Puffing up her shoulders, she resumed dancing.

During the second chorus, she picked up a canister of air-freshener and, holding it like a microphone, began mouthing into it. We laughed. Her rhythmic gyrations grew ever more animated. By the third chorus, she was strutting up and down the length of our sitting room, one hand on her hip and the other round the canister, looking adorably theatrical. My mouth didn't know whether to hang open in awe or to laugh. As the song came to an end, Rob and I gave her a rousing round of applause and she took a bow. She was now laughing too and my heart swelled: I loved the way she could laugh at her own antics.

'That was fantastic!' I said. 'Where did you learn to dance like that?'

'Dunno,' she said, shrugging.

'And those sexy hips, well, I don't know if we should allow it!' I joked, and began chasing her around the room.

A little while later, Alex lay curled in my arms as we listened to one of Rob's Simple Minds tracks. 'You ought to be on TV,' I said to her. 'You could make lots of people laugh then.'

'Yeah, I'll be funny,' she stated drily.

'Maybe you should start singing and dancing lessons.'

'Yeah.'

I squeezed her tighter. 'I love you.'

'I love you,' she replied, burrowing deeper into my chest.

A week later, while watching television with Alex, I reached down beside the sofa, grabbed a tissue and sneezed loudly into it, which made her laugh. Through bloodshot eyes and with a bunged-up nose, I glared at her with mock affront. 'Not funny!' I said. She giggled even louder and I gave her an affectionate squeeze. It was nice to snuggle up and escape another game of ghosts.

I turned my attention back to the TV and a programme we'd not watched before – *Letterland* – known to any mother of recent times as a story peopled by characters representing letters of the alphabet. A moment of drama was unfolding on the screen. Robber Red was trying to steal Kicking King's crown. Jumping Jim and Oscar Orange looked like they might save the day. I snatched a furtive glance at Alex whose eyes were glued to the screen. My interest was piqued and I pondered the moment. In the five months Alex had been with us, we'd not, until now, discovered anything on TV capable of holding her attention for more than a couple of minutes. Either she'd resigned herself to the fact that I really was too ill to play, or she was actually enjoying the programme.

When I glanced at her a little while later, she was mouthing the names of the *Letterland* characters. A small thread of excitement fluttered through me and I averted my gaze quickly so as not to distract her.

The following day, still streaming with a cold, I walked into WH Smith and bought a *Letterland* jigsaw.

'What now, Mummy?' Alex asked eagerly. She was kneeling on the floor, her eyes darting across the remaining jigsaw pieces scattered on the carpet.

'Now let me think,' I said, adopting a look of serious contemplation, 'which piece comes after Robber Red? I think it might be Ssss . . .'

'S for Sammy 'Nake!' (She still couldn't pronounce her 'S's.) She dived onto the relevant piece, slotting it perfectly into the jigsaw. 'It fits!' she shrieked again, her face flushed with effort and delight.

'High-five!' we shouted in unison, and slapped each other's palms in triumph.

'What piece now?' she asked.

'Hmm . . . that must be t – t – t—'

'Ticking Tess!'

She found the piece and slotted it in.

'High-five!'

A few minutes later she'd completed the jigsaw for a third time and I was ecstatic. In five months she'd not managed to learn one nursery rhyme, yet today, in just over an hour, she'd learnt all the sounds and shapes of the alphabet.

I was still grinning when Rob came home later that evening.

'You're looking mighty pleased with yourself,' he said.

'Mighty pleased with Alex, actually,' I said, and filled him in on the afternoon's jigsaw game.

'That's brilliant.' Rob's tone was heartfelt.

'I know. It took Daniel longer to learn his alphabet.'

'Maybe this will give her the confidence she needs.'

'I hope so because I don't think she even knew she had it in her. You should have seen how pleased she was with herself.'

'Good for her,' Rob leant across and planted a kiss on my cheek, 'and good for you, too.'

I couldn't wait to tell everyone.

January gave way to February and my optimism proved short-lived. A week later we were back on the carpet playing a different game: one that I'd devised as a diversion from the *Letterland* game, which she could now do with her eyes shut.

Unfortunately, this game wasn't proving quite so successful and I was beginning to regret ever contemplating it. I could feel the now all too familiar exasperation ballooning inside my temples. How hard was it to learn the colours red and blue?

Alex lifted a plastic beaker to reveal a red Smartie and then a second to reveal a blue Smartie. Sporting an encouraging smile, masking my growing desperation, I met her gaze. She was sitting cross-legged on the floor, frowning at the two Smarties.

'So which is the blue one?' I asked.

'Um . . . Um . . .' She reached out gingerly and pointed at the red one, 'Is blue.'

I felt my shoulders slump and I closed my eyes against her cowering stare. When I opened them, aside from a nervous flutter, her eyes hadn't moved from my face.

'No, Alex, it's red,' I corrected her evenly. I picked up the Smartie. 'Red, red, red — like Robber Red,' I repeated, pointing to the lone jigsaw piece that lay on the coffee table. 'Remember?'

She nodded.

I picked up Robber Red. 'Red,' I said, holding it in front of her with one hand, 'and blue.' I picked up the blue building block and flashed that in front of her. 'Robber *Red, blue* block.' I repeated the action. 'Robber *Red, blue* block. Red, blue, red, blue . . .'

I watched her trying intently to log the two colours. As always, I was hopeful she'd get it next time. After all, we were only playing with two colours, having long ago removed the green and yellow Smarties from the game.

'Come on Alex,' I urged her, 'let's see if you can get a Smartie in your bowl.' I gestured at the empty plate beside her, still awaiting a correctly guessed Smartie. Then I concealed the two Smarties under their respective bowls. 'OK, let's see if you can find the blue Smartie.'

She was attempting to dislodge a frayed piece of carpet.

'Alex, please concentrate,' I implored, my tone weary. She stopped instantly, then lifted the first of the bowls. Underneath, in all its glory, lay a blue Smartie. She alternated her look of concentration and timid uncertainty between my face and the Smartie. I held my breath.

Nothing.

'What colour is it?' I asked, a stiff smile of encouragement pinned to my face.

'Mmmm . . . er . . .'

'Yes?' I willed her.

'Um, is it, um . . .' Her eyes were now locked onto mine.

'Look at it,' I implored.

She did. 'Um, is red?' she eventually whispered.

The balloon that had been slowly swelling inside my head over the past few months finally popped. Rolling forward onto my knees,

I dropped my forehead onto the carpet. When I sat back up, my eyes were tear-filled. I grabbed the wretched Smartie, and thrust it in front of her eyes. She flinched in terror.

'Red, did you say? Red? What, like the red blue block? Or like the blue Robber Red! God!' I cursed, slapping my forehead. 'What is it you can't learn?' Then I dropped my head back onto the carpet.

She'd not moved a hair on her body, and as the silence began to fill every last corner of the room so I began to flood with guilt and self-loathing. In one short minute, I'd managed to violate every rule in the adoption and special needs handbook. Me. The one with all the patience and understanding in the world. The one who would accept her learning difficulties when others wouldn't, who understood how important the formative years were for a child's ability to learn and develop, and who would never ask anything of Alex until she was ready, until she was emotionally more secure. I looked up in shame. Her eyes were a well of tears poised to fall.

'I'm really, really sorry, I should never have got angry. I know how hard you find learning. I should never, ever have shouted like that. I'm so sorry.'

A single tear spilled onto her cheek and ran down her face. I shoved the game aside and pulled her onto my knee. 'I promise we won't do any more learning until you're ready, OK?' She flung her arms round my neck and began to sob. It was the first time I'd heard her cry and the sound tore at every guilty bone in my body. I rocked her gently until at last the tears abated.

'Can we play ghosts?' she asked, wiping her cheek. A long string of mucus hung precariously from her nose, to which she seemed oblivious.

'I'd love to,' I replied, grabbing a tissue.

I prised open an eye to a dark room, yearning for the day when I could start at a more civilised hour. I rolled gently over to see the time. Alex knew that unless someone was ill or sad, no one would be getting up before six a.m. It was five forty-seven. Before burrowing down for another thirteen precious minutes of oblivion, I sneaked a quick glance across the landing and into her bedroom. I frowned and my heart did a double beat. Instead of seeing Alex prone in her bed with her light on waiting for a new day to start, she was sitting upright, cross-legged, her arms folded across her chest, staring straight into my face.

'Oh, hello,' I whispered, throwing her a limp wave.

She uncurled an arm and fluttered it at me.

I lifted myself up onto an elbow.

'Are you all right?' I whispered.

She nodded.

'Do you want to come into our bed?'

She nodded again.

'Come on then.' I smiled, beckoning her over.

A grin spread across her face and relief washed over me. She scrambled off her bed, skipped across the landing and climbed under the duvet.

'Did you sleep well?' I asked.

'Mmm,' she muttered, and draped her arms around my neck. Clinging tightly, her body began to twitch with eager affection.

'Aaghh,' I said, feigning a choking fit. She giggled, and when I tickled her tummy she relaxed her grip. I flexed my neck into a more comfortable position.

'Mmm, that's nice,' I said, snuggling down. Alex had clearly been unsettled by my outburst the day before and was looking for reassurance.

Chapter Six

I cupped my eyes and peered through the window of the pre-school. Alex stood in the centre of a farewell ceremonial circle, looking as animated as ever. I smiled. She faced each of the children in turn, and with exaggerated pomp, presented them with a lollipop. The children were giggling.

When it was over and the pre-school was being dismantled for the Easter holidays, Mrs Graves, a rotund lady in her early sixties, found her way to the back of the hall where Alex and I were waiting. Under one arm, she carried a small cardboard box, her other was outstretched in greeting.

'Mrs Allen, thank you so much for waiting,' she boomed. She'd run the pre-school for over thirty years.

I returned her smile, though I'd always suffered with an overwhelming sense of deference when faced with anyone in authority – it didn't matter whether it was a policeman, a teacher or a midwife.

We sat down, then Mrs Graves, resting the box on her lap, turned to Alex. 'Why don't you go and see if Stephanie needs a hand putting the dressing-up clothes away,' she said.

Alex sidled closer to me, but I nudged her gently away. 'Go on, love,' I said.

When Alex didn't move, Mrs Graves flashed her one of her stern looks. She moved instantly, but in the opposite direction.

'No, not to Mrs Squires, to Stephanie,' Mrs Graves corrected her. Alex looked momentarily bemused. 'Over there, where the dressing-up box is.' She pointed in the right direction and Alex, finally understanding, skipped across the sun-filled hall to the young assistant.

Mrs Graves puffed a sigh of relief and we both laughed. 'We've been very pleased with her, you know,' she announced, 'she's been a delight. She's happy and friendly and, unlike some of the little mites we have here, very well-behaved.'

I beamed. 'That's great. Thank you.'

'Don't thank us. It's a credit to you that she's settled so quickly.'

I brushed the compliment away. Although proud, I was not entirely convinced we deserved it.

'Do you think she's ready for school?' I ventured.

Mrs Graves paused. 'As ready as she can be,' she said. 'Of course she's still got a long way to go before she catches up, but with the right support, I'm sure she'll be fine. She's counting to ten quite happily now and she knows her letters. I would suggest, though, that you get the Statement* process started as soon as possible. She will need extra help in the classroom for a while at least.'

I was pleased to hear that. Rob and I had been wondering how the school would cope with Alex's learning difficulties.

'Does she occupy herself?' I asked. I was intrigued to know whether or not it was just us she shadowed.

Mrs Graves reacted as though she thought it a strange question, but she nonetheless shook her head. 'No, she still needs an adult with her, but I'm sure she'll start working independently fairly soon,' she said. 'I've always believed that confidence gives us our wings. Alex is no exception. She obviously just needs a little more time than the rest of us.'

I nodded my agreement: Rob and I had been telling ourselves the same thing.

'Anyway,' she continued heartily, 'all the while she's producing such *wonderful* work . . .' Grinning, she handed me the box.

I flicked through the piles of paint-encrusted papers, trying not to dislodge any of the pasta pieces, beads, cotton wool, milk tops and general odds and ends that adorned the eclectic array of papers. The sight delighted me. I couldn't wait to pin them onto our walls for the world to see. Before I could comment, we were distracted by a

---

* A Statement of Special Educational Needs is a document compiled by the Local Education Authority (LEA) setting out the child's needs and any special help they require which cannot otherwise be met by the school's own resources, e.g., a set amount of hours a week of one-to-one assistance paid for by the LEA. The statement is reviewed and adjusted, as necessary, once a year.

noisy bout of giggling that started up near the stage. Alex was evidently trying to don the costumes as quickly as Stephanie was attempting to put them away. Strangely irritated by the sight, I glanced at Mrs Graves for some kind of validation, but she was watching the unfolding scene with an air of gentle amusement.

I turned away quickly. I didn't want her reading my uncharitable thoughts and instantly felt ashamed. I adjusted my expression to match hers then Alex, dressed as a hula girl and wearing a long blonde wig, began gyrating around the stage. I silently conceded that, as at home, it was very amusing and, ignoring the noise and excitement, I asked how Alex was getting on with the other children at the pre-school, none of whom she'd ever mentioned. Although she occasionally played with the children in our street, her learning difficulties hindered their games and they often tired of her hyper-exuberance. More and more now, they tended to leave her alone.

'She prefers the company of adults,' Mrs Graves admitted, 'but with encouragement, she will play with the others. In fact, we've been surprised by how well she can interact with her peers. Socially, I don't think she's got any problems,' she concluded, her tone packed with understatement.

The discussion drew to an end and I thanked her for everything she'd done for Alex.

'It's been our pleasure,' she said.

We shook hands warmly before I said my goodbyes to the other assistants. There was a lump in my throat, but I was confident we'd soon be enrolling the second of our adopted children – Rob and I were already making plans.

I watched as, unprompted, Alex embraced each of her teachers before saying goodbye. It was clear from the length of time they held on to her, and from their muttered sighs, that Alex had made a big impression on all of them.

They were still waving at the window as we turned the corner. Hand in hand, Alex and I babbled all the way home.

As I tucked Alex into bed that evening, I asked her if she'd decided yet on her 'treat'. It had been a long tradition that Daniel could choose a treat for having done well at school. She looked up at me, her expression working overtime as she considered her choice. I waited. And waited . . .

'I can't think,' she chuckled eventually, so I suggested a trip to the zoo.

'Yeah!' she shrieked.

'That's sorted then,' I said, bending down to kiss her. 'And well done again – I'm proud of you.'

Alex smiled.

'Please can I go outside and play now?' Daniel implored.

I put the shopping list to one side and glanced at my watch.

'Daniel, you have been playing with Alex for precisely eighteen minutes,' I said, my tone clipped and exasperated.

'But she won't play properly.'

'Well, find something that she *can* do. I've been with her all morning. I need to get on.'

I picked up the list.

'But I want to play "it" with the others outside.'

'Then take Alex with you,' I said, my mind trying to focus on whether or not to add eggs to the list.

'They don't like it when she has to join in.'

'Play your own game then.' The irritation was creeping back into my voice as I struggled to concentrate on the groceries.

'But,' he huffed, 'she can't play "it" properly.'

'Well, have you taught her?' I asked absently.

'Mu-u-m . . .' he beseeched, as much as to say of course I have. '*Please* can't I play with the others?'

I snapped. 'No, you cannot!' I slammed the list onto the kitchen table and glared at him. 'I want you to stop being so selfish and go and play with Alex. It's not her fault she finds things difficult. You should know that by now. If the others won't play with her, that's their problem, but you, Daniel – I expect you to be more patient. It's not often I ask you. Now off you go,' I said, gesturing angrily at the door. 'I don't want to see either of you for the next hour.'

With a final huff, he slunk miserably out of the kitchen.

'Jesus!' I hissed to myself, 'one hour was all I asked!'

*

Later that evening, as I settled down to the latest Martina Cole, I first re-read the poem inscribed on my laminated bookmark.

HEAVEN'S VERY SPECIAL CHILD

A meeting was held quite far from earth
'It's time again for another birth,'
Said the angels to the Lord above
This special child will need much love.
Her progress may be very slow.
Accomplishments she may not show
And she'll require extra care
From the folks she meets down there.
She may not run, or laugh or play.
Her thoughts may seem quite far away.
In many ways she won't adapt
And she'll be known as handicapped.
So let's be careful where she's sent,
We want her life to be content.
Please LORD, find the person who
Will do this special job for you.
They may not realise straight away
The learning role they're asked to play,
But with this child sent from above
Comes stronger faith and richer love,
And soon they'll know the privilege given
Their precious child so meek and mild
Is HEAVEN'S VERY SPECIAL CHILD.

© Edna Massionilla (1981)

I tucked the bookmark back in its place, dropped the book onto the floor, and stared hard at the ceiling. Why could I not relate to the poem?

'What do we all want?' Rob asked, peering up at the menu boards as we queued in McDonald's.

'Cheeseburger Happy Meal,' Daniel said.

'I'll have a quarter-pounder with cheese,' I said.

I deliberately didn't look at Alex, who was taking her time choosing. Today was her treat and I'd vowed to be patient with her, for all our sakes.

'Mmmm . . . Chicken Noggets,' she said.

My vow broken, I snapped. 'What are they called again?' I asked stiffly, unable to stop myself and knowing I'd regret it.

Her brow creased in an effort to remember, her eyes fixed on mine. 'Chicken noggets,' she said in a tiny voice.

'Chicken *noggets?*'

She nodded; Rob and Daniel braced themselves.

'Alex, how many more times do we need to tell you they're called Chicken Nuggets?' I asked, my head pounding. 'NUGgets. Ug! Ug! Ug! Can you say it for me?'

Silence. Her eyes wide on mine. More silence and then . . . 'Nurgits,' she said.

'Thank you.' It would have to do.

I asked Rob to take the children to find a table, then I joined the longest queue I could find and tried to re-compose myself. My stomach was churning with competing emotions. Noggets, Nuggets, so what? But I was angry and disappointed. Why did she always have to get it wrong? I'd invested my time, a hundred times over, trying to help her say it correctly – wasn't that what I was supposed to do?

As I tried to make sense of Alex's learning difficulties, a thought, a seedling of doubt, crossed my mind. *Maybe she's faking it?* I shook my head to banish the thought – it was ludicrous but I couldn't get rid of it – and her ineptitude certainly secured her the attention she craved. But then an image of her timid bemusement came to mind and I reconsidered. No. It was genuine. No child could pull off that level of acting. So, what *was* it?

I had another thought: maybe there was a 'learning switch' that had to be triggered within the first three years, after which it would be too late. I tried to recall anything I'd read suggesting such a thing but, as always, I came to the same conclusion: Alex's mind was still too unsettled to absorb and retain information. As long as she was happy, she'd eventually calm down. Feeling marginally better, I collected the food, found my family and sat down.

'So! Are we all excited about the zoo?' I asked, attempting to steer the day back on course.

The table erupted into a relief of excited chatter. Alex wanted to see the 'cocodiles', she told us, and launched into a bumbling discourse about nothing in particular.

'Sounds lovely, Alex,' Rob interjected five minutes later. 'Now eat up before your food gets cold.'

Alex picked up a fry and bit off the end. I swallowed my annoyance. Then I felt a leg brush against mine and Daniel chuckled.

'Alex, your food,' I reminded her after an interval.

Alex and Daniel exchanged furtive sniggers. When Rob and Daniel had finished their food, they busied themselves with the plastic toy my son had received with his meal.

I reached across the table for my apple pie. Alex was staring at me.

'What is it?' I asked her tersely.

Her gaze dropped instantly. She knew how much I disliked her staring; I'd hinted at it enough times. Although there was nothing sinister in her stare – in fact, I believed it was nothing more than a habit she'd picked up from her birth mother – I nevertheless longed for it to stop. It bored a hole through me every time.

Alex picked up another fry and, keeping her head bowed, bit off a piece. I bit my tongue until I could bite it no longer.

'Just because I asked you not to stare, doesn't mean that you need to keep your head down, and please, for God's sake, eat up.'

Her head shot up obediently and she stared stiffly to one side as though she had a cricked neck. I couldn't win.

'Mel, why don't you and Daniel go to the playground and have a wander around the shops,' Rob suggested tactfully. 'I'll finish up with Alex and we'll meet you back at the car.'

'Thanks,' I said bleakly, and Daniel and I walked silently out of the restaurant.

'Are you all right, Mum?' he asked.

'Yeah.'

I spent the rest of the day purposefully distanced from Alex and deep in thought.

I motioned Rob to follow me out of the kitchen where I'd insisted Alex do some drawing at the table.

We walked to the farthest corner of the sitting room. 'Please don't go back to work tomorrow,' I whispered, giving him an imploring look.

He gave me a sad smile. 'Listen, it's only three days and then it's the weekend, and then Alex starts school.'

'I know, but three days? That's an eternity at the moment.'

We stared silently out of the window.

'Maybe you just need a break. You're with her constantly and I know how exhausting that must be.'

'I'm not tired,' I insisted, 'at least, not in that sense.' I wanted to swipe the expression of sympathy from Rob's face. He didn't understand.

'I know she might have some brain damage,' I continued, 'and I know she missed out in her early years. What do you think I keep telling myself every time I have to look into her frightened little eyes? I also know she needs a ton of attention but, well, it's more than that. She – she's—'

I couldn't get myself to use the word 'insatiable', nor could I admit that I was beginning to dread each day; that I was feeling choked to the end of my patience every minute of every day, because Alex was everywhere I turned: needing, talking, giggling, touching me, flitting – or staring. I couldn't tell Rob that she was like an entity that required constant feeding but never seemed to grow; that my whole life had been turned on its head by a situation I could never have foreseen; that I would have sold my soul to see Alex throw a tantrum, to retreat into a sulk, to be *normal*.

So, instead, I told Rob I was being silly and that it was only a matter of time.

'Why don't you ask Tess if she could have the children for a couple of days? She's always offering.'

'I might do,' I said, knowing that such a luxury came with a price – another bucketful of her gushing over Alex. Nevertheless, it was a small price to pay for a couple of days in my own space, and I resolved to ring her first thing in the morning.

'Alex knows we're talking about her,' I said, as we moved away from the window a little while later.

'She can't hear us.'

'You wanna bet? That child doesn't miss a thing. If I hadn't insisted on five minutes alone, she'd be flitting behind the door right now.'

'Now you're getting paranoid!'

But when we sauntered back into the kitchen, Alex's sheet of paper was blank, save for one solitary and misshapen circle she'd drawn on it.

Rob poured us both a large gin.

Chapter Seven

*I*t was Alex's first day at Hollybrook School and already we were running late.

'OK Alex, quickly now,' I called up the stairs, 'I want to take this photo.'

My words had barely escaped my mouth, when I heard Alex begin her thunderous descent. With lightning speed she arrived at her destination – the fireplace, backdrop to all our posed photos. A deafening silence then followed as she waited patiently for me to do the job.

I rummaged feverishly through the top drawer of our bureau for the camera. 'OK, let's see a big smile,' I said, spinning round to face her. My smile collapsed.

'I thought Daddy had dressed you,' I yelped.

'He did,' Alex whispered, her proud pose having given way to timidity. One sock was stretched above her knee, the other bunched around her ankle. Her shoes were on the wrong feet and a thick rim of white toothpaste adorned her mouth. But, most bizarrely, she looked as if she'd stuffed an inflatable ring inside her skirt. I knelt down and pulled her stiff, new, oversized red school jumper from under the waistband of her grey skirt.

'So *why* are your shoes on the wrong feet?'

'They were too tight.'

With a sigh, I ripped open the Velcro and yanked off her shoes. 'Next time they're too tight, just tell Dad, OK?' I implored.

She nodded, willing and compliant.

'And please, please, *please* remember to wipe the toothpaste off from round your mouth – that's why we put the wet wipes there.'

She nodded again, her eyes firmly fixed on mine.

I sighed silently at this second nod of consent. How I was beginning to despair at her look of timid compliance. Its intensity was unnerving and it never bore any results. How I would have rejoiced at a display of petulance, I thought, aware of the irony of my wish.

I pulled up the loose sock, smoothed down her now orderly uniform, and watched as she again took up her pose by the hearth. Feeling flat, I took a couple of snaps. It was small consolation that I knew Alex would look adorable in the prints.

'Go and wait for me by the door,' I said, the pictures done with, and called to Daniel that we were leaving in two minutes. Gathering together the last bits and pieces, I felt a sudden urge to cry. Why did every eagerly anticipated moment with Alex turn sour? Gripping her new lunch box, I swallowed the lump in my throat. If we didn't leave soon, we really *were* going to be late.

As usual, Alex skipped ahead for most of the walk, peering backwards every thirty seconds with a cheery wave. If she was feeling nervous, she didn't show it.

'You'll look after her, won't you?' I said to Daniel. 'At least until she settles in.'

'Mum,' he implored, exasperated. It was the fourth time I'd asked him.

I smiled down at him apologetically. 'Thank you.'

As we reached the school, Daniel gave me a hurried kiss before propelling himself through the gates to join his friends.

'Daniel?' I yelled after him.

'I won't forget,' he called back, and then he was gone.

As Alex and I walked through the school gates, we were greeted with encouragement and smiles from the other mums. During the previous seven months of Daniel's school runs, she'd managed to amass a large collection of adoring mothers who had clearly been anticipating her first day as much as we had. She was their real-life Orphan Annie, who repaid their concern and adoration ten times over with her enchanting looks, her soft voice and her bountiful smile, and she'd just doubled her worth by wearing her brand-new uniform.

We had almost reached the classroom where, amidst all the attention, I almost failed to notice Alex's growing tenseness beside me. Taking both her hands in mine, I knelt down to face her.

'Are you feeling a little nervous?' I asked.

'Um, yes.' Her eyes flickered rapidly between my gaze and the door.

I pulled her almost rigid body close. This was a first. Alex had always embraced the new and unknown so confidently.

'Oh love! You're going to be fine,' I said, my heart swelling. I did my best to fill Alex's head with as many comforting thoughts as I could think of. Someone had evidently told Miss Turley, for suddenly she was standing beside us.

'Hello Alex,' she said gently.

Alex pulled herself instantly out of our embrace. I saw her nervousness transform itself into coyness and I knew the moment was gone.

With a reassuring nod to me, Miss Turley took Alex's hand and led her into the classroom. Alone in the corridor, I wanted her back. The moments before had felt inexplicably good. I considered suggesting to Miss Turley that I sit quietly in her class until Alex had settled in. However, as I raised my hand to knock on the door, I paused. Through the glass I saw Alex settling herself on Miss Turley's lap and already making her laugh. Feeling redundant and strangely disappointed, I sloped away and, by the time I'd reached the gates, I'd managed to talk myself out of my despondency.

It would come, I told myself firmly, whatever *it* was.

Another month, another weekend. Daniel was upstairs with Bradley and Erin. Unable to join in, Alex was now playing an excruciatingly slow and painful game of snakes and ladders with me. Just when I thought I might explode with the strain of it, the doorbell rang. It was Jude, Bradley's mum.

'Are you hot?' she asked, frowning at my crimson face.

'A little,' I replied airily, envying her serene, immaculately made-up face, and asked, 'Would you like a glass of wine?'

I regretted the question immediately. God, I must be desperate: we'd known each other for five years and never yet shared more than a cup of tea. Jude was a nice lady, very nice in fact, but she was quiet, and aside from our children we had little in common.

'Just a small one, dinner's nearly ready,' she replied politely.

She followed me into the kitchen. As I pulled the cork from a bottle during the ensuing uncomfortable silence, I caught Alex flitting by the door. She began making large eyes at Jude.

'Out!' I ordered, pointing an insistent finger at the door, and before Alex's crestfallen face could pull on any more of Jude's heartstrings, I ushered her out myself to the sitting room. There, I attempted to redeem myself from my display of ruthlessness by suggesting amiably, and loudly, that I put on a video for her.

However, when I returned, Jude threw me a 'bless her, poor little mite, she could have stayed' look. It stung. I suppose in different circumstances I might have shrugged it off, remained unperturbed by the fact that Jude didn't understand. But I was desperate for approval and acutely ill-disposed to reproach from others, however paltry or insignificant. It had always mattered to me what people thought, so, how to justify my actions to a woman who so evidently found Alex utterly adorable and thoroughly beyond reproach?

As Rob and I had learnt to our cost recently, venting our frustration about Alex's attention-seeking and learning difficulties was not a luxury afforded us without a price. We weren't stupid. We knew how 'perfect' Alex came across to others but, in recent weeks, I'd been unable to suppress those frustrations and had braved voicing them to Tess and her boyfriend, Ben. It hadn't gone well. Of course, neither of them had openly challenged my thoughts – we were far too 'nice' a middle-class family for such candour – but their misgivings had been obvious. Griping about Alex was as inappropriate as griping about a free fortnight in a five-star hotel in the Bahamas as far as they were concerned, and now here I was, faced with Jude and my urgent need to justify myself. She had witnessed too many moments like this recently, and our once easy acquaintance was becoming more strained by the day.

'You must think I'm awful,' I began. She made a polite gesture of denial and I shook my head. 'No, if I were you I'd think the same,' I continued. 'In fact, I'd be calling Social Services!'

She laughed, but she was kind, and for the next few minutes she listened as I attempted to defend our short-tempered moments with Alex. I underlined her unremitting need for one-on-one attention, her inability to amuse herself even for a minute, the early mornings and the incessant chatter. 'I understand why,' I said. 'What I don't understand is why she's not settling down. There's been no sign of a let-up; in fact, if anything, her needs are escalating. And it's not just the attention, she's still unable to learn anything.'

But by now I'd lost my objectivity and had lapsed into exasperation, beseeching Jude to understand my frustration. I told her about the hours we'd spent teaching Alex how to use the TV and video; the hours we'd spent trying to coax her into enjoying her vast array of toys; the hours we'd spent showing her how to play games; the hours we'd spent trying to teach her to count; the hours . . .

'Maybe you should stop teaching her,' Jude said, damming my flow of words.

I flinched. The overtones in her suggestion sliced me to my core. I knew precisely what she was alluding to and was poised to defend myself yet again, to explain that Alex's inability to learn related to more than just her ABC, that it affected everything she did bar breathing.

But Jude continued.

'When I was a child,' she said, 'I went through a phase where I couldn't learn a thing. My parents had split up. I'd moved house, moved school and just felt unhappy and out of sorts. People – my parents, my teachers – would ask me stuff I'd been taught, but for about a year, my mind would go blank. Completely and utterly blank. The more frustrated they got with me for not being able to respond, the blanker my mind went, and the blanker it became, the more I panicked.'

Comprehension began to trickle icily through my bones.

'It was a vicious circle,' she concluded.

I sat cold and still, staring reflectively at my glass. She was right. When I looked up, she gave me a small reassuring smile, but it was no consolation. A string of images began coursing through my head, each one as hot and shameful as the next. Hour after hour in front of a blank TV showing Alex the buttons to press on the remote; showing her which way up to insert a video; showing her how to button her tops; how to brush her teeth; how to use a knife and fork; how to move a counter on the roll of a dice; how to write her name . . .

Suddenly the images stopped and the focus of my reflection

changed. 'Except that doesn't explain why she can't copy onto paper,' I said, shaking my head.

Jude frowned.

'It's one thing being unable to recall what you've been told, but it's another being unable to reproduce what you can see,' I said. 'We've been trying to teach Alex how to write. All she's had to do is to look at a letter and copy it. We've spent hours on it. Rob's tried, I've tried, and the school has tried.'

'Does she just refuse?'

'Oh, God, no! Alex would never refuse anyone anything.'

'Maybe she's dyslexic.'

'We've thought of that, but if so, she must be verging on dyslexic blindness or whatever they might call it. I once spent an hour and a half trying to get her to draw the number four.'

As soon as the words left my mouth, I regretted them. Jude looked at me aghast. And yes, I'd been pretty horrified myself after the event, knowing I'd subjected Alex to an hour and a half's harrowing tutorial on the shape of the figure four. Yet time itself had not been an issue. Not only was Alex immune to boredom, but she'd put so much effort into trying to write the number that each failed attempt looked sure to lead to success at the next attempt. It was only when I'd looked at my watch, appalled at the time, that I'd brought the 'session' to an abrupt end.

'I'd stop trying if I were you,' Jude said. 'Let the professionals deal with it.'

I looked hard at her. Maybe she was right. A brain freeze would certainly explain many of the problems. I wasn't convinced about the dyslexia, but maybe Alex had some bizarre eye-to-hand coordination disorder. In fact, there could be any number of malfunctions going on inside her little brain of which I, in my paltry few months of limited research, could have no understanding.

I made up my mind. 'You're right,' I said emphatically. 'I am going to stop. As of now.' I pulled a piece of white paper out of the pile that lay on the floor and wrote, in large bold letters: I WILL NOT DO ANY MORE TEACHING WITH ALEX and signed it Melanie, May 1998. Then I pinned it onto the wall.

I debated whether or not to tell Alex but decided I would. She might have problems in some areas but natural intelligence was something she carried in abundance. She'd register soon enough that I'd stopped 'teaching' her. I wondered briefly what we'd replace our time together with, but dismissed the thought. Jude had given me something concrete and positive with which to move forward. Alex needed more time emotionally. Meanwhile, I'd leave it to the school to decipher the rest.

'Bradley! Erin!' Jude called up the stairs.

Her children bounded down, followed by Daniel and — I felt myself grow hot — Alex. Jude and I traded a look of alarm. In order to move from the sitting room to the stairs, she would have had to pass the kitchen door. Had she heard anything? And, if so, how much?

Jude threw me a reassuring look, but I wasn't confident. I'd never met a child who could flit around a house with as much stealth as Alex. I searched her face for any sign that she'd overheard my griping and felt myself relax. She was helpless with laughter as she and Erin swung each other round the base of the banister.

As soon as Jude and her children had left, I sat down with Alex and apologised for not being patient enough with her. Then I showed her the note on the wall and read it to her. 'Until you're ready,' I said, 'I promise there'll be no more learning. OK?'

She fixed me an Alex smile and nodded. Her expression told me nothing.

I took a sip of coffee and waited eagerly for my computer to fire up. I should have done this a long time ago.

I typed 'What is Foetal Alcohol Syndrome' into Google and clicked on Search.

Wow! Over a million hits. Then I set about researching.

I established very quickly that if Alex's brain had been damaged by alcohol exposure whilst in the womb, she would be classified as having an alcohol-related neurodevelopmental disorder (ARND) — not Foetal Alcohol Syndrome because her physical growth pattern and facial features had not been affected.

Then I began researching the signs and symptoms of ARND and mentally ticking off the boxes:

Hyperactive? Yes. Poor memory? Definitely! Short attention span? Sometimes. Speech and language difficulties? Yes. But poor communication? Absolutely no! Poor reasoning skills? My gut said no. Poor judgement? Again, I was inclined to tick the 'No' box. Difficulty following directions? Yes.

Then I moved into the realm of behavioural problems:

Inappropriately friendly with strangers? I took a moment to reflect on that one. Yes, I supposed so. Immature social behaviour? My head said yes but my gut said no. Lack of control over emotions? Easy, no. Temper tantrums? No. Difficulty learning from consequences? Absolutely!

And so on.

Two hours later, I'd learned as much as I reasonably could. As I closed down the computer and gathered up the printouts, I felt a lot better. There was no doubt that Alex had some of the traits associated with ARND, and I promised myself that, from now on, I would remember this. Equally, there was no cure, and I had to accept that she would struggle for the rest of her life.

It would be another couple of years before we'd learn the truth about her condition.

Simon Davies crossed his sandalled feet beneath him and welcomed everyone, in particular Miss Turley, who'd come to talk about Alex's progress at school. It was exactly nine months since Rob, Daniel and I had first met Alex, and this was our third review meeting.

The patio door stood open in the small hope that a breeze might pass through Mallard Close. Our old electric fan strained to move what little air there was. Alex sat snuggled between Rob and me, and we continued to paint a picture of the idyllic family. These meetings were now just a formality.

Simon, as always, began with Alex. Alex, as always, exuded contentment, making everyone smile.

He then moved on to Miss Turley. She expressed much satisfaction, indeed, delight, with Alex's progress. Alex was a pleasure to have in the classroom; she tried very hard in all areas of the curriculum, had made many new friends, and was polite, friendly and well behaved.

Murmurs of satisfaction. Alex dropped her eyes and smiled demurely.

With some tactful wording, Miss Turley explained that Alex was now on the Special Needs Register, but she was confident that her effort and hard work would pay off and she would soon catch up. With Alex present, I was not surprised that she refrained from voicing her only real concern – which she'd voiced with us the previous week – about the high level of attention Alex continued to seek from the adults in the school. 'We still can't persuade her to work on her own, but no doubt that'll come,' was what she'd actually said.

Next it was our turn. Again, had Alex been out of the room, we might have tentatively voiced some of our own concerns. Earlier, in fact, Rob and I had briefly considered engineering a few minutes alone with Simon or Mary, but had binned the idea. There was nothing they could offer us that we didn't already know. Alex *would* eventually settle down. Rob and I had no problem covering the cracks.

Finally, Simon turned to Daniel, who'd been primed to speak truthfully, but whenever possible positively, about Alex. He brought smiles too, as he told the meeting that he liked Alex, that she was funny; and that she drew pictures for him.

All that was needed now was a round of applause.

What we got was the go-ahead to adopt.

For a moment I thought I'd misheard.

'Does that mean we don't have to wait the full eighteen months?' Rob asked.

'I see no point in dragging things out just for the sake of it,' Simon replied.

My trickle of delight grew to a surge, which threatened to propel me off the sofa into a victory stance with both fists punched in the air. I looked over Alex's head to find Rob smiling broadly at me. We gave Alex a big squeeze. She feigned suffocation and laughed. Daniel laughed too.

Then, with one last round of congratulations, everyone rose to their feet, gathered their belongings, and made their way cheerfully to the front door.

Miss Turley was the first to leave – she still had her classroom to tidy up.

Next it was Simon. 'It's been a pleasure to be involved with this placement,' he said, offering us his hand for a final time. We thanked him.

After scooping Alex into her arms for an emotional embrace, Karen followed Simon out with the promise that she'd try and make it for the 'big day'.

Finally it was time to say goodbye to our beloved social worker, Mary, who'd become such a huge part of our lives over the past few years.

'Thanks for everything,' I said.

'Call me when you're ready to do it all again.'

We both laughed. 'Give us a few days,' I joked.

And then there were just the four of us: Daniel kneeling on the path engaged in trying to entice a beetle onto his hand, Alex hopping on and off the front step, and Rob and I, watching Mary's car recede and barely able to grasp that our dream was about to become a reality.

Chapter Eight

July sunshine, and I was outside scrubbing the winter mould off our paddling pool when Daniel appeared, about to burst into tears.

'What's happened?' I asked, looking for any blood or bruises.

He held out an arm and unfurled his fist to reveal a ball of paper.

'She scrunched up my certificate.'

Had Alex ever been naughty or unkind, my instinct would have been to run into the house screaming blue murder at her. If nothing else, it would have allowed me to give vent to the exasperation I was already feeling towards her that morning. But Alex had so far never misbehaved. Ever.

I gave Daniel a consoling hug and attempted to iron out the creases on his scout certificate. 'Are you sure?'

'She says she didn't do it, but it wasn't all scrunched this morning.'

'Where is she now?'

'Hiding under her duvet.'

Daniel followed me into Alex's room.

'Alex?'

The lump under the duvet didn't move. I flung back one corner to meet her terrified gaze. I dangled the certificate in front of her.

'Did you do this?' I asked evenly.

'Um . . .' Her eyes flickered at Daniel before returning to mine. Silence.

'Yes or no?'

'Um, yes.' The voice was soft and frightened, but the stare remained rigid.

'Why?'

'Er . . . I didn't know.'

Silence.

'Didn't know what? And can you please speak up!'

'I didn't know what it was.'

I considered the likelihood. She'd been with me when we'd collected Daniel from Cubs. Was it possible she'd not seen the certificate? No. Daniel had done nothing but talk about his achievement during the journey home. But had Alex actually *seen* it? Maybe not . . . it had been her turn to sit in the front of the car. What about when we got home? I stopped debating with myself. This wasn't the point.

'If you didn't know what it was, why did you scrunch it up?' I asked.

'Um . . . Um . . .'

'Stop staring at me and look at the paper, if you can't remember,' I said wearily.

Her gaze shot to the paper. She stared at it until I thought I might explode.

'Alex!'

She jumped. 'Um, I thought it was rubbish paper.'

'Rubbish paper?' I'd never heard the phrase before, but I knew what she meant. I also knew she was lying. Desperate to tear myself away from her eyes, I took the easy option.

'Maybe you thought it was rubbish paper, or maybe you just didn't like the certificate. Only you know the answer. Either way, it was not your paper to scrunch up,' I said. 'From now on you're not to touch anything in Daniel's room unless he says you can. Understand?'

Her eyes didn't waver, but she nodded.

'Good. Now what do you say to Daniel?'

A slight hesitation, then, 'Sorry.'

'OK,' Daniel responded graciously, and returned to his bedroom.

I considered having one of our 'talks' with Alex but opted out. For a start, I wasn't sure what I could say. Had any other child ruined the certificate, I would have discussed jealousy with them, possibly even anger, and then tried to bolster their ego with examples of their own special achievements. But with Alex? She'd never shown jealousy or anger, and Rob and I always did the talking. Until Alex's speech improved and she was able to express her thoughts, our words of guidance to her would continue to be based entirely on conjecture. Anger and jealousy were big subjects to play about with on that basis.

Nevertheless, as I pulled her door to, I was fairly confident, even hopeful, that jealousy had been her motivation and, if so, who could blame her?

I returned to the scrubbing. Alex needed her own certificate and I resolved to find a way of achieving this.

'Mum,' Alex called cheerfully out of our bedroom window, a few minutes later, 'can I help you?'

I sighed. It was going to be a long summer holiday.

We stood radiant before the world, midway up the imposing stone steps of the Court House on 4 August 1998.

'OK, you happy lot, say cheese,' Dad said, signalling with a raised finger that he was ready. Click. At that moment, the camera captured the real beginning of our new life together. The four Allens. The four Musketeers. The whole, perfect four of us.

We ate lunch in the most expensive restaurant in town.

We've got to get out. Now! The place is filling up like the porthole of a sinking ship. *Where's the exit?* I scan the cave: our escape is behind us but blocked by a ten-foot-high sheet of water, inert, but poised to cascade into the cavernous chamber any minute now.

Look again! There's another opening ahead. I start wading towards it as quickly and fluently as I can, but something is slowing me down. Weeds anchored to the floor are coiling themselves round one of my ankles. I shake off Alex's hand and grab at the weeds, tearing them off. The water's rising, and Alex's hand has found mine again – hers so warm against my own which is arctic. She looks calm, but I can barely breathe for fear.

We make it into the next chamber, which is colder and darker. There's an opening ahead, but it's so hard to move. I feel sluggish and the weeds are stronger this time. Now I'm angry. 'Get off me!' I shriek, clawing at the weeds. Without a word Alex kneels down to help. Her composure is surreal and the weeds quickly relent.

'Thanks,' I say, at her self-effacing smile, and pull her into the next chamber, labouring through the still rising water. No amount of exertion can bring warmth to my bones. I see Daniel perched precariously atop a boulder. He looks frightened, and I'm fighting the weeds again to get to him. I shake off Alex's hand in frustration. 'Stay here!' I command, and she complies.

I coax Daniel off the damp and slimy rock and search the cavern for an escape. There are several openings and Alex's eyes are fixed on one of them. She knows. 'Is that the way out?' I ask. Alex looks at me for a moment, but doesn't answer. 'Is that the way out?' I repeat. My pleading frightens her, and bemused, she stutters, 'Um, um, um . . .' *Oh God, hurry, hurry!* 'Um, um, um,' Alex continues. *Tell me!* I start pointing frantically at the hole, imploring, 'Is that the one? Is that the one?' By now I'm screaming.

Rob emerges from the blackness of the walls. 'Darling, shouting won't help. This isn't Alex's fault,' he says. His tone is loaded with calm disdain. I want to cry.

And then Alex takes my hand and the water is gone. The weeds are limp and lifeless and she's leading me to the opening, which is radiating light, but I'm more terrified than ever, and the fear is swelling with every step.

Wake up! Wake up!

Alex and I are almost at the opening. I can't yet see what lies beyond the hole, but it's terrifying. Then I'm alone and standing over it, teetering on the edge of a gaping, bottomless abyss, and gravity is pulling me relentlessly forwards . . .

Wake Up!

With an iron will, I launch myself into consciousness, my heart pounding against the mattress. My sheets are saturated, but for a while I lie coiled and still, willing myself to calm down, and keep my eyes resolutely open.

Our illuminated clock read five thirty-six a.m. I'd saved myself from the abyss, but not from Alex, who would be awake by now.

I shook off the aura of the nightmare and sat up, casting a tentative glance across the landing and into Alex's bedroom.

She was lying on her side, her eyes awaiting mine.

With nerves still jangling from the dream, I shuddered. For once I didn't smile at her, but acknowledged her with a tired nod of the head and slipped back under the damp duvet.

I lay there until the alarm went off an hour later. Alex never made a sound.

It was six forty-five and it was Dad's fifty-fifth birthday. We were taking the train to the seaside for a day of fun, fairground rides and then the circus. I groaned and burrowed back in my bed.

After careering into Alex on the stairs for a third time, I ordered her to wait in her bedroom until we were ready to leave. Twenty minutes later, the four of us were gathered by the front door with fifteen minutes to get to the station, park the car and buy our tickets and chocolates.

'Eek!' I exclaimed, as I bent down to pick some encrusted food off Alex's fleece. 'What have you done? You're all back to front!' The label on her fleece was peeping out from under her chin, her shoes were on the wrong feet and she had Ready Brek caked across her face. Par for the course.

Startled, she looked herself up and down and stared at me nervously. I took a deep breath and hauled the fleece over her head. I frowned at a mysterious-looking fold running down the centre of her blouse. It took a moment of fiddling to ascertain that she'd managed to button up her blouse inside out.

'Just get in the car,' I ordered. 'It'll have to wait.'

We made the train with a minute to spare.

Once we'd established ourselves in some seats, I led Alex into one of the empty sunlit luggage compartments. 'How, exactly, did you manage this?' I asked, fumbling with the buttons on her blouse.

'Um, I dunno.'

Once properly dressed, Alex watched impassively as I knelt on the floor to see to her shoes. I sighed. We'd tried every trick in the book, from marking the soles of her shoes, to binding them together with elastic bands ready for use. We'd even tried ignoring her dishevelled turnout, but that had proved equally ineffective. I recalled now the moment we'd chosen to say nothing: Alex had left the house in the February chill wearing socks and flip-flops – again on the wrong feet. We'd watched in disbelief as she marched down the hill, crushing great banks of icy leaves beneath each indifferent step. The stares we'd received from passers-by ensured we wouldn't be repeating the experiment.

Now, having delivered a finishing pat to her shoes, I braved a look at her scabby face. I pulled out the packet of extra-strength baby-wipes, now a permanent fixture in my handbag, and started attacking the cereal cement. Pick, rub; pick, rub; pick, rub. Alex didn't flinch. I gingerly gathered up the used wipes and, with nowhere to deposit them, resorted to placing the soggy clump in my pocket. I took a step back and gave Alex a head-to-toe inspection. She looked all put back together again, if not a little raw in the face.

I ushered her out of the carriage.

The murky feelings I'd been harbouring on the train were instantly swept away by a childlike pleasure as we stepped onto the pier. The smell of fish and chips; the sounds from the amusement arcade which had the floorboards bouncing beneath my feet; kiosks selling tokens; booths announcing Tarot readings; neon signs – some broken, others a frenzy of flashing light. Teenagers milled around – girls in tiny skirts and boys looking moody beneath baseball caps; the call of vendors vying for custom and promising big wins or the thrill of a lifetime. And at the end of the pier I could just make out a giant claw-like structure signifying the rides Daniel had been looking forward to all week. In an instant, I was lifted by a sudden sense of optimism that today might be fun after all.

I was roused by a tap on my shoulder. My sister had arrived with her boyfriend, Ben.

'Who's up for jellied eels?' Tess asked and we laughed.

We were joined shortly afterwards by Matt, Lilly, Tim and Dad. After a muted rendition of 'Happy Birthday', which Dad acknowledged with a theatrical bow, we headed off along the pier.

As we wended our way, I looked at Daniel and smiled. His eyes were as wide as saucers and he was practically skipping with excitement. Then I glanced across to Alex. She was hanging off the end of Matt's arm, pleading to be lifted onto his shoulders, and Matt was happy to oblige.

An hour later we'd exhausted the rides and Dad suggested a quick visit to the small pier museum before stopping for fish and chips at the Seaview restaurant. And it was in the museum that the fun suddenly stopped.

Where the essence of Alex's relentless high spirits had been swallowed up in the hubbub of noise on the pier, they became acutely evident in the relative hush of the near-empty museum. The effect her giggling had on me was like being dragged from a deep sleep by a dousing of icy water, and I resented it. She was with Lilly who, although she couldn't help being amused by Alex, was clearly trying to calm her down – to no avail. Eventually, I could bear the noise no longer and strode over to where they stood by one of the small exhibitions. I knelt down to face Alex and held a finger to my mouth indicating silence.

'You can do all the giggling you want to outside, but not in here, OK?' I said.

As usual, she held her gaze a fraction longer than felt comfortable. Then she dropped it and nodded. Lilly ruffled her hair affectionately and whispered 'Good girl.'

However, I'd not moved five feet away, when Alex stifled another giggle. I wheeled round and, ignoring Lilly's horrified expression, took Alex's arm, pulled her to her feet, and mumbling an apology to Lilly, marched us off to some seats in the corner of the room. I sat down feeling hot and conspicuous, Alex now motionless beside me, her sticky hand clasped tightly around mine. Without glancing at her, I knew she would be looking crushed and servile. A bit like my hand, I thought.

She would not let go of it even after we'd left the museum until, feigning the need to look for a tissue, I managed to shake it off. She continued to walk compliantly alongside me, and as soon as I'd replaced the tissue, she found my hand again. I glanced down at her and she threw me a sweetly tentative smile. Where once I'd found it endearing, it now made me uncomfortable. I gave her a gentle nudge.

'Go on Alex, off you go,' I said. 'Lilly's waiting for you.'

A brief flash of hurt crossed her face and then she was gone – into the arms of Lilly, who scooped her up into her maternal bosom and carried her the last stretch to the restaurant. Lilly didn't see the several impassive but lengthy stares that Alex proceeded to pin on me from over Lilly's shoulder.

Over lunch, Alex flitted between the three tables we'd procured, entertaining everyone in her usual buoyant and charming way. I watched her in silence, bitterly questioning in my mind how a person with so little speech and almost no conversation could hold court for hours on end. It made no sense. She was never still, bouncing from lap to lap, her eyes sparkling with flirtation and wit. She held eye contact better than any adult I knew and her touch was seductively subtle and loving.

It was no accident that Rob and I sat up at one end of the table with Daniel and Tim, who were playing noughts and crosses on a napkin. Daniel was never going to match Alex's charm and outgoing sociability. Indeed, Rob and I had taken to explaining to him why he must never try; why he *need* never try. Thankfully, his friendship with Tim endorsed our words. At a time when I truly felt I might be losing the plot, I needed all the endorsement I could get. When there was a break in the conversation, I took the opportunity to smile gratefully at Tim and he smiled back.

After lunch we headed for the games arcade, a darkened chamber lit by row upon row of noisy interactive games, flashing neon colours from floor to ceiling. It was a boy's paradise.

'Not so fast,' I said, grabbing the back of Alex's jumper, 'you can stay with me.'

Rob intervened. 'It's OK,' he reassured me, 'I'll keep an eye on her.'

I shook my head, depleted of compassion and coiled like a spring. Anyway, I wanted Rob to enjoy the games with the boys without the distraction of Alex jabbering and giggling, or pressing the wrong buttons or hanging off their trouser legs.

'OK, but only for ten minutes. Then I'll take over,' he said.

'Would you like me to take her?' a voice spoke over my shoulder. It was Tess, and her tone was anything but gracious.

'No, thank you.' I moved hastily on.

'Mel, why are you behaving like this?' Tess whispered, hot on my heels and determined to have her say. 'It's Dad's birthday. It's not every day we get to be together like this, and we're all trying to enjoy it.'

'Thanks for reminding me! Now if you don't mind—'

'—and just because you're in a bad mood, doesn't mean you should take it out on Alex,' she continued.

Her clipped and icy tone rendered me instantly small and unable to reply. When I refused to meet my sister's eye, she bent down to Alex and said sadly, 'I'll see you later.' Then she turned on her heel and left, no doubt to dwell on her pity for my daughter and stew over her irrational and ungrateful sister.

I wanted to follow her out, to make her understand – convince her that Alex wasn't quite the embodiment of innocence she appeared to be. I wanted Tess to hug me, say how sorry she was and promise her unfailing support ever after. That, however, was not going to happen, as I knew from experience. Besides, Alex was attached to my hand and no doubt savouring this little nugget of conflict. So, with a heart pounding with anger and hurt, I walked Alex over to the nearest game I could find.

But playing with her was like playing with a lump of dead wood: passionless and fruitless. In fact, had anyone bothered to look, they would have noticed that Alex had been equally uninterested in everything she'd seen or experienced so far today.

We regrouped outside before moving on to the dodgems. Rob and I trailed at the back of the group, subdued and strained. For my part, I felt precariously close to imploding.

'Look at her,' said Rob, shaking his head in despair. Ten metres ahead, Alex was engineering herself a swinging session along the walkway with Ben and Matt, her raucous hilarity piercing our moment of peace. 'Aren't they just the teeniest bit tired of her by now? She's been hanging off their arms since we arrived,' Rob continued.

'Actually, she hasn't. She's been moving from person to person, always clever enough not to outstay her welcome,' I sneered.

Rob shot me a look.

Where had that come from? I felt a stab of shame. 'OK, that was mean. I'm sorry.'

But *was* it mean, or did I speak an element of truth? I forced the thought from my head. No way!

'Maybe we should send Alex round to theirs for the weekend,' Rob suggested.

'Wouldn't that be bliss!' But my smile wilted as I remembered reading in Alex's records that the Radfords had asked for respite care for Alex and belated empathy crashed over me. But I didn't *want* to empathise: the Radfords weren't us. We were younger, more patient and more compassionate than they. Weren't we? An icy finger of doubt invaded my thoughts but I dismissed it. We *had* to be!

'C'mon, let's catch up,' I said, with renewed resolve, 'they'll think we've done a runner.'

'Now there's an idea!' he said, turning playfully on his heels.

Smiling, I yanked him the other way. *Nice thought though!*

Benji's Travelling Circus Tent was pitched in a large field just outside the town. We were one of the last groups to enter, and rather than cram ourselves in with the masses at the foot of the arena, we opted for some seats in a deserted back corner of the stands: a perfect spot to spread out and enjoy the show. I'd been to the circus once before, but I'd been seven at the time and had just a vague memory of that day. When Tess had suggested the circus for Dad's birthday, we'd all jumped at the idea. Fortunately, so had Dad, and as I settled back into my seat my shoulders finally began to drop as, bit by bit, I lost myself in the weird and wonderful world of the circus ring.

Ten minutes into the show, the clowns in super-sized spongy shoes were dropping plates and tripping perfect somersaults over each other. It took a while for a squeaking noise behind me to fully register over the din of audience laughter and amplified drum rolls. It was the squeak of a spring-loaded seat flapping up and down with ever increasing persistency. I knew instantly to whom the seat belonged.

Three rows behind me, Alex locked eyes with me. I beckoned her over and she clambered noisily over to the seat directly behind me and next to Tess.

'Please stop playing with the chairs,' I said, evenly.

'They not cumptable,' she said, startling me somewhat with her unprompted excuse.

'Then watch the show. It will take your mind off the chair.'

She fell quiet for a few minutes, but then very gently and with metronomic time, Alex began tapping the back of my plastic seat.

I spun round. 'Please stop that, Alex.'

Her eyes became huge, she twitched and the tapping stopped. I turned back to the show, determined to try and enjoy it.

I don't know whether it was the sound, or the microvibrations on my back that next pricked at my awareness. By then, the princess who couldn't sleep for a pea wedged beneath a mountain of mattresses didn't seem quite so pathetic after all. I could have donned a space-suit and still felt her scratching the back of my seat.

I tried to ignore it, but failed.

'That's enough!' I hissed, indicating that I wanted her to sit next to me. With her now well-known look of abject terror, Alex clambered over the seat and fell in a clumsy heap on the chair beside me.

'Sit up,' I snapped. 'Properly!'

I could feel Tess's eyes behind me, boring a fiery hole into the back of my neck. I kept my own grimly fixed on the scene in front of me – a dazzling display of acrobatics – but saw it shrouded in a crimson haze of rage.

The minutes passed and Alex didn't move. The ringmaster announced another act and a man on a twenty-foot unicycle pedalled into the arena to a huge round of applause. Still Alex didn't move. I risked a sideways glance at her. Her eyes were facing the arena but were as lifeless as glass. More minutes passed. No reaction.

Move, dammit!

She didn't. In fact, waiting for her to stir had rendered me paralysed too. I shuffled on my seat as if to break the freeze for both of us. Eventually, I was only spared when Tess tapped Alex on the shoulder to ask if she was enjoying the show. Barely turning her head, she gave her a sweet smile and nodded. Then, loose again, she leant across and started whispering to Daniel.

At this point frustration, disappointment and fury took over. I grabbed her under her arm, yanked her upright, then had her tumbling over legs and bags to the stairway. There, I ordered her to sit.

I then stumbled back, managing a few knee-jerk apologies on the way, and had just collapsed into my seat when the show came to its spectacular end.

For a few moments, I was paralysed by a deluge of molten shame that had me pinned to my seat. There was nowhere to look but down. I fumbled around on the floor, assembling our bits and pieces, dropping tears beneath me. I was acutely aware of a hubbub of excitement, which drained away in our party as those fortunate enough to have escaped sight of the earlier debacle caught sight of Alex's tiny figure on the bare metal stairway.

There followed a deafening silence, filled I assumed with a frenzy of quizzical gestures, shrugs, nods and silent mouthings of *I'll tell you later.*

I made sure I was the last one out of the aisles where Rob was waiting for me on the stairs. He took me in his arms and I cried.

'They must hate me,' I said, when the tears had stopped.

"Course they don't,' he said, and held me some more.

'Where is she?' I asked.

'Tess took her.'

I groaned. 'This is a nightmare, Rob.'

He pulled himself out of the embrace and we looked hard at each other, letting the words that we both knew to be true sink in. I willed Rob to speak, but he didn't. He understood, and yet he didn't; his gut instincts told him, but he was primarily an onlooker. His take on Alex didn't include neurotic thoughts the way mine did. Rob's personal nightmare was seeing his wife unravelling and the chaotic and unwelcome demise of our once tranquil life. He dropped his head for a moment. When he lifted it again, he looked dispirited but resigned. 'What are we going to do?' he asked.

I'd already decided. 'Talk to Alex.'

He raised a cynical eyebrow.

'Properly this time,' I assured him. 'I want to find out what's going on and I want to hear it from her. Her thoughts, not ours. I want to know how she really feels. If she's hiding stuff, which I think she is — correction, I *know* she is — I want to find out what it is.'

Rob nodded. People in overalls had begun to file onto the arena floor to clear it and only a handful of spectators lingered in the stands. 'Come on,' he said, 'let's get out of here. We'll get home, put the children to bed and open some wine. Tomorrow, we'll start again.'

I managed a smile. That sounded nice.

We emerged from the tent to say our goodbyes. The atmosphere surrounding my family waiting by the exit for us would have been no less tense had Rob and I approached brandishing baseball bats. To make matters worse, Alex wore the expression of one who'd been cruelly battered.

Rob stuck faithfully to my side as we did the rounds. Only Tim and Matt could look me in the eye. I'd never been so relieved to get away from anywhere.

'Why did Alex have to sit on the stairs?' Daniel asked, as we headed back towards the station. 'Tess said she felt sorry for her.'

I tensed, indignant. 'Did she really?'

'She said it to Uncle Tim'.

Well she shouldn't have! I wanted to retort. Instead, I stopped walking, looked Daniel in the eye and simply said, 'Tess doesn't understand.'

'Yeah, she doesn't have to live with her,' my gorgeous son said, raising his shoulders and eyebrows dramatically, and copying my all too familiar phrase.

'No, she doesn't,' I said, laughing gently. Daniel couldn't fully understand either, but somewhere he did.

As the train chugged out of the station, Daniel launched into a sparky account of everything he'd enjoyed the most. He'd barely listed three things when Alex interrupted with a vapid comment about the amusement arcade games. In a flat tone, Rob told her we weren't interested.

Alex flushed and didn't speak again until the train pulled into our stop.

Chapter Nine

The following day, as soon as Rob and Daniel had left for football practice, Alex and I sat down at the kitchen table with a jar of pens and some paper. I was eager to talk, but reluctant to make the fact too obvious. So, for a while, we chatted around vague subjects. I found a way in when, for nothing better to say, I commented on her drawing, 'That's good. What is it?'

'Um, a round fish.'

'Is it swimming in the sea?' I asked cheerfully.

'No,' she said simply.

'Did you see any fish in the sea yesterday?' I asked, and watched as her face creased in a fruitless effort to remember. 'I didn't see any either,' I said eventually. 'In fact, I didn't see very much at all yesterday. How about you?'

Unless I was mistaken, her eyes darkened. 'I did,' she answered softly.

'Did you enjoy the day?'

'I 'joyed it.'

'Oh good, because I didn't. Not all of it, anyway.'

Her mouth twitched as she sussed where the conversation was going.

'You see, I think you were cross with me' I said evenly.

Silence.

'In the museum,' I continued, 'when I said you couldn't stay with Lilly, and in the games room when I asked you to stay with me.'

Silence.

'Am I right?'

Silence.

I knew I was prompting her, just as I'd sworn I wouldn't. But I'd sensed an unusual and uneasy shift in her demeanour. It was nothing

I could qualify, but I knew I was on the right track. 'Is that why you didn't want me to watch the circus?'

Silence.

'Alex?'

Then the shift was gone. 'Um . . . yes,' she said, her tone flat and unemotional.

Did she mean that? Or was she simply agreeing because the affirmation was what she knew I wanted to hear? I searched her eyes for clues, finding none, but I wasn't deflated. The earlier shift had not been wishful thinking. She *had* acted out of anger yesterday.

However, the truth still had to come from her, unprompted. Alex needed a positive experience under her belt, of opening up, even letting go. Only then would she discover that honesty didn't hurt – at least not any longer, not in our house. She'd discover that a pain shared was a pain halved. She'd discover that she could trust us with her pain, and most importantly, that we wouldn't love her any less for it. Liberation was hers, if only I could persuade her to open up. If only . . .

Five minutes later. Alex had asked politely to be excused and was now on the toilet singing to herself. I was staring dully at her vacant chair, none the wiser. Unless I was prepared to turn this 'talk' into an ordeal (in which I waited stubbornly for minutes on end for her to offer her own answers) I had no option but to prompt her.

When she returned, we shared a Kit-Kat, and a giggle over my drawing of a clown. Then I tried again.

'Do you understand why I asked you to sit with me in the tent?'

'Um . . . yes.'

'Why?'

'You were angry.'

It wasn't the answer I'd expected, but it was bang-on. 'Why do you think I was angry?'

'I, um . . . I dunno.'

'I think you do.'

This time I let the silence linger. I had to know she understood. Alex broke her stare to look at the ceiling, the floor and the garden, as she pondered the question with great effort. Still I refused to speak. And then, bit by bit, the effort on her face began to strain until, quite suddenly, I felt compelled to smile. It was as though a shroud had been lifted. I was now wholly confident that the effort she was putting in to find a response was fake. I knew it and so did she. I cocked an eyebrow and her eyes darkened.

'I was making noise,' she admitted dully.

'*Lots* of noise,' I corrected her, 'so I got angry, which made you angry. I understand that – no one likes to be told off – but Alex, anger has to stop somewhere. And the only way to do that is to *say* that you're angry. Making someone angry because you're angry with them doesn't work. Look what happened yesterday.'

She nodded.

'Love, we need to know how you're feeling. If you can't tell us, just stick your tongue out at us, or bang lots of pots and pans; anything, just so long as we can see and understand. Because then we can talk about it.' I put my hand gently over hers and gave it a small squeeze. Then I placed my other hand on her arm and began stroking it. 'We know you had a horrible time when you were little and you had to live with so many different mummies and daddies. Dad and I understand that everything must have made you very angry, so it's really important for—'

'When Tess coming?' she asked, her question crashing into my train of speech. Derailed and deflated, I took a full breath, dug out a flat but neutral tone, and said, 'On Friday, I think.'

'Yay!' She raised a celebratory fist. 'Am I going to school on Friday?'

I stopped stroking her arm. It felt suddenly mechanical and unnecessary.

'Yes, Alex, you are going to school on Friday,' I said, stressing each syllable with a tired familiarity. She had no concept of time and we'd long since given up trying to enlighten her.

She began asking lots of excited questions about what she might do with Tess and I knew the 'big talk' was over.

Despite a sense of unfinished business, I was pleased nevertheless that we'd managed to cover some ground. At the very least, she should now know it was OK to show her true feelings.

'Do you want to help me lay the table for tea?' I asked Alex one November morning, tripping over her feet as I crossed the kitchen to put the potato peelings in the bin.

'Yes.'

'Great.' I pulled four knives, forks and spoons from the drawer and arranged one set on the table. 'Fork on this side, knife on this side and spoon across the top. Can you do the same with the others? Thanks.' I returned to the stove.

A few minutes later she piped up, 'I finished.'

'Well done,' I said absently, as I took four beakers from a cupboard and took them over to the table, saying, 'Next we put the—' I stopped dead. Two of the place settings were slightly askew but otherwise perfect. The third had the knife and fork upside down. I wanted to congratulate her on the first two but a sense of uneasiness stopped me.

'Please could you do that one properly?' I said.

I felt compelled to watch. She picked up the three pieces of cutlery and this time put the knife and fork the wrong way round. Innocent mistake, I thought. We've all done that. Patiently, I corrected her. This time she replaced the knife and fork correctly, but put the spoon on its front. The all too familiar stirrings of perplexed frustration began to seep into me and I slapped my hand on my forehead.

'That's not funny, Alex,' I said, my heart thumping in the knowledge that I was about to be jettisoned into a realm of her behaviour I'd long suspected existed: that rather than just being incapable, she was purposefully needling me. As she fumbled with the implements, I scrutinised her face. She looked a hundred per cent bona fide confused, and frightened of messing up. Several times she glanced at me with her eyes pleading for assistance. My conviction wavered. If this was a performance, she was Meryl Streep. This was not a child acting, surely? Yet, the law of averages said, brain-freeze or not, she had to get a 'hit' at some point. So far she'd managed two out of two misses, which, I realised with sudden clarity, was the story of her life. The pain etched on her face was now swelling to intolerable proportions and once again I was forced to relent. I took the implements from her and talked her through the setting a second time, asking her to confirm she understood.

'Yes,' she whispered, giving me a cowed look.

My convictions continued to yo-yo and the atmosphere was strained. Turning away and moving to the sink, I busied myself with a head of broccoli for several agonising minutes during which I became aware that all movement by the table had stopped. When I could stand the suspense no longer I turned round. Alex was standing stiffly beside the setting, waiting for me. I went to her. The fork had been balanced perfectly – on top of the knife!

My world seemed to list, before coming to rest on a different axis. I had been plunged into that other realm and suddenly found myself laughing, not roaring hysteria, just a small wry laugh laced with a measure of relief.

'Oooohkaay . . .' I said, finding her eyes. She looked just off centre of my eyes – a rarity for Alex – and her rigid posture twitched a couple of times. This was the moment when we fused our understanding. She knew, and I knew she knew. Nothing would be the same again. Then she squared up her gaze and her eyes went blank. No emotion, no sheepishness, no remorse, not even an impish smile. Nothing. Just blank.

My confidence faltered and I forced myself to look deeper – a human being couldn't just switch off. But then I detected something glinting in the deep blackness of her eyes. Was it defiance? Alex dropped her gaze and I decided it was. I needed to think and told her I'd finish laying the table.

As soon as she'd shuffled out of the kitchen, I slumped onto the chair and buried my head in my hands. Then, when I'd fully confronted the reality of the situation, I began to re-evaluate.

We would start again, I decided, and this time we'd do it properly. We knew now what we were dealing with, and it *wasn't* the slow but happy-go-lucky child who'd first been presented to us. *Loving* – yes. *Sociable* – yes. *Funny* – yes. *Beguiling* – yes. *Hyper* – yes. *Learning difficulties?* Not always. *Attention seeking* – Yes! Yes! Yes! *Angry?* Instinct told me she harboured an ocean of pent-up anger. *Manipulative* – you only had to see the way she commandeered attention and batted her large, not quite so innocent, eyes.

She was no different to any other damaged child, I acknowledged, feeling a surge of optimism. But then I corrected myself.

There was one exception – and I let the significance of the fact sink in – she was an astonishing actress. The realisation wasn't a comfortable one.

I picked up the phone, dialled Rob's mobile number, and asked him to come home early. We needed to talk.

And then we needed a plan of action.

ACTION PLAN
STOP. THINK. REACT.
DO NOT GET ANGRY!
NO MORE EXPLANATIONS – SHE'S HEARD THEM A
    HUNDRED TIMES ALREADY.

Then we began to list all the things Alex did for attention and/or to stir up our anger:

Fumbling & confusion
Learning, working the TV, homework, etc.
Talking 'at' us
Diverting attention away from Daniel, etc.
Disrupting with 'niceness' e.g. offering me my hairbrush before
    I've even finished breakfast
Staring
Repeating
Slow eating
Exaggerated use of knife and fork
Hysterical laughter (when no one else is laughing)
Walking strangely

The list, which we'd barely started, was making bizarre reading. Had we shared this list with anyone, they'd no doubt have been horrified at our lack of tolerance – cruelty even. So be it. Alex's behaviour might not have been conventionally naughty, but it was equally destructive, mind-bendingly so. If we didn't start to resolve it soon, Rob and I would end up in a funny farm somewhere, which would be no good to anyone. When we'd exhausted the list, we began jotting down ideas for tackling them:

Fumbling and confusion: Remember her learning difficulties.
Does the gut say she can do it? If yes, explain *only once*!

Learning, working the TV, homework etc.: Remember her learning difficulties.

Explain slowly and carefully *once only*. Then stop! If she can't do
it, leave the task.

In the scale of things, the ABC etc. is not important right now.

Talking 'at' us: If talk/question is really daft, ask: Why do you
want to know?

End conversation dead when she says 'I don't know.'

And so the list went on, until we were finished and satisfied that
we'd got it fair and right.

We crawled into bed at one in the morning, confident of a new
start. Our only regret was that we'd not opened our eyes to things
sooner.

Chapter Ten

I walked nervously into the school hall for my end of term consultation with Alex's teacher. She clearly adored Alex, and all day I'd been rehearsing what I might say to her.

'Hello, Mrs Allen,' said Mrs Soane. 'Take a seat.'

I smiled and sat down on the chair opposite, wiping my damp hands across my jeans. It didn't help that Mrs Soane, a middle-aged lady with a pinched face and nondescript short, grey hair, set little store by the parents of her pupils. She considered most of us to be inept adults who'd fallen, ill-equipped, into parenting, requiring the teachers of this world to pick up the pieces and show us how it should be done. The children, though, loved her.

She began pulling out several sheets of paper from the files in front of her. 'You must be very proud,' she said, with unusual generosity.

I forced a smile. 'Thanks,' I mumbled, now doubly dreading voicing our newly discovered insight into Alex's learning difficulties. I decided to wait until after she'd said her piece.

It was the usual: Alex is friendly and gets on well with everyone; she's very helpful in class, polite and well-behaved; she tries very hard and loves drawing . . . and so on. It was only at the end that she mentioned the learning difficulties and Alex's heavy reliance on adults for help and reassurance. But that was only to be expected, was her conclusion.

I'd heard it all before, and by the time she'd finished her tribute my face ached from smiling so hard. The effort left me exhausted and I was more than ready to thank her and leave, but I had not yet said my piece. Tentative, but curious, I asked Mrs Soane how my daughter's reading, writing and numbers were coming along. There was a pause as she considered her answer. It was improving, she eventually said. I asked her to be more specific. Another pause. She explained that Alex was still catching up, *of course*, but that once she'd learnt her alphabet, she was confident *the reading would come* and that once she could control a pen, *the writing would come* and, finally – and this was said with much satisfaction – *she was now almost always able to count to ten.*

I frowned. Eight months ago, she could count to ten. And eight months ago she knew her alphabet. Then the frown dissolved as I was suddenly tempted to smile. Not just at my wry scepticism at the news, but also from a strange sense of gratitude that we were not the only victims of Alex's emotional gamesmanship.

Mrs Soane asked me if there was anything else I wanted to discuss.

I took a deep breath and cleared my throat. 'Well, er, yes there is – something quite important that we've learned recently. About a month ago. Well, longer ago than that actually, although we weren't sure then—' *Jeez, Mel, just spit it out!* Mrs Soane was staring at me with a patient but bemused smile on her face. I got a grip.

'We think Alex might be faking some of her learning difficulties,' I said, loud and clear. 'Not all of them, of course, but there have been several occasions when . . .' I faltered. How did we explain these situations? 'For example, I asked her to help me lay the table . . .' I began. Mrs Soane, despite her frown, was all ears and I recounted the episode with the knives and forks. 'The mistake was so blatantly not a mistake,' I concluded.

Mrs Soane surprised me by smiling sympathetically. 'Hmm, that certainly sounds like she might have been stringing you along. Children can be quite devilish, you know, especially when they know they can get away with it.'

'Pardon?' I spluttered.

'I remember how much I used to hate being called in to lay the table for my mother.'

She was missing the point entirely. Alex never had to be 'called in' – she was rarely more than a few inches from my side. 'It's not the defiance we're worried about,' I said. 'It's the fact that she was able to *fake* being unable to do it. It's the fact that she looked so frightened and so desperate to get it right, when in fact she wasn't desperate at all,' I said, jabbing the table with the side of my hand emphatically. 'Now we're wondering what else she might be faking and how we tackle the issue – as a team – because I think she might be pulling the wool over *all* our eyes.'

I stopped and waited, willing her to at least consider the idea.

'Are you suggesting that Alex underachieves deliberately?' she asked.

'Yes. Well, not all the time, no. She really has got learning diffi-culties and, obviously, she's got a lot of catching up to do. But yes, that is what we're saying.'

There followed a lengthy and uncomfortable pause and then she shook her head.

'No, I don't think so,' she said. 'I've seen nothing to suggest that Alex isn't doing the best she can. She's eager to learn and she's co-operative. It concerns me that you might be looking for answers that aren't there. Not everyone is as bright as Daniel you know.'

'She put the fork on top of the knife!'

'I'm not disputing that, but I can assure you she's done nothing of the sort here,' she said, pitying me.

I bit the bullet. 'A year ago she could count to ten. And she knew every letter of her alphabet.'

Mrs Soane looked puzzled, faltered, but recovered her smile, sug-gesting she'd located the explanation. 'Pre-schools don't assess educational standards the way we do.'

It was my turn to falter.

'Be proud of what you've achieved with Alex,' she continued by way of consolation. 'She's happy and she's settled. It won't be long before she catches up, of that I'm sure,' she said.

Not for the first time, I noticed that Alex's developmental disor-der was being wholly overlooked.

She continued. 'And, yes, she's bound to play up from time to time. I imagine laying the table was the last thing she wanted to do,' she snorted.

Oh, if only she knew!

At this point, I should have stood my ground, but I buckled. I didn't want to add Mrs Soane to our growing list of non-admirers. That list was already too long. I'd sown a seed of doubt if nothing else and, besides, we had an action plan now that we were sure was going to work, and that would eventually start reflecting in her school work. Yup, we could do this on our own.

So I pretended she was right and I told her I was probably tired. At which point she softened and produced a warmer and more compassionate smile than I'd seen on her face before. Being the parent of such an adorable child brought its rewards.

'What are you doing? Let go of his tail!'

I launched myself across the floor and pulled Alex's arm away from Scooter. Then I picked up our cat and began gently stroking him. I couldn't get myself to look at Alex, who I knew would be standing rigid with fear beside me. When finally Scooter started purring, I placed him on the sofa, then I turned to Alex, furious.

'Don't ever, EVER, pull Scooter's tail again!' I shouted.

Alex cowered. It was too much for Scooter, who scampered from the room.

'What on earth do you think you were doing?' I demanded. The image of Alex holding Scooter's tail high in the air, yanking him backwards on his front legs, blackened my insides and filled me with dread. Had she hurt Scooter before and, if so, for how long had she been doing it? No wonder the cat never went anywhere near the girl. *Oh, God! I should have kept a closer eye.* 'If I ever catch you doing it again, you will not be allowed anywhere near him. Understand?'

She looked about to dissolve in her own fear.

'Understand?'

She jumped. 'Yes.'

'Good, now get to your room. I don't want to see you until lunchtime.'

The house froze over in silence.

Later that night, I reaffirmed our love for her and she responded sweetly.

Daniel lifted his head from the last of his Christmas cards. 'I've finished. Can I go round to Bradley's now?'

'Yes, but be back in an hour,' I replied, returning my attention to my own pile.

'Can I go to Bradley?' Alex asked.

I didn't look up. 'When you've finished.'

Silence. I sensed no movement, only her eyes boring into me. '*Have* you finished?' I asked.

'Um, no,' she whispered.

'Well, you'd better get on then.'

For ten painful minutes, as I tried desperately to focus on my cards, the only sound that filled the room was Alex's pen scraping her four-letter name on each of the twelve cards in which I'd already written the recipients' names and the words 'Love from'.

'I finished,' she said finally.

I took a deep breath and picked up the top card on the pile. Experience told me to expect the worst, yet I also knew she was longing to join the others outside. I opened the card and, without a flicker of emotion, closed it again. Then I picked up the next and then the next until I'd seen all twelve. All of them had been erratically signed incorrectly, and on the last two she'd even managed to turn on its head the letter 'A' in her name. She clearly wasn't longing to play enough, I thought wryly.

'Thank you. Now you can do them again,' I said, gathering up the pile of cards and dropping them in the bin beside me. This was part of our 'new start'. No more Mr and Mrs Nice. Then I counted out another twelve cards and placed them in front of her. Lastly, just in case, I picked up the scrap of paper on which I'd earlier written '*A l e x*' and placed it purposefully in front of her.

'There you go, that's how you write your name,' I said.

The room was plunged once more into an uneasy quiet. After a while, all movement from her stopped. Before she managed to bore a hole right through me, I asked, 'Have you finished?'

'Yes,' she whispered.

'Sure?' The dread I felt at having to look at the cards lay heavy inside me.

'Yes.'

'And you've written your name properly in all of them?'

'Yes.'

'Good,' I said, hopeful. I picked up the first and then, with an inward sigh, worked my way swiftly through the other eleven. *Didn't she want to play with the others?*

'And again,' I said, keeping the irritation from my voice. I passed her twelve fresh cards, thankful I had bought an extra pack.

Silence descended once more.

'I finished,' she said a while later, but this time there was an ominous tone of dread to her voice.

By now my nerves were raw. I'd written umpteen of my own cards, but had someone asked me what I'd written, or to whom they'd been addressed, I would have drawn a blank. Alex, as ever, eclipsed my every move, and had it not been for the 'new start', I would have happily signed the cards for her and walked her round to Bradley's myself.

I scanned the cards and threw them into the bin, all thoughts of the action plan left behind as I demanded belligerently, 'Don't you *want* to play outside?'

'Yes,' she whispered, sounding desperate.

'Then please do them properly.'

This time I watched her. She picked up the pen, hesitated; placed the nib on the card, hesitated; lifted the pen, hesitated. Then, almost reluctantly, she placed the nib at the very top of the card. *Bang!* All control left my body as I slammed my hands down on the table, then, before I could stop myself, swept the table's entire contents – cards, envelopes, pens and a glass fruit bowl – to the floor.

'For goodness' sake!' I shouted. 'I paid for those cards and you've ruined them. Happy now?'

'Um . . . um . . . no . . .' she cowered.

In the ensuing silence two hearts hammered, both of us on the edge of tears. I tore my gaze from the mess and fixed it on Alex.

'So why won't you write your name where I asked you to? And properly? I know you can!'

'I can't!' she retorted, with a punch of passion we'd never heard before.

For a moment, I couldn't speak. 'Why?' I implored, a little frightened now.

She dropped her head. 'Um, I dunno.'

'Answer me, for God's sake.'

She jumped, lifted her head and two large tears sprung from her eyes, one of them spilling over and falling down her cheek. She didn't make a sound.

Oh God! She can't do it! She wasn't acting. Guilt extinguished the hot ball of fury, leaving me scorched inside. What had I done? So she'd written her name at the top of the cards instead of the bottom. Had I made myself clear enough? Had I even stipulated where she should sign her name? No, I hadn't, yet . . . *No Mel, it's obvious to you. You've written a thousand cards in your life. She's probably never written one. AND she's developmentally delayed! Remember?*

'I'm sorry,' I said, shaking my head in disgust and shame. 'Sorry I frightened you like that.'

Alex began to cry.

'Come here,' I said, standing up and brushing aside some of the debris on the floor. I knelt at the foot of her chair. Her tears dropped onto my knees. Like a woman pleading for her life, I flung my arms round her tiny shoulders. 'Sorry. It won't happen again, I promise.'

Later that evening, still hot with shame, I wrote and signed her cards. So it was with much relief to find that, in the morning, her usual high-spirited chirpiness had returned. I welcomed the sound that ricocheted round the house. Rob, Daniel and the school would hopefully never know of my appalling loss of control.

It would be confirmed years later that Alex had not been acting. Her fear was genuine. She couldn't write those cards. For now though, our lives were about to be dragged deeper into our own confusion.

Chapter Eleven

I found a seat near the front of the school hall next to Tracey. Amidst the hubbub of the growing congregation of parents, we waited for the play to start.

'Is this her first Nativity play?' she whispered, as Mrs Steele struck the first chord on the school piano.

'Yes.'

'What is she?'

'A bunny, though you wouldn't know it,' I said. Costume-making was not my forte.

Tracey smiled. 'Is she nervous?' she asked, as the hall fell silent. I had no idea. 'Yes,' I whispered.

The door opened and a procession of children dressed in an array of costumes began filing in. 'There she is,' Tracey whispered, excited.

Despite the throng of children seating themselves on the stage, I found Alex immediately. It hadn't been difficult as she was staring right at me, a small smile on her face, fluttering her hand at me every few seconds in tiny frantic waves.

Tracey found her and melted on cue. 'Aw, bless, she's waving at you.'

'Yes,' I said, straining to match her enthusiasm. Even here, I felt that my daughter had me trapped. I waved back.

Five long minutes later, the last of the children had filed in and taken their places on the benches. Alex was still waving, her eyes not moving from mine. *Please let this play start soon*, I thought. When my mouth finally collapsed under the strain of smiling at Alex, I turned to Tracey.

'Where's Jasmine?' I said, feigning interest.

'Oh, somewhere at the back,' she said indifferently. 'Look, Alex can't take her eyes off you.'

With a shudder, I turned my head to face the front, and keeping my eyes a fraction off-centre from hers, I resumed smiling at her. This was going to be a long hour.

When at last the play had come to an end, I felt ready to detonate. My jaws were aching, my head was pounding and my back was still smarting from the prodding fingers of the mothers behind me, who'd felt it necessary to point out, throughout the play, that Alex was smiling and waving at me. *I know!* I wanted so much to shout, *if you were concentrating properly you'd notice that she hasn't yet stopped smiling at me.* I smiled back, graciously.

Walking into the playground afterwards was like stumbling into freedom after undergoing something gruellingly claustrophobic. I walked briskly to my car, ahead of the other mothers.

Rob and Daniel went to the play that evening. Before they left, I warned Rob about the waving and the staring.

I was draining a large glass of wine when they returned.

'I see what you mean,' Rob said, after putting the children to bed. 'It was horrible.'

'Why d'you think she does it?' I asked.

Rob shrugged his shoulders. 'Nervous, insecure? I don't know.'

I cocked an eyebrow. 'Alex? Nervous? No way. This is about master and slave. She's the master and we're the slaves. She waves, we wave. She jumps, we jump,' I responded bitterly.

Rob stared hard into my face – could I be right?

The following day it was Daniel's school play. I was grateful to find the school had laid mats at the front of the hall for the younger siblings who'd come to watch. Keeping my eyes to the front, I walked Alex down the centre aisle to the mats.

'Look, there's Jasmine. Why don't you sit next to her?' I suggested, propelling Alex towards her classmate.

'I don't want to.'

I stopped dead in my tracks at her emphatic declaration and frowned curiously at her. 'Why not?'

'I sit with you.'

Sensing the first tentacles of stranglehold tickle at my temples, I shook my head. 'This is where the children are meant to sit. Look.'

I pointed at the twenty or so youngsters perched at our feet. She didn't say anything, so I started moving us deeper into the throng towards Jasmine.

Alex dug her heels in. 'I don't want to.'

My temples began to throb as those tentacles tightened their grip, freedom slipping away from me. 'If you sit with me, you won't be able to see anything,' I tried.

'I want to.'

I deliberated for a moment. Could I make her sit at the front or was she feeling insecure and needing me? But she knew Daniel's school and several of the children on the mats were from her own school, including Jasmine. She wasn't shy. I made up my mind.

'I want you to sit here. You'll be able to see much better, and if you need me, I won't be far away, OK?'

She stared bleakly at me and sat down next to Jasmine.

I found myself a seat midway down the hall, on an aisle where Alex could find me if she needed to.

I picked up the programme sheet and began searching for Daniel's name in the cast list, but halfway down, I realised I'd not digested a single name. Daniel could have been playing every part and I'd not have noticed, thanks to my preoccupation with Alex. I shook off the guilt I was feeling about her and resolved to enjoy Daniel's moment. God knows, he'd taken a back seat for long enough.

Any residual hope that I might enjoy the play, however, was extinguished when, a few minutes later, Jude approached me wearing a grave expression.

'She's crying, Mel,' she said.

I shot out of my chair. 'Thanks,' I said, and walked briskly down the aisle of shame to where Alex sat bowed and sobbing.

Muttering words of reassurance, I picked her up and carried her on my hip back down the aisle and past the sea of concerned faces.

Alex sat still in my arms for the next five minutes, as I tried desperately to understand what had prompted her reaction. Once the play had begun, however, she started wriggling, eager for a better view of the stage. She didn't stop until the play finished. My only confirmation that Daniel had been in the play was a comment from a friend on how swashbuckling he'd looked in his pirate's costume.

Tap-Tap-Tap-Tap-Tap-Tap.

I caught Rob's eye across the small kitchen table: he was searching for the source of the noise too.

Tap-Tap-Tap.

I glanced briefly at Alex, but the noise didn't seem to be coming from her.

Daniel was absorbed in the delight of scooping up long strands of bolognaise-covered spaghetti and sucking them into his mouth. The tapping wasn't coming from his quarter either.

It was Boxing Day, our second Christmas with Alex, and unfolding as a mirror-image of the frantic and chaotic Christmas we'd shared a year ago – with one significant difference: with the new action plan came a rule that there would be no unnecessary talking until we'd finished eating what was on our plates. That such a formidable rule controlled our dinner table, once so vibrant with conversation, horrified me. However, after a year of Alex's excruciating and laboured eating habits, accompanied by her almost relentless, insipid chatter, we'd been left with no option. Particularly as we were now ninety-nine per cent sure that this behaviour was intended to disrupt.

Tap-Tap-Tap. The silence was almost as deafening as the tapping.

Tap-Tap-Tap. Ah! There it was! A flicker of movement in one of Alex's legs: up and down, up and down, surreptitiously working the sole of her shoe on the lino. I looked up. Her eyes were fixed on me.

'Please stop that,' I said, my tone deceptively calm. The noise stopped, but it was a couple of seconds before she dropped her gaze, her expression as always, timid but otherwise unreadable. She looked at her bowl, still brimming with food, raised her fork and stuck it lamely into the spaghetti. She pulled out a morsel of minced meat and carefully placed it in her mouth.

Sticking to the action plan, we said nothing. We didn't tell her to hurry up or to stop playing with her food or remind her that it would go cold. The speed at which she ate was now up to her, but she knew that she couldn't get down until she'd finished.

On paper, this part of the plan had seemed the perfect solution for two reasons: firstly, it did away with the inevitable raised voices, and secondly, if we *were* mistaken about the attention seeking and she in fact did suffer with an undiagnosed digestive problem, she would be spared from being irreparably scarred with food issues.

In practice, however, the rule was proving no more soothing to our nerves. Right now I had a scream trapped and ballooning inside me. I dropped my gaze, white-knuckled my fork and spoon and continued to eat, consoling myself with the fact that this torture could not last indefinitely. One day soon, Alex would come to trust that she was staying for ever. This would give her the courage she needed to start revealing her emotions, and her anger would no longer be channelled into attention seeking and – *staring*.

I ignored the eyes that were fixed blankly at the top of my lowered head and shovelled down the rest of my food, eager to dispel the silence. Rob had evidently been of the same mind for we broke out simultaneously into meaningless chit-chat, feigning normalcy and cheeriness. The air in the room slackened with relief. As soon as Daniel had finished, the three of us left the table. Alex needed only an additional few minutes to gobble down her remaining mountain of spaghetti.

'Mum, I can't find my fossil,' Daniel yelled from his bedroom.

Just then his fossil landed at the bottom of the stairs and I looked up to see Alex's legs scurrying round the top of the stairs and into the passage.

Debating what to do next took a few minutes. There'd been several incidences recently of things going missing, only to be found later in places they didn't belong. We were fairly certain that Alex had been the one to move them, but she always denied knowing their whereabouts with such conviction that we had no option but to believe her. This was the first time I'd caught her in the act.

I entered Alex's bedroom. 'Have you seen Daniel's fossil?'

'No,' she said, quite innocently.

'Sure?'

'Yes.' Had I blinked I'd have missed it – a solitary twitch at the corner of her mouth while her eyes were otherwise engaged in glue-ing themselves unwaveringly to mine.

'Absolutely sure?' I asked, keeping my voice even. 'Think. It's the one he found last weekend.'

I watched as Alex moved seamlessly into a concentrated effort to remember. She frowned; she thought intently and then she frowned again; she thought some more and eventually shook her head. The performance had been flawless, neither shifty nor over-cooked.

'I haven't seen it,' she said, during my struggle to find my voice.

I composed myself anew, raised an eyebrow, and smiled. 'Thank you. Now you can go and pick up the fossil you just threw down-stairs and give it back to Daniel, and when you've apologised, I want you to stay in your room and think about the lie you've just told me. There will be no TV tonight.'

A darkness crossed her otherwise vacant eyes and she went downstairs to retrieve the fossil.

Although awake, I was enjoying a few minutes of luxuriating in the warmth of my bed before getting up to make breakfast. Rob was snoring peacefully beside me. Even the sun was shining on this cold December morning.

Don't do that, Alex! You'll hurt him.

I shot out of bed, grabbed my dressing gown and ran downstairs to where the children were watching TV. Daniel was stroking Scooter. Alex was nowhere to be seen.

'She wouldn't let Scooter get out,' Daniel said in distress.

'Out where?' I asked.

'Out of the room. She kept pulling his tail so he couldn't get out.'

I scanned the room furiously, detecting a shadow of movement behind the sofa. Marching over, I swung the chair aside to reveal Alex hunched up small behind it.

With the memory of my loss of control a few weeks ago still fresh in my mind, I kept my breathing and my voice controlled. 'Well, that's decided that then, hasn't it?' I said. 'Until I'm sure you won't hurt him again, you're not allowed in the same room as

Scooter. Understand?' She nodded deferentially and I continued, 'If Scooter walks in, you walk out.'

I looked into Alex's big, black eyes and found nothing there. No emotion, no anger, nothing at all. Yet I'm sure it must have been there somewhere. She simply nodded. I turned away with an uncomfortable sense of revulsion and, as I stepped into the hallway, I heard Alex whisper to Daniel, 'I hate you, you made Mum hear.'

It brought me to a grinding halt. I'd never heard her speak like that and I returned to the sitting room where I ordered her to say sorry to Daniel, which she duly did. Marching her up to her room, I tersely explained how it had nothing to do with Daniel.

She gave me one last dark and empty look as I closed the door on her.

I crawled back into bed to think. Sure as anything, the action plan wasn't working. In fact, if anything, it was making things worse, because suddenly Alex was being banished or silenced for just about everything except breathing. More worryingly, the atmosphere in the house had taken on a strangely taut and subdued air, which wasn't doing any of us any good. Despite her destructive behaviour, she still needed – deserved – far more attention than this action plan allowed her. In hindsight I realised it had been far too harsh, so I thought on.

The idea, when it came to me, lit up inside my head like a beautiful firework. A star chart! For a moment I was dumbfounded as to why we'd not considered the idea before but was quick to realise that, until recently, we'd not perceived her behaviour to be 'naughty' – I could count on one hand the occasions she'd been overtly disobedient. And I'd only recently begun to get the full measure of her destructive intentions.

I'd also never considered the idea because I wasn't a great believer in bribing 'goodness' from children. Clearly, that was because I'd never needed to do so. Daniel had been blessed with a stable life and an easy-going temperament. The thought of losing an evening's TV, or not being allowed out to play, had always been incentive enough. Alex, however, for obvious reasons, was a different kettle of fish. She, more than anyone, needed an incentive to show acceptable behaviour – at least until it came willingly to her.

Rob began to stir beside me and I gave him a big smile. A star chart was just what we needed.

Chapter Twelve

*I*t was Rob who came up with the idea of calling it a Smiley-Faces Chart, which somehow softened the disciplinary essence of it. It would help Alex to focus more on behaviour that made people happy or unhappy than to focus on behaviour that was 'good' or 'bad' – in our opinion words that were both unattractive and patronising.

'If we do a chart for Alex, we have to do one for Daniel,' Rob pointed out.

'You're right.' I felt a little sheepish for not having thought of that.

So, a chart each it was. One half of the chart would be allocated to smiley faces, the other half to sad faces. Initially, we'd opted for a chart which focused only on positive behaviour, but we were not yet confident that Alex fully understood the negative impact her attention seeking had on us. It made more sense to give her a sad face when she interrupted than a happy face for not interrupting.

Once the smiley faces column had been filled, they could choose a treat. There would be no punishment for a column full of sad faces. However, that chart would be thrown away, and with it any smiley faces already amassed, and they would start on a new chart.

'What sort of treats are we going to give them?' Rob asked.

'Why don't we let them decide?'

The following day, we talked to the children about the charts.

Daniel, brimming with ideas for his treats, thought it was a great idea.

Alex appeared to like the idea too, but was unable to think of any particular treats she might want. She decided to give it some thought.

We also asked them to think of things they thought might be

deserving of a smiley face. Daniel's list included not whinging when he had to come in for tea, reading more, putting his stuff away, and helping around the house.

Alex's list was trickier to compile. She never whinged, her room was always immaculate – a trait that had initially delighted us, but now served only to remind us that she had no interest in the toys and books that filled her shelves; she was only too eager to help around the house, and she couldn't read. In the end, her final list included things like managing to dress herself; eating her food before it had gone cold; remembering to clean her mouth; walking safely next to us when we were near a road and playing by herself without being asked to do so.

By the time we went to bed, the two charts had been drawn up. Tomorrow was the first day of a new year. We were ready to go!

The following day, 1 January 1999, Alex achieved her first smiley face. For the first twenty minutes into a New Year's Day stroll through the woods, she had remained glued to our sides, step for step. Eventually, when we realised Alex's position at our side was a misinterpretation of the previous day's smiley faces list, Rob and I had assured Alex that it was OK for her to run ahead with Daniel. The rule, we reminded her, applied only when we were near a road.

Nevertheless, a deal was a deal, and when we got home we watched ceremoniously as she crayoned the first smiley face onto her chart.

The next two days saw the chart otherwise empty. There had been many opportunities to add sad faces, but we resisted. We wanted the chart to be a positive experience, so the following day, afraid that the chart might have been forgotten, we gave Alex a smiley face for eating faster than she had the day before.

Two days after that, we felt compelled to remind Alex that when the smiley faces reached the bottom of the page, we'd be taking her to the cinema.

'Now, if you eat that up quickly . . .' I suggested, willing her on to finish her quarter-eaten, now cold pizza. She gobbled it up, and breathing a big sigh of relief, I added a third smiley face. She then grabbed a tissue and managed to wipe the top layer of pizza residue off her face and Rob quickly added a fourth to the chart.

'If you go on like this,' Rob declared, 'you'll reach the bottom by the end of the week!'

'Yeah! Then I can go to the films and have ice-cream.'

When Alex turned her back, Rob and I traded exasperated smiles, but at least she'd grasped the concept.

Nine days into the chart experiment, I gave Alex her first sad face. Ostensibly, it was for 'forgetting' that I'd asked for fifteen minutes of peace while I drank a cup of coffee, and for subsequently flitting around outside the kitchen door until my time was up. If I were honest though, I'd given it as a churlish response to the indifference she was already showing this damn chart.

'I thought you wanted to go to the cinema,' I said to her the following day.

'I do,' she whispered timidly.

'So why are you not eating up? Why are you making that silly scraping noise with your knife on the plate' – my voice was rising in pitch – 'and why, *why* have you been staring at me for the last ten minutes?'

I shot to my feet, grabbed the nearest pen, and with great emphasis drew four large sad faces in a column on the chart. Then I pointed to Daniel's chart and did exactly what I had promised myself I wouldn't. 'See that? Daniel's nearly finished his line of smiley faces. If I have to add one more sad face to yours, you will not be joining him at the adventure park. Understand?'

I didn't wait for her doleful nod but marched out of the kitchen.

The day after this little battle, I did all I could to distance myself from Alex before and after school. Rob made the breakfast, and in the afternoon I feigned a headache which meant Alex had to watch TV. Otherwise, I would have been forced to carry out my threat. Daniel, who'd continued his quest for smiley faces by hounding me for chores, would be going to the adventure park tomorrow.

However, with only a few daylight hours remaining, Alex made the task of ignoring her behaviour impossible. I caught her in the bath, very deliberately pouring water from a bath-toy onto the bathroom floor. She hadn't heard me come downstairs from my bedroom. Everything inside and around me turned red. For months I'd been on my knees, mopping up water 'accidentally' sloshed over the side of the bath and washing towel after towel after towel.

'What, may I ask, are you doing?'

She jumped in shock and stared at me with paralysed eyes. Despite the frequency with which she went in for looking cowed, frightened, abject – even terrified – I was now witnessing what I judged to be her first genuine display of terror at being caught in the act of doing something so obviously wrong.

'Mmm, er ... Um ...' she stammered, her face crumpling, 'I dunno. I was, um ... putting water, um, on the floor.'

'I know that! Why?'

'Um ... I dunno.'

My mind was a jumble of questions. I didn't know either. 'Right, get out of the bath now! I want this floor bone-dry in five minutes. Then we'll talk.'

Five minutes later she was standing erect as a soldier by the bath, her expression having been downgraded to its more customary timidity. Still shocked, but having got a grip on myself, I wrapped her in a bath towel and marched her into the kitchen. I shoved her into a chair.

'Well?' I said, challenging her for an apology.

'Um ... um ...' she mumbled, seemingly fear-stricken.

'I'm waiting,' I said, hands on hips and glaring at her expectantly.

More mumbles and hesitancy.

'What do you say?' I prompted her, but got the same response again.

I slapped a hand onto the table.

'What do you say?'

She looked as though she might disintegrate. 'I dunno.'

I spun round, ripped her chart off the wall, put it on the table and, with a marker poised over the sad faces column, said, 'Say it!'

'I don't know.'

I drew a big sad face inside the column. That was the adventure park gone. 'Say it!'

'Um . . . um . . .' she mumbled, tears falling onto the table.

Shaking with upset and frustration, I drew another sad face. Then another. And, meaningless though they now were, another.

'Say it,' I cried, fists clenched, my head ugly and disconnected.

'Er . . . I put . . . um . . . water on the, um, floor.'

It was like a kick in the stomach and the slits of my eyes opened slowly as the horrific truth dawned on me: *she hadn't understood.* Alex had not known that I wanted an apology.

I stood mortified, imprisoned in a nightmare of my own making and too frightened to apologise this time. She must never know what a bitch I'd just been. She'd hate me for ever.

'Don't ever do it again!' I said. Then, terrified of who I'd become, I turned on my heel, stormed past a white-faced Rob and grabbed my keys, calling out that I needed some air and that I'd be back later.

I wanted never to return.

Twenty minutes later I stood, shoulders slumped, on Sophie's doorstep. She gave me a hug and led me into her front room. She guided me into one of her sofas, knelt down beside me and with deep concern said, not for the first time, 'Mel, you've got to ask for help.'

'I know.'

By now, we could assign the opinions held about Alex by all our friends, family and acquaintances into one of four categories:

1. She's absolutely adorable – end of story.
2. She looks sweet enough to me, but if Rob and Mel say there's a problem, I believe them.
3. There's definitely something not right about her, but I can't put my finger on it.
4. She unnerves me.

The vast majority of people sat in the first two categories. Sophie fell into the third group and, like her, those in the last two groups were there because they were reacting to their instincts. This was why, I believed, the children who knew Alex fell into the fourth category — children react instantly and instinctively to others, unrelated to the amount of time spent with them. And Sophie, too, had felt there was something odd from day one.

She returned a few minutes later with a bottle of wine, two glasses and a bowl of Doritos.

'It's all very well asking for help, but what would we say?' I picked up where we'd left off.

She popped the cork and began to pour. 'The same as you've told me.'

'Which is what?' I pleaded. 'I can't remember. One day I'm telling you she's the problem, the next I'm telling you it's me. One day I'm telling you categorically she's winding us up, the next, like tonight, it's me with the problem again.' She handed me a glass and I took a large gulp. 'God! You should have seen me earlier. I was like one of those soap opera psychos,' I said, and recounted the whole hideous episode. 'I was sure she was just being defiant, but ding-dong, wrong again!'

'How do you know she wasn't?'

'Because of the look on her face. She was in tears, and I mean genuine tears.' I burned with mortification all over again. 'Oh God, what I have done!'

'So you screwed up. Big deal. She's been through far worse, she'll forget.'

'I'll pay for it tomorrow, though.'

'Stop beating yourself over the head—'

'No!' I corrected her, '*she* will make me pay. She'll be at my feet all day, sucking me dry, making sure I don't get anything done. Jabbering, jabbering, jabbering until all I can breathe is her. She'll—' I stopped spewing, but Sophie's eyes were sympathetic, non-judgemental.

'It was never going to be easy,' she said.

'It was never going to be like this,' I replied.

'OK, so she's a little unusual.'

'Unusual is an understatement. In all the books we've read, all the courses we've attended, nothing — and I mean *nothing* — could have prepared us for Alex. She's . . . she's . . .' I struggled to find the right words, but couldn't. 'Oh, I don't know what she is. I mean, some-times she's everything we could have hoped for, but right now I'd gladly swap her tomorrow. God, that sounds awful, doesn't it?' I grimaced. 'But at least with a screaming, foul-mouthed monster who wiped poo all over the walls, we'd know what we were dealing with. With Alex, we haven't a clue. We know she's angry, but only because we can feel it,' I said, laying my hand on my heart. 'But then again, we might be wrong. We're not, but we might be.'

Sophie looked confused.

'Exactly!' I said. 'Nothing makes sense any more. My eyes tell me she's a vulnerable, timid little girl, desperate to please, to be accepted, to be loved and to love back. A little girl with a hideous past that's given her the problem of developmental delay. But my gut tells me she's also an angry, secretive little girl who occu-pies our every waking thought and who's intent on destroying us.'

'Oh, Mel!'

'Paranoia? I could write a book on it. I pace the floor sometimes, thinking she's some evil person reincarnated. Then I pace about cursing myself for such hateful thoughts, knowing I've got it hideously wrong, and I wonder what the poor mite did to deserve *two* terrible mums.'

I took another gulp of my wine, hoping to blot out the memory of Alex sobbing on the chair, innocent and frightened.

'The problem is that I don't know what to trust any more, my gut or my head. They've both let me down,' I said. And so, it would seem, had my heart. But I kept that part to myself.

Sophie got up and perched beside me. She put an arm around my shoulder. 'I don't know what to say.'

'Neither do I. In fact, I haven't got a bloody clue.' I closed my eyes and shook my head. 'It does scare me. I think I understand, yet when I look at her and see her frightened little face, I don't understand. Why, if she's so eager to comply — and I mean she'd stand on her hands and pick her nose if we asked her to — does she do the same thing to wind us up, over and over again? It makes no sense. Is she that dense? It's almost like we speak a different lan-guage, yet . . .' I paused as I thought about her anger — '. . . she *knows* what winds us up: she did *not* lay that knife on top of the fork by mistake and she did *not* pour water onto the floor by mistake.'

Sophie offered me a crisp and I continued talking, waving it about as I gesticulated.

'How do we know when she's being destructive and when she isn't? How do we know which are learning difficulties and which aren't?'

I stopped, took a breath, and we sat together in silence for a while, neither of us with any answers. Eventually Sophie asked the inevitable – a question I'd posed to myself only recently.

'Do you regret adopting her?'

'God no!' I said. 'She's only been with us for eighteen months. It's going to take longer than that to fix things.'

'But you will get some help, won't you?'

'I'm going to give the Post-Adoption Centre a ring tomorrow. Apparently they're the people to deal with.'

'Good,' she said, and the conversation moved to Daniel and Rob. 'How are *they* coping?' she asked.

'Fine,' I assured her. 'Daniel's almost detached from it. Alex shows hardly any interest in him. It's me she wants to be with. Fortunately, he's got his mates in the close and spends most of his time with them.'

'And Rob?'

I shrugged. 'You know Rob, always positive.' Sophie raised an eyebrow and I continued. 'Obviously he'd like to see Alex more settled and he'd like his wife back to her happy, cheerful self, but he's convinced it's only a matter of time.'

'Mel, you and Rob are OK, aren't you?'

'Oh God, of course,' I said, but when she continued with her look of dubious concern I added, 'Sure, there are times when I wish we were on the same wavelength, but only when I'm feeling particularly sorry for myself. The rest of the time I just want Rob to be happy. This adoption, after all, was my idea.'

'Mel!' she exclaimed. It was the first time I'd admitted as much even to myself, and it had taken me by surprise.

'It was.'

'He could have said "no".'

'I know, but let's be honest,' I said. 'Rob's not the kind of guy to say no, especially as he was being browbeaten by me into believing that we'd make perfect adopters.' I stopped to grimace. 'Remind me again – *why* did I think we'd make great adopters?'

She chuckled. 'It started with a little book, if I remember correctly.'

'Maybe I should have stuck with rescuing unwanted puppies.'

The book had been entitled *A Family of My Own*, and I'd read it obsessively as a child. It had been about a mutt of a dog in a pet rescue home, who'd waited longingly until the very last page to be adopted by a loving family. It had sown the seed of my desire to rescue 'unwanted' children. After that, whether by coincidence or fate, every second person I met seemed to have been adopted. My first real boyfriend had been adopted, my closest friend at work had been adopted, as had two others in our office, and one of my bosses had adopted two children.

When I was in my late teens I discovered my favourite cousin had been adopted and then, just when it seemed I'd exhausted my share of adopted people, I met Rob. Though not adopted himself, his parents had fostered several children while Rob and his brother were growing up. I'd known then that we were meant to be. Of course, it had taken a little more persuasion on my part for us to adopt, including the reassurance that I also wanted birth children of my own.

A year to the day after we'd married, we'd been blessed with Daniel. Two years later we'd tried to conceive our second, but after a year and a half of trying without success, we'd decided that fate had intervened and that we were destined to adopt sooner rather than later. Six months after Daniel's third birthday, we were filling out our first application forms.

'We're never dealt more than we can handle,' Sophie said now. 'You're strong. You'll find a way through this.'

I said goodbye an hour later, feeling much better and saner but, nevertheless, the thought of walking through my front door sat like a rock in my stomach.

*

The following day, I rang and spoke to a Mr Stephen Radshaw at the Post-Adoption Centre. We talked, or more precisely, I talked, for over half an hour, at the end of which he suggested a course of three or four sessions with him so that he could assess our needs and help move us all forwards.

Chapter Thirteen

Stephen Radshaw looked nothing like I'd envisaged on the phone. He was a slight man with very little hair and a high forehead, and wore thick spectacles. However, what he lacked in physical stature he more than made up for in confidence as one of the leading child psychologists in the field of adoption.

After a hail of hearty greetings, he showed us in to the Family Room and gestured for us to sit down. The room had one large sofa and three chairs. I was tempted to sit in one of the chairs away from Alex, as it was crucial that Mr Radshaw wasn't swayed in any way by her displays of affection – love was not the issue right now – but Rob and Daniel were already seated, and Alex had left me a space on the sofa. I sat down and she duly snuggled into my side. Mr Radshaw then eased himself into one of the single chairs opposite, crossed his legs and gave us a world-beating smile.

'Nice to meet you all finally,' he said. 'I'm Stephen Radshaw – call me Steve.'

He began by asking the children if they knew why they were there. They both nodded. We'd prepared them last night, saying we would be meeting a special man who was going to try to make things better for us all.

'Good,' he said. 'I see lots of families like you who are finding things a bit too tricky to sort out themselves: families who have lots of love to give, but who don't really understand how scary it feels to be living with a *new* family.'

Alex's cheeks flushed and she gave a little smile.

'It's my job to help them to understand,' he continued. 'It's also my job to help you, Alex, understand why you're feeling the way you do. To understand why sometimes those feelings make you do things that confuse your new family and sometimes make them angry.'

Mr Radshaw continued talking, breaking off only occasionally to ask questions that often required little more than a 'yes' or 'no'. He spoke positively and empathetically, with an air of confidence that immediately relaxed and absorbed us. As promised, what he said was designed to make us understand both ourselves and each other. The skill with which he chose his words was masterful, so that at no time did anyone have to leave the room. Never once was any one of us made to feel in any way bad or shameful about their thoughts or past behaviour.

After the first ten minutes, I began to grow a little concerned that he might not offer us anything we didn't already know, but then he introduced the word 'control'.

He talked about Alex's desperate need to be in control in a world where once she'd had no control. Her life would have been very scary, he explained, and she had been helpless to change this.

He described how fear would drive the anger that followed all attempts we might make to take back the control. He talked about the mountain of trust that Alex would need to build before she was comfortable with relinquishing control to us, and told us that most children had confidence in their parents' decision-making because they had been shown a million times that their parents knew best. In Alex's case, she'd been shown the very opposite. Telling Alex *we* knew what was best was like telling a man who had been paralysed in a sky-diving accident that sky-diving was safe. Sky-diving *is* safe, he said, but only in the right hands and with the right equipment. Alex had to learn that she was now in safe hands and that we possessed equipment she could trust. That would take considerable time.

The need to be in control, he added, could manifest itself in many ways. Telling a child like Alex what they could and couldn't do was tantamount to taking away their control. Whereas the majority of children might respond with petulance or sadness, children like Alex become angry – angry because the parents are trying to take charge of their 'safe' world and thus, in their eyes, change it. As importantly, this meant taking charge of a world that the parents invariably did not understand.

'Would you hand over control of your world to someone who didn't understand it?' he asked us.

I shook my head, now filled with new insight. Alex's attention seeking was not just about anger; it was also about control.

Rob spoke for both of us when he asked, 'How will we learn to understand Alex's world, if she won't show it to us?' Rob went on to describe how Alex didn't show us her true feelings.

Mr Radshaw told us that Alex needed to trust us before she'd allow us into her world. 'It isn't a pretty world,' he said, 'and before letting you in, Alex will require total confidence that, firstly, you can cope with what you find there, and secondly, you will know what to do with it.' He also explained that hiding her true feelings was keeping those emotions safe from assault. 'Children like Alex have had their emotions abused too often, and therefore build a protective shell around themselves. Any "unauthorised" attempts to penetrate their defences are fought tooth and nail. Have you read *The Primal Wound*?' he asked.

'No,' I confessed, sheepishly. *The Primal Wound* was the bible of the adoption world and I was awash with shame that I'd never bothered to read it. This was yet another mark of my once smug complacency.

'Read it,' he said simply, then turned his attention to Alex once more. 'I don't suppose it's much fun being only seven and having to manage all that control, hmm?'

Alex, who, uncharacteristically, must have wriggled free of my arm at some point in the last twenty minutes, and was now pressed against the edge of the sofa, gave a small nod.

'You know, though, don't you,' he continued to address Alex, 'that Mum and Dad do need to be in charge? They may not yet understand exactly how you're feeling, but it is their job to keep you safe and happy and to prepare you for the big wide world. So you understand that when they ask you to do something you might not want to do, they're doing it because they love you and want what's best for you?'

Mr Radshaw let the words hang and Alex dutifully nodded.

'Good.'

Finally, the consultant turned to Daniel with all the right words of advice and understanding for him, too, even making him laugh. 'I think Alex's very lucky to have a brother like you,' he remarked. Daniel beamed.

And then, with a quick glance at the clock, the consultation was over. I fumbled around in my bag for my diary, eager for our next appointment with this wise and reassuring man. I had my pen poised, but instead Stephen Radshaw threw us a broad smile, and said, 'I don't think we'll need the other two sessions.'

'But all the things we discussed on the phone. What about them?'

'Mr and Mrs Allen, I'm sure there are many more issues than we've addressed today, but I think you'll find they'll soon resolve themselves now you understand the root of the problem. Besides, the most important issue in a case like yours is that the channels of communication are kept open. From the gist of your phone call and on the evidence of today, I would say you are achieving just that.'

I could feel myself relax again, letting his faith trickle into my diminished pool of confidence. 'OK, but—'

'—but if you need me, you've got my number,' he reassured me, with another smile.

Once the children had bounded into the courtyard, and Rob and I had thanked him, he said, 'Just remember that the anger and sense of powerlessness you experience when Alex is in control is nothing compared to the emotions she's having to deal with when she's *not* in control.'

We understood.

That evening I dug out our copy of *The Primal Wound*, and began to read. By the following evening, I was furious with myself for not having read it until now. Had we read it, we could have spared Alex and ourselves months of pain and confusion, and even, perhaps, a trip to the Post-Adoption Centre.

As soon as Rob walked in the door one evening a couple of weeks later, I beckoned him upstairs.

'Alex spat at Daniel today,' I told him.

Rob's eyes widened, he frowned, and then he shrugged, 'Well, good!' he said. 'Better out than in.'

'What, the spit or her anger?'

We both pulled a face, but in truth we were delighted. Alex's recent naughty behaviour was a sign that we were taking back the control. For now, she was having to fight for it.

The following afternoon, a wet Friday, Alex stood at the door waving goodbye to her classmate, Jasmine. Jasmine was only the second girl we'd had home for tea since Alex had started at Hollybrook. The visit had been reasonably successful and I still lived in hope that one of the girls might one day return the invitation.

'Can I play with Daniel and Billie now?' Alex asked, as soon as I'd closed the door.

Since Daniel and his friend had been allowed to play uninterrupted for the past couple of hours, I felt that was all right. 'Yes, if they agree,' I replied, and she bolted past me and up the stairs.

For the next quarter of an hour, I could hear Alex-induced shrieks of laughter coming from Daniel's room, but suddenly he appeared downstairs clearly exasperated.

'Mum, can you tell her to go away?' he pleaded, 'she's being disgusting.'

I sighed, put down my magazine, and followed him upstairs. There were still yelps of excitement coming from his room. I pushed open the door to find Billie darting round the room with Alex in hot pursuit. It looked harmless enough.

'She's putting spit on us,' Daniel explained.

Alex, unaware until now that I was in the doorway, froze in her tracks. She had globules of spit hanging off her chin, and Billie was wiping his face with his sleeve.

My stomach gave an angry lurch.

'That is disgusting! And very naughty! What on earth are you—? Oh, forget it, if you can't play nicely, please leave the room now.'

Alex remained paralysed.

'Now!' I repeated, pointing furiously at the door.

Nothing.

'Now!'

When she still didn't move, I felt the first stirrings of horrible unease. She always did as she was told. What was I going to do if she continued to hold her ground? If she simply refused to budge? The silence stretched interminably. My glare was beginning to waver from the strain of maintaining its authority.

'Now. Please.'

'I don't want to,' she said suddenly, calmly and without petulance.

I kept the surprise from my face. 'Too bad,' I said. 'I warned you about spitting.'

As the silent stand-off continued, my outstretched arm was beginning to ache. Billie and Daniel were watching in fascinated but nervous anticipation and in the end I had no alternative. I marched across the floor and took her arm, but to my surprise, she pulled it back. So I grabbed her wrist more firmly and gave it a gentle tug. However, instead of following me, she dropped to her knees and began furiously twisting her arm out of my hand.

'No!' she screamed suddenly.

I was stunned out of all my anger. My heart began pounding against my chest as my mind reeled with a mixture of shock and fear. This was the moment we'd all been waiting for, I was sure of it. 'Daniel, you and Billie go downstairs,' I said quickly.

'I hate you!' Alex screamed at me, stopping the boys in their tracks. I urged them on and they scurried downstairs. 'I hate you! Get off me!' Alex continued. She was thrashing and writhing beneath me as I began dragging her out of Daniel's room. Her legs connected several times with my shins and I winced silently. Then, just as I'd managed to pull her across the threshold, she spat at my legs – a spray which left a trail of saliva hanging from her mouth. She looked deranged as she spat again. Trying desperately to maintain my composure, I kept pulling.

We'd reached her doorway, when she suddenly emitted a guttural hiss, a sound more animal than human such as I'd never heard before. The hissing grew louder and more guttural with every passing moment. Fear was coursing through every vein in my body. I'd never seen anything like it and I realised I was way out of my depth. Even so, I knew I had to hide my feelings. Alex had to know we could cope with whatever she threw at us.

'I understand you're angry,' I said, citing words from a psychology book, 'but it was wrong to spit.' Then I released my grip, hoping she'd calm down, but she was beyond all control. As she continued to hiss and writhe, I took hold of her once more and dragged her the final few feet into her bedroom.

'I hate you!' she screamed again, as I closed the door on her.

For the next few minutes I stood in the passage, my mouth dry and my body shaking, wincing as object after object was hurled against the back of her door. Then I stumbled into our bedroom and closed the door. Just as I'd sat on the bed, wondering what to do next, the violence from Alex's room suddenly stopped. I pricked up an ear, waiting for the noise to resume. Nothing. The coward in me was relieved, but I also knew Alex would be suffering. I crept across the hall and put an ear to the door. I could hear nothing. In fact, bar the thumping of my heart, the silence was acute. I considered entering, but as she wasn't crying, I opted to leave her alone for a few minutes.

So I went downstairs, found the boys and reassured them that all was well, then drank a glass of water. Though still shaky, a strange sense of relief began to wash over me. Alex had finally let go; she'd at last felt able to show her anger, just as Mr Radshaw had predicted. My mind replayed her outburst and I shuddered. She had been nothing less than a pressure cooker exploding, and it was a frightening reminder of how little we knew about our daughter.

With a sudden sense of urgency, I went back upstairs and knocked on her door. Silence. I knocked again. Still there was no sound and I grew anxious as an unwelcome image of Alex hurling herself out of her window popped into my head. I dismissed it, reminding myself she was only seven years old, but I turned the handle and pushed open the door.

I flinched. Alex was sitting cross-legged on the bed with passionless eyes, waiting for me. Her floor was bare, all the objects she'd hurled having been removed and put away.

'Are you all right?' I forced myself to say.

She nodded but for once didn't simper back, for which I was grateful.

'Well, when you're ready, can you come downstairs and apologise to Daniel and Billie?'

'Yes.'

As I turned to leave, I said to her, 'Alex, I think it's good that you were able to show me that you were angry. I'm proud of you.'

Her mouth twitched and I closed the door.

Later, I recounted the episode to Rob.

'I don't know what was more frightening, the hissing and the spitting, or the way she managed to take back her self-control,' I said.

'Mel, it's a start.'

'I know. Thank God! And I know this sounds strange, but for those few raging minutes, I felt more in control than I've done since she moved in.'

'Yeah, because you could see exactly what you were dealing with.'

Sadly, it would be the one and only time Alex would ever show her anger to us.

Chapter Fourteen

I woke up to a head beautifully empty, but the moment didn't last long. In fact it took less than a second to remember who I was and that I'd downed a bottle and a half of wine the previous night. It took my head and stomach a further second to catch up. I groaned silently, but even that hurt.

I slipped quietly out of bed, forced a smile at Alex who was lying in bed raring for the day to start, and tiptoed downstairs where I swallowed two Paracetamol with half a litre of water. Then I climbed back into bed and waited for relief.

An hour later, still feeling fuzzy and nauseous, I was not amused when Alex started chewing loudly on her crumpet and butter. Even less so when the butter threatened to dribble from her chin onto her school shirt. I grabbed a tissue and swiped away the grease. Alex flinched, but otherwise kept her eyes blank. She was demanding our attention, winding us up and she knew it.

We finished breakfast and at last it was time for school. Alex came bounding down the stairs, her hair gathered together like a fountain on the crown of her head.

'Like it,' I said, forcing cheer, but admiring her style.

'I look funky!'

We slapped hands. 'Come on then, Funky, let's go.'

Getting into the car was always an arduous and ungainly routine for Alex; indeed, she made it look like a Herculean task. For me, it was one more frustrating blood-boiler I was forced to endure at least twice a day.

As we pulled out of Mallard Close, Daniel turned on the radio. The noise jangled my sensitive head, but was preferable to the noises coming from behind. Thankfully, Alex gave up trying to compete, and supplanting one attention-seeking ploy with another, she began opening and closing the electric window. Today, however, she was on a loser: I needed the fresh air.

After dropping Daniel at school, I knew I had only twenty more minutes to endure before I could retreat back into my house and nurse my aching nerves. Alex mumbled something.

I turned the volume down on the radio. 'Sorry?'

The only word I could pick up was 'fairies'.

'Alex, please speak up.'

'I, um, play fairies and we skip.'

I switched off the radio.

'You what?' I said, trying to hide my irritation.

'I played . . . um . . . skipping . . . fairies.'

'That's nice,' I said, wearily. 'When was that?'

'At school time.'

'That's nice.'

Had it been another child talking, I would have been keen to hear their tale. Alex's stories, however, were not only uninteresting, but the tone of her voice when she spoke suggested a lack of interest in the story herself. Only when she was holding the floor and making people laugh did her tone sing. Hence, I had now tentatively included Alex's vapid chatter in the ever-expanding list of tactics she used to stay the centre of attention and, consequently, in control.

I switched the radio back on.

'Are we [*mumble*] up [*mumble*]?' she asked.

I hit the mute button again.

'What?'

'Are we, um, picking up Erin and Bradley after school today?'

'Yes, it's Wednesday. Now please can I listen to the radio?'

Within seconds the back seat began to rock and roll. I managed not to rise to the bait until, as she was turning a hundred and eighty degrees to take a crisp bag off the parcel shelf, she accidentally kicked my elbow through the central console.

'Enough! Now sit still!' I ordered. Then I prepared myself for the painful, paralysed silence that would ensue until we got to school.

When I dropped her off she planted a saliva-sodden kiss on my lips.

'Have a good day,' I said cheerfully. 'Love you.'

I went home, walked straight upstairs, and crawled back into bed, but sleep didn't come because I wasn't tired, at least not mentally. It had been only half past nine last night when I'd fallen into my drink-aided slumber; an hour before Rob returned home from football practice.

This wasn't me. A bottle and a half of wine . . . on my own? How had I sunk to such depths? I'd always been such a positive and buoyant person, sated only by life itself. Drinking was something I did at parties, never on my own. Yet right now, if I wasn't careful, drink would become my lifeline. In a day-to-day existence gobbled up by the demands of a troubled and exhausting child, the sedative lure of alcohol was proving increasingly tempting. In fact, on particularly bad days, it was proving essential if I was to maintain a semblance of normality with Daniel, and to a degree with Rob.

Rob knew things weren't normal, but only in the sense that his daughter was still no less demanding and, as a result, his wife was still exhausted and marginally overdoing the wine consumption. I was happy for him to believe that: I needed him to stay upbeat and positive. The thought that his life might be irreparably damaged by this adoption was terrifying but, as dramatic as that may sound, it was the way I felt. I'd already deprived Rob of a life in his homeland, and unless I made this work, he'd surely regret ever meeting me. So, though I moaned and at times showed my neurosis, I was careful always to prove to him that I could cope; that I wasn't going to require a straitjacket and a padded room.

So, it was fortunate then that Alex targeted me rather than Rob on whom to vent her troubled emotions. Why she chose me I wasn't entirely sure, but my guess was that it had something to do with my being the mother figure and that she resented me for not being her birth mother, Michelle. With me the one most likely to take control, she felt she couldn't relax her grip for too long in my presence.

I understood that. I did! What I didn't understand was why it was taking so long for her to trust that we were no threat to her; that if she'd just allow us to, we could show her what happiness and peace were all about. I rolled over under the duvet and stared across the passage into her sterile bedroom. What were we doing wrong?

I could think of a multitude of sins we'd committed prior to meeting Stephen Radshaw, but in the six weeks since then, I truly believed we'd barely faltered.

We'd ceased resenting Alex's need to be in control; we were infinitely calmer when reacting to her attention seeking and negative behaviour; we'd stopped trying to teach her anything, despite our continued suspicion that some of her alleged ineptitude was no more than an angry refusal to learn; we constantly reassured her of our love for her, and when she *really* went for it, surprising us with the level of her covert destruction, we told her even that wouldn't stop us loving her. Hand in hand with our new understanding of her feelings, wherever possible – that is, whenever there was no doubt that she was playing up – we were now much firmer with her. I recalled now a journey to school last week when I'd told her that, unless she had something interesting to say, I wasn't interested either. Glancing at her reflection in the rear-view mirror, I'd witnessed her genuine surprise, and two small red patches had sprung to her cheeks. Nevertheless, she'd resumed her jabber within twenty-four hours. So *why?* Why, aside from that solitary outburst of violent rage, had we seen no trace of an improvement?

I turned over, dispirited by the image of her bedroom, and let my eyes rest on the gentle movement of the clouds outside. Was it just a matter of time? Were we being too impatient?

Suddenly, a small bell rang inside my head, heralding the memory of some pertinent words I'd once heard: *It took me three years before I could say I loved my daughter.* Brutally honest words spoken by our social worker, Mary, two years ago – and fifteen years after adopting a three-year-old girl of her own. The relationship she had with her daughter now was as close as the one she shared with her birth children.

I smiled in memory of the no-nonsense, plain-speaking Irish lady who filled such a special place in our hearts. And I said a silent word of thanks to her.

Then I did my sums. Alex had been with us for two years – we had a whole year to go!

I flung back the duvet and went downstairs. In the kitchen, I drank a cup of strong coffee and came to a decision. If we were in for the long haul, and I felt we were, I needed a distraction that would take me away from the house and all that it represented. I needed a job.

The following day I dug out and dusted down my CV and started applying for job vacancies advertised in our local paper. A week later, I was offered the position of finance assistant at our local university. The hours were nine a.m. till two p.m., Monday to Friday, term-time only, and I would be starting next week. I couldn't wait!

I clapped loudly and Alex took a bow.

'I think I'll call you Ginger from now on,' I said.

'Who's that?' Alex said, wrinkling her face.

'Ginger Rogers,' I smiled at her.

'Who's that?'

'A famous dancer, that's who.'

'I'm not a famous dancer.'

'No, but you could be. You're good enough,' I said, lining up the next track on the LP, 'or you could be a famous actress.'

'No, I couldn't.'

'If you wanted, you could.'

'I don't. That's silly!' Her eyes were almost playful.

Is it? I thought silently, smiling at her dramatic and animated expressions. *Not from where I'm sitting.* Not only was Alex's mimicry and story-telling funny, but it appeared to spring from an innate talent. With a bit more speech therapy, performing would be effortless.

After joining her on the floor for S Club 7's 'Reach', I watched in awe her rendition of 'Diamonds Are a Girl's Best Friend'. She had me laughing until my sides hurt.

I loved our moments together like this. These were the moments when I felt genuine affection for my daughter; when I felt we connected. These were moments when all my concerns for our fragile relationship transformed into conviction that one day we'd be exceptionally close.

I loved her.

An hour later when Alex, her teeth brushed and her pyjamas on, crawled into bed, I crawled under her duvet with her. I waited for her jittery body to calm down and her loving arms to relax their grip round my neck. Then I asked her if she'd like to join the local singing, dancing and drama club. I'd been intending to wait until her speech had improved and she'd learnt at least to recite a nursery rhyme, but now I was beginning to think that maybe the classes might encourage her speech.

'Ummmmmm . . .'

'I think you'd enjoy it.'

'I would like to,' she said quietly.

I smiled. 'Good. I'll ring the teacher tomorrow.'

'And tell her about me.'

It took a moment for me to understand what she was saying. 'Of course! I'll tell her what a star you are.'

'No, I'm not!'

'You are!'

'I'm not!'

'Are!'

'I'm not!'

'Are! Are! Are!' – and I began tickling her tummy. 'Are! Are! Are!' She writhed in a fit of giggling until I stopped.

'I'm gonna kill you,' she said.

It had been said so quietly I almost missed it.

I pulled away and my eyes shot to her face.

'Ha! Ha! Tricked you!'

I let the breath out of my lungs and managed to find a smile. 'Very funny, young lady.'

The following day, I tracked down the number for Little Troupers. I spoke to a Vanessa, who ran the club, and told her about Alex's learning difficulties, but I also told her how well she could hold the floor when it came to entertaining.

She told me all about one of her pupils who had Down's syndrome and said that she'd love to accept Alex into her classes. She could start next week.

'Still up for Friday night?' Gabby called out as I left the building.

'Can't wait.'

With a final wave I skipped into the car park, feeling happier than I'd done in years. Spring had come, and I loved my job. I'd only been at the university for two weeks, but already I felt as much a part of the place as if I'd been there ten years. The girls in the main office were lovely. We were all of similar age and only one, Megan, had no children. Instead she had a wonderfully acerbic wit, and kept us entertained with delicious fantasies of gruesome mishaps that might befall the thin-lipped assistant to the college dean.

As I climbed into my car, still smiling, I realised I'd not thought of Alex once all day.

Chapter Fifteen

*M*rs Soane accompanied Alex out of her class and into the playground where I was waiting. She had an arm round her shoulder.

'We've had a bit of an upset today, Mrs Allen,' she grimaced apologetically.

'Is she all right?' I asked, alarmed.

'We've had a few tears,' she explained, and pointed to a dinnerplate-sized wet patch on her silk blouse, 'but she's all right now.' She went on to explain that Alex had repeatedly pulled books off the bookcase during class and that, eventually, she'd been forced to raise her voice to her. 'I think she was just shocked,' she said with a cloying squeeze of Alex's shoulders.

Any sympathy I'd been saving for Alex evaporated on looking at her huge, black, blameless eyes and at her gushing remorse. My blood began to simmer. When was Mrs Soane going to wake up and see that no one said no to Alex? That pulling books off the shelf was nothing more than good old-fashioned attention seeking, and that the timidity she responded with when told off was just . . . was just Alex! I forced myself not to say the word 'fake', as she'd proved me wrong before.

I painted on a smile and assured Mrs Soane that I understood, although, lest she'd forgotten, I also felt compelled to remind her that Alex should not have been pulling books off the shelf in the first place.

She waved a dismissive hand. 'Alex gets a little confused with the rules sometimes.'

I breathed hard.

Alex found my hand as soon as we'd exited the school gates, but I yanked it away. As I strode down the alleyway, she scuttled alongside me no more than an inch away, bumping into my thigh. When I tripped over her foot a second time, I ground to a halt.

'How many times have I told you not to walk so close?'

'Um, lots,' she said with frozen rabbit eyes.

'Well, stop doing it then!' I yelled.

Just then, two mums from the school turned into the alleyway. There followed a hideously awkward moment as the echo from my shouting bounced sharply off the walls. Then, lifting their eyes, one mum fired me a look of disgust while the other gave Alex a look of sympathy. I stood stock still as they walked on muttering and tutting to themselves.

We arrived at Daniel's school and he and Bradley climbed in the car. We'd barely reached the end of the road when Alex's finger-poking antics and inane laughter had hit hysterical proportions.

I was sure she was laughing at me.

'She's crowding us,' I whispered to Rob in our bedroom as he was changing into a pair of jeans after work.

'Sorry?'

'Alex doesn't hover two inches from our side because she needs to feel secure. She's doing it because she's angry,' I explained, my conviction tumbling from my mouth.

Rob gave his head a little shake. 'What do you mean?'

I explained. 'In the playground today, I told her she couldn't eat a second lollipop until after tea. She spent the next five minutes glued to my side. She mirrored me step for step. And I *mean* step for step – you know that game we used to play as kids when you repeat everything someone says just to wind them up? That's what it felt like.'

He looked at me hard, trying to make sense of this, but I knew I was right.

It was time for new school shoes.

Daniel and Alex scanned the displays and chose the ones they liked best, after which we found an empty seat and waited for an assistant. Peering into my bag, Alex found what she was looking for and turned on her large, pleading eyes. Who could deny such eyes!

I reached into my bag and pulled out their 'Friday' sweets. Alex ripped into her packet of blackcurrant Chews.

'Not all of them,' I reminded her.

When she'd eaten two-thirds of the packet and an assistant still hadn't become free, she turned her eyes on me once more.

'Can I have some more? I'll eat my tea—'

I was going out with the girls that night and I was in a good mood. 'Go on then.'

She put her head down and mumbled something.

My jaw dropped.

'What did you say?' I asked.

She froze. 'Um . . . nothing.'

'You did!' I exclaimed, with a disbelieving smile. 'You said "well done". Didn't you!'

'Um . . . yes.'

'Why?'

'Er, I like the sweets.'

Stunned at the brazenness of her comment and the volumes it spoke, I was left speechless. I had just been congratulated for giving her sweets! An assistant arrived in the nick of time.

'Ooh, sweets! Can I have one?'

I was spared from having to say anything further.

Six weeks after Alex had started at Little Troupers, I got the phone call I'd been expecting from Vanessa – she'd already hinted that Alex was struggling to keep up.

'I'm sorry,' she said, 'maybe if you left it a year—'

'No, don't worry. I don't think she was enjoying it that much anyway,' I said, without implying criticism of her classes. She had a waiting list a year long.

'May I say something?' Vanessa asked in a tentative voice.

'Sure.'

'Alex's adopted right? Has she got, well, emotional problems?'

I was taken aback but felt far from offended. 'Yes. How did you know?'

'Alex has a way about her that reminds me of my adopted son.'

'I didn't know you'd adopted a child.'

'Thirty-five years ago, but I haven't seen him for fifteen years. I don't tend to brag about him.' She chuckled drily.

I expressed sympathy and then, desperate for her thoughts, asked her to elaborate on Alex, declaring her the first person outside our home to pick up on her problems.

'I think it's the staring that first made me suspect. My son used to do the same when he was angry.'

Angry! 'How did you know Alex was angry?' I asked.

'Because she only stares at us when we're too busy to give her one to one. My son was similar – he hated being ignored, if that's the right word. I also think Alex may be overplaying the "I can't do it" bit. I've watched her, and there's nothing so slow about her that she can't learn two lines from a song.'

I was flooded with gratitude. 'I can't tell you how relieved I feel to hear you say all this,' I said. 'There've been times I've thought we were going mad; that we were the ones with the problem.'

'These kids are very good at playing the innocent. My son was the same. Outside the home he was all sweetness and light. Inside, he was a monster.'

'Did he hide his emotions, too?'

She gave a wry laugh. 'God no! He threw the most awful tantrums I've ever seen, just about every single day. Always when he couldn't get his own way.'

'Where is he now?'

'Who knows? Last time we heard, he was in prison for arson,' she said. 'We used to bail him out, but not any more.'

How awful, I thought, and though I was sure Alex wouldn't go the same way, I touched wood anyway.

We talked a bit more about her son, then she asked if we were getting help for Alex. I told her about the Post-Adoption Centre and their confidence that in time she'd settle down. Vanessa made me promise that, if ever we felt the problem was too big to handle, we'd bring the professionals in. I assured her we would. Then she advised me not to allow ourselves to become wrapped around Alex's little finger, because she didn't think Alex was quite the self-effacing little thing she appeared to be.

'What do you mean?' I asked, stunned again by her perceptiveness.

'It was something she said at the end of her first class,' she began. 'Just before you collected her, she approached each of my four assistants and thanked them for being "good teachers".'

I winced. The comment left a similar taste to the one she'd made to me in the shoe shop. 'I'm sorry,' I said.

'Don't be! I just thought it was an interesting comment to be made by a child like Alex, and certainly not one I've heard in all my years of teaching.'

After reiterating my gratitude to Vanessa and saying goodbye, I replaced the receiver and punched the air, jubilant that we'd finally found someone who could see through Alex's butter-wouldn't-melt demeanour. Surely, it wouldn't be long before the rest of the world caught up. Then I rang Rob with the good news.

'Mum, my teacher gave me some homework.'

'OK, let's have a look.' As Alex was still so far behind at school, it was rare that she was given homework other than reading and writing practice.

She pulled out a piece of paper from her pocket, scrunched to within an inch of its life.

I studied the sheet. It had the seven days of the week printed down the first column and the remaining columns were entitled *breakfast, snack, lunch, snack, dinner*. It was the *Diary of What I Eat* homework.

'So what do you have to do then?' I asked, engaging her in conversation.

She pointed at the sheet. 'Um . . . this.'

I smiled at her misunderstanding. 'No, what do you have to do for your homework?' I asked, my breezy tone falling away.

Alex stiffened into her familiar pose of timid confusion and I felt myself being propelled into that place I hated so much. A vortex of frustration and doubt, steered by Alex's spinning finger. *Don't let Alex wrap you round her little finger* . . . Vanessa's words rang in my ears, and I dug my heels in, bringing the journey to a grinding halt. I returned to the starting point, smiled sweetly at Alex, and ran a final check.

'Did she explain the homework to you?'

'Um . . . I think so.'

Which meant yes. Good.

'Well then, you'll know what to do, won't you?' I smiled. It was so much easier to smile outside of the vortex.

I turned round and resumed peeling the potatoes, but from the corner of my eye I could see Alex had remained stock still, one hand on the chair, staring at me.

'What?' I asked, feigning innocence.

'I, um . . . I don't know how to do it.' Her voice was so small and imploring that a bubble of doubt broke through my defences. I popped it.

'I'm afraid I can't help you,' I lied, 'because neither do I. So you're going to have to try to remember.'

I picked up the kitchen knife and began slicing the potatoes, cranking up the volume on the radio. As I began sashaying around the floor, I could feel the stirrings of something powerful grow inside me. I wasn't altogether sure it was a healthy feeling, but that unwavering stance and those staring eyes weren't pushing the usual buttons, so I allowed the feeling to build.

'Have you remembered yet?' I shouted nonchalantly over the radio, a few minutes later.

She shook her head.

'OK, well let me know when you do.'

Daniel came in. 'What are you doing?' he asked, clearly unnerved by the strange atmosphere in the kitchen, particularly the sight of his mum dancing around the kitchen wielding a knife.

'Waiting for Alex to remember what her homework is,' I said brightly.

He looked down at her homework sheet lying on the kitchen table. His eyes lit up. 'Oh, we did this one,' he said. 'This is the one where you have to—'

'Yes, thank you, Daniel,' I said, 'but I'm waiting for Alex to tell me.'

Alex's eyes grew dark but otherwise remained expressionless.

Daniel looked confused and I ushered him out of the kitchen with the promise to Alex that I'd be back.

'Why can't I tell her what the homework is?' Daniel asked.

'Because she already knows.'

'But—'

'But nothing, Daniel,' I said. 'I know this might be difficult to understand, but I think Alex's cleverer than she pretends. I think she knows what the homework is, but doesn't want to say it.'

'Why?' he asked.

'I don't know, but it's something we're trying to figure out.'

I left Daniel watching TV.

Alex didn't appear to have moved an inch.

'So, have you remembered yet?'

'Um, no.'

Five more minutes passed, and I was still surprisingly calm. Not so long ago those same five minutes would have passed by like an hour in a Chinese torture chamber, but today, I could have conquered the world in half the time.

When Alex coughed, I turned round. She still hadn't moved. I stopped stirring the gravy. 'Have a look,' I suggested, pointing to her homework sheet. 'That might help to remind you.' My voice was sounding syrupy and contrived.

She frowned briefly at the sheet and then re-pinned me with her stare.

'Still don't know?'

She shook her head and I knew instinctively she was raging.

'Oh well, it looks like you're going to have to ask your teacher to explain it once more.'

She struggled for a beat before saying, 'I don't want to.'

As always, her declarations of 'wanting' or 'not wanting' took me by surprise. 'Why not?'

'Um . . . Mmmm . . . I dunno.'

I do. You want me to tell you. I held strong. *Sorry, not this time, Alex.* 'I can't help you on that one, but I can help you with the homework, if you can tell me what it's about.'

'I can't,' she said eventually.

'Then you'll have to ask your teacher to remind you.'

The battle raging within her was almost tangible. She knew that if she left now she'd have lost the battle for control, but she could also sense the unbending shift in my demeanour. In fact, I believed she could sense, with every perceptive bone in her body, that I'd never felt as much in control as I had tonight. Alex, better than anyone, understood the essence of feeling in control, and she knew I had no intention of relinquishing it; she knew that she could smash a glass on the floor right now and I'd still smile sweetly.

Holding the stare until the bitter end, she marched swiftly out of the kitchen.

I smiled to myself. Riding high in the battle for control was a hugely powerful sensation, and it helped me to understand Alex a little bit more.

The following afternoon, Mrs Soane took me to one side, looking tight-lipped and uncomfortable.

'Alex was upset this morning. She said you wouldn't help her with her homework.'

Blood rushed to my cheeks. 'Did she tell you *why* I wouldn't help her?'

'No, only that you wouldn't help her.'

I paused. 'That's not strictly true,' I said. 'She couldn't tell me what the homework was about, so I suggested she ask you to explain it again.' My tone dropped away, hollow.

'The sheet was fairly self-explanatory, Mrs Allen.'

What could I say? Not much, except to apologise and to promise to read the sheet more carefully next time.

I left her office, shamed but maddened. One—nil to Alex.

Chapter Sixteen

*T*hat summer Alex received her first school report. She could almost count to ten and knew most of the letters of her alphabet.

Dad had given Daniel a spud gun. However, when Rob caught Alex pointing the potato-loaded gun an inch from the back of Daniel's unsuspecting head, he told her that if he caught her aiming it so close again we'd be forced to take it away. Less than twenty-four hours later, I found her repeating the exercise with Scooter. Enraged, I grabbed the gun from her and told her that until she could be sensible with it she was not allowed to touch it.

When Alex came in to tea later that day, she sat in the wrong chair. My chair.

During tea, she managed to drop her drink on the floor twice. I mopped up the mess.

Later, she got a book stuck behind the wardrobe in her bedroom. Rob fished it out.

Then she began bouncing a tennis ball on her bedroom wall. Now I *knew* she was angry.

I walked into her room and sat down beside her on the bed. 'Do I guess that you're angry?'

Her eyes bored into mine.

'Because I took away the gun, right?'

Her stare wavered.

'Do you remember why we took the gun?'

''Cos of Cooter.'

I nodded. 'So why are you angry?'

'Um . . . you took the gun.' Her voice was flat, but her eyes were dark.

'But we warned you.'

Not a twitch.

I sighed, weary and perplexed. 'Alex, if a robber robs a bank, should the police send him to prison?'

'Um . . . yes.'

'And when he's in prison, what will he feel, angry or sad?'

'Um . . . angry.'

'Angry with whom, the police or himself?'

Pause. 'The police.'

I was beginning to despair. 'Why?'

''Cos he's in prison.'

My despair continued. 'But he was naughty. He knew that if he robbed a bank, he would go to prison. Just like you knew that if you used the gun dangerously, we'd take it away.'

Nothing. I tried a different tack. 'If I shot you with the gun that close, it would hurt, wouldn't it?'

'Yes.'

'And if I did it twice, would you like me for doing it?'

'Um . . . no.'

'How would you feel?'

Pause. 'Angry.'

'And if you could, would you take the gun away from me, so that I wouldn't hurt you again?'

'Um, yes.'

'And how do you think I would feel when you took the gun away?'

'Um . . . angry.'

I gave up.

Life at home was not improving. In fact, it took an unsettling lurch for the worse when Alex turned her attentions to Daniel. My guess was that, with our drive to remain calm and 'understanding', Alex was sensing a loss of control over me and Rob, so began to target Daniel. Not, I believed, because she disliked, or even necessarily resented him, but because she sensed how precious his wellbeing was to us and she knew we'd jump to protect him.

It took us a while to cotton on to her change of tack and to the fact that Daniel was now the object of her 'mind games' – as we now referred to her attention-seeking behaviour. They seemed fairly innocuous at first: nothing more than disturbing a homework session or causing disruption when he had a friend to play. We were not even particularly alarmed when she began to stare at Daniel during mealtimes, but when she woke him for the third time in a week, I finally jumped. The jump had been as unrestrained as that of a lioness protecting her cubs against attack.

It was during breakfast that I discovered Alex had disregarded our previous two requests not to wake Daniel and had switched on his light at five-fifteen in the morning under the pretext of trying to locate a missing book. I exploded. All the constructive advice from Mr Radshaw and the textbooks went out of the window yet again.

I grabbed Alex and marched her upstairs to her room. 'I want every book out of here and onto our bedroom floor, now,' I ordered. 'And just in case you're tempted to use your toys to wake Daniel, I want them on our floor as well,' I said. My rational side was warning me that my behaviour was extreme, but I ignored it. 'And if you *ever* wake him again, you'll be sleeping downstairs. Understand?'

This was not a pointless threat: I knew instinctively that she'd hate to sleep downstairs.

She nodded feverishly.

Emptying her room would take a while, so Rob took Daniel to school. When I thought enough time had passed, I went back upstairs. Her room was empty. She'd even taken the posters off her wall, which really irked me, and my pique increased tenfold when I entered our room to find all her stuff stacked neatly on top of our bed. If she could act on the 'everything' bit of my earlier command, why could she not tell the difference between a floor and a bed?

'In here, now!' I shouted. In a fraction of a second she was at my side, rigid, and staring with terrified bewilderment at me. 'Get these things off my bed and onto the floor.' She picked up the first stack of books and scanned the room with nervous confusion. 'The floor,' I said firmly, pointing to a spot by my wardrobe. Instantly, she scampered over and put the books down. I didn't move until our bed was empty again.

Then, with a quick phone call to let the office know I was going to be five minutes late for work, I drove Alex to school. For the first time in months, I didn't kiss her goodbye.

At work, Megan asked if I was OK, that I'd not seemed myself that morning. Work was my Alex-free zone, so I lied and said I had a headache.

Just after lunch, I received a call from the school secretary asking me to collect Alex. She'd been violently sick over her bumblebee outfit during rehearsals for their summer play.

She looked pale when I arrived but I have to be honest and say I strained to make a suitable fuss of her. Even when she threw up into a small plastic bowl on the journey home, my emotions were conflicted and I was unable to muster the required amount of sympathy.

'We'll be home soon,' was all I said.

When we arrived home, I walked slowly with her to her stark and empty bedroom.

She pulled the duvet over herself, looking horribly small and vulnerable. I smoothed her duvet down automatically rather than devotedly. 'Here's the bowl, if you need it,' I said. 'I'm going downstairs.'

I stumbled down the last three steps and landed on my knees at the bottom. I admonished myself for being so unsympathetic. I felt sick, numb, hateful, hopeless and stupid. *Now who's the bloody adult?*

In the morning, Alex still had a temperature, so I rang to say I wouldn't be in to work. Alex and I had just settled down to watching some TV, when Jude knocked on the door unexpectedly. She'd locked herself out of her house and wanted the key we kept for such emergencies. As I was rummaging around in the drawer for it, the phone rang. It was Daniel's school, saying he was feeling sick and could I pick him up?

'I'll sit with her, if you want,' Jude offered.

I returned twenty minutes later to find Jude descending our stairs from the direction of Alex's bleak bedroom. My stomach dropped.

'She told me she couldn't find her Noddy book.'

'Oh! Yeah,' I fumbled. *Think!* 'It's in our bedroom. With all her other stuff. Er, I'm doing a spring clean.'

I think she believed me. My only concern now was that neither Alex nor Daniel had overheard my lie.

Two—nil to Alex!

Over tea, I managed to engineer an apology from her. I asked her if she was ready to say sorry to Daniel for waking him.

'Yes,' she replied.

By the time she went to bed, her shelves had been replenished and I'd made a vow never to underestimate her again.

The following morning, Rob rang his mum to say we wouldn't be going to Australia this summer. The excuse he gave, that I was newly employed and unable to take the time off work, was lame. Gabby could have covered for me, but we had no option. He promised her that he'd fly over in October for ten days. Then he retreated to his garage.

Chapter Seventeen

*I*n August of that year, beneath a deep-blue Mediterranean sky, Matt and Lilly finally tied the knot.

'Congratulations big bro!' I said, curling my arms round Matt's big-bear chest.

'Lucky, aren't I?' he grinned.

'Yes,' I said, 'and so is she.' We stood for a moment, arm in arm, admiring his radiant wife, who'd never looked more beautiful than she did today.

'Do you think you'll ever move to Spain?' I asked. 'I mean, look at it!' Our eyes drifted over the backdrop of majestic mountains, so close we could almost touch them, and across to the serene blue waters of the Mediterranean Sea visible beyond the taverna.

'Maybe one day,' he said. 'Someone's going to have to take over this place when Lilly's parents go. It's been in the family too many generations to let it go.'

A few minutes later, Matt was 'borrowed' for some more photos and I took a moment to myself to soak in the atmosphere. The guests were milling around or seated at festive tables in the courtyard, sheltered by a vast canopy of trailing vine. The sun was beginning to dip and the evening's festivities would soon be starting.

My eyes came to rest on a table in the far corner, and I felt an unpleasant jarring in my stomach. My eyes were surely deceiving me! I squinted for a sharper picture and, sure enough, there was Alex, sitting perfectly poised at a table full of people we'd never met. They looked to be Spanish and there were no other children amongst them.

I didn't know what to think or how to react. The sight of her so composed in the company of total strangers set my emotions spinning. Part of me wanted to turn away and forget I'd witnessed the scene, but as I edged closer for a better look, I noticed that none of the others appeared to be talking to her. In fact, even from twenty feet away, I could sense the awkward atmosphere. I felt suddenly ashamed that Alex was my daughter and equally angry that she was unsettling their moment.

I began to make my way over to the table but had barely covered the distance when a hand shot out from a nearby table blocking my path. It was Tess.

'Are you OK?' she asked. 'You look flushed.'

'Look at her,' I said despairingly, my eyes glued to Alex. 'Those poor people don't know where to look.'

'What *are* you talking about?'

'There!' I pointed. 'Alex . . . sitting with a table full of strangers who probably don't even speak English.'

'Ah, bless.' A sentimental smile filled her face.

'It's not, "ah, bless!" for Christ's sake. How would you feel if a child of yours imposed herself like that?'

Tess recoiled. 'Cut her some slack, Mel, she's only being sociable.'

'Do you see anyone talking to her?'

Alex's ears must have been burning because she suddenly turned round and gave us a small wave. Tess waved back; I stood like stone.

'No,' she said coldly, 'but she likes being around people. Anyway, better that way than if she was timid as a mouse. And yes, for what it's worth, I'd be delighted if a child of mine grew up as confident as Alex.'

I gave up. And when, later, Alex took to the floor and entertained the guests with her moves and her laughter beneath that beautiful face, I turned away.

I wanted my mum.

The following morning I learned that one of Lilly's relatives, who'd been at the table, had earlier asked Alex to stop ripping the foliage off the vine canopies. This was yet more evidence, as far as I was concerned, that Alex 'crowded' anyone who attempted to control her.

Two days after the wedding, we arrived at the Coral Waters Aparthotel – three-star, 'family-friendly' – on the Costa del Sol. We had made a last-minute booking to coincide with the wedding, and it had not been an easy decision. For starters, we had cancelled Australia: how would Rob's family react when they discovered we'd gone to Spain instead? But we'd pushed aside our guilt. The flight took only two hours, we were already in Spain for the wedding, and we would only be away for a week – short enough to survive if the holiday turned out to be a disaster. And lastly, but most important, in Spain we were anonymous. We would be staying in our own apartment and answerable only to ourselves. The consequences of Alex's behaviour, should she continue to play up, would not be felt by anyone else.

We dumped our bags in the tiny sun-baked apartment and decided on a quick dip to cool down before unpacking. As Rob and I located the swimming costumes and the sun-cream, Alex initiated a game of 'it'. As she and Daniel charged around the apartment, tripping over bags, and bounding off sofa beds that had seen better days, Rob and I grimaced. There was barely enough room in the apartment for the four of us to draw breath, let alone play boisterous games. I could see we'd be spending most of our time by the pool.

That afternoon, Daniel found a friend, Max, whose parents we befriended later in the evening over several glasses of rum and Coke. Fascinated and smitten by Alex, Anne, Max's mum, quickly took her under her wing. For the next two days, after which they were flying home, we barely lifted a finger, and I slowly began to unwind.

But then they were gone, and we felt ourselves being catapulted right back into hell, only this time with no escape. Even here, with a glorious pool, miles of sandy beach and warm waters, Alex had eyes for nothing and no one but us. Rob was getting his first real taste of Alex and I didn't know whether that was a good or a bad thing.

Meal times in the restaurant became an ordeal as we tried to contain Alex's eating games. When we could no longer tolerate the Siberian glances of the waiters, whose hearts were clearly bleeding for the sweet, friendly little girl who was being made to endure her meals in near silence, we retreated to the confines of our apartment where, in temperatures reaching ninety-five degrees, we prepared the remainder of our meals in a kitchenette no bigger than the upstairs toilet at home.

Time spent at the pool proved no easier. Alex's attention-seeking games, so covert that they were indiscernible to the guests in the neighbouring sunbeds, drove us to crests of anger not reached before. When we finally broke and ordered her to remain quietly beside us, she would sit motionless, wearing her wounded expression and choosing neither to read nor to play her Game Boy. Reclining in the sun with Alex frozen like a statue only inches away played havoc with our nerves and earned us the scorn of the watchful guests around us.

On the morning of the fifth day I awoke with a certainty that neither Rob nor I had enough in our tanks to see us through the next two days. And yet we had no way of refilling them. We had no jobs to escape to, no Sophie or football practice where we could let off steam, no school to give us some respite, and no bedroom where we could hide away and refuel. The only feasible option was to split into two pairs, Rob and I alternating shifts between Alex and Daniel. That way, we hoped we could top up the tank just enough to see us through the next shift.

Rob pulled the short straw and got Alex for the first shift. He opted to take her for a game of mini-golf and then an ice-cream. Daniel and I chose the pool.

I hated to admit it, but the relief when they left was immense. As was the pleasure I experienced from being alone and unwatched with Daniel. We splashed and giggled and dived in the pool. Eventually, when our hands were wrinkled and prune-like, we decamped to our sunbeds to eat ice-cream and play cards.

When Rob and Alex arrived back for lunch, my son and I were enjoying easy chatter about school and friends, catching up on what felt like two years of news. I was tempted to trade a couple of years' worth of washing-up if Rob would only take my next shift, but he was clearly running on empty.

Lunch drained some of my reserves and I knew I was going to have to breathe very deeply to get through the afternoon with Alex. Rob and Daniel arranged to hire bikes for a couple of hours and explore the resort; I decided on the beach, where the chances of being recognised from the hotel were minimal.

My first task, though, was to reapply Alex's sun-cream, a task so onerous I was almost tempted to stay in the apartment and watch TV instead. This ordeal had begun when we first arrived on the holiday. Initially, she'd merely giggled and writhed when we attempted to apply the cream. After a while, the 'joke' wore thin and we'd demanded she keep still, which she duly did with textbook precision. Once we'd tired of shuffling circles around her on our knees, we toyed with the idea of letting her apply the cream herself, but having seen how she applied soap to only one side of her body, or shampoo only on the crown of her head, we decided the risk of sunburn wasn't worth taking. So here I was now, asking her to move.

I gritted my teeth and, squatting on the floor with Factor-30 glooping down my arms, I asked her to turn around. We were used to the drill by now and the inevitable sparks of adrenalin began flying across the air between us. She made a quarter-turn, leaving me just her right shoulder.

'All the way round,' I said.

Looking suitably confused, she made a three-quarter turn the other way, offering me her left shoulder instead.

Suddenly, I felt a psychic shift in my head; a disengaging almost, of mind and body, and when I spoke my voice was robotic. 'Please, Alex, no more.'

She vacillated between left and right for a moment too long, and my patience was suddenly gone. I snapped and, at that same moment, Daniel bounded through the front door to fetch his hat which he'd forgotten to take.

I grabbed Alex's shoulders, twisted them round a hundred and eighty degrees and, exploding with anger and frustration, screamed at her: 'Stop it! Stop it! Stop it! Just fucking stop it!'

Only Daniel's anguished cries brought the terrible moment to an end.

For a long moment I tried to draw breath. When it came, the horror of my actions hit me like a tank: the aggression I'd inflicted on Alex and the pain I'd inflicted on Daniel.

'Go and get Dad,' I managed weakly.

When I finally found the courage to look at Alex, she was staring down at me – flushed, dry-eyed, but otherwise inscrutable. She had vivid finger marks on her shoulders – were they an indication of how violently I'd seized her? Suddenly, I couldn't remember the moment, and I was scared. Very scared. How badly had I hurt her? I told her to wait for Rob in the bedroom and was relieved beyond belief when she scurried, unimpaired, across the living room and disappeared into the bedroom.

I collapsed onto the floor and began to pray. I prayed for forgiveness. I prayed for Alex and I prayed for Daniel. And then I prayed for help.

The following day, I woke up feeling bleak and sullied. The mood over breakfast was sombre and at ten o'clock we explained to Alex that she would be going to the Kids' Club for the day. She took the news like she did almost everything in life – with acquiescence.

After dropping her off, I set about making amends to Daniel, but he didn't need much persuasion, and again we were forced to question why he so readily accepted the way we behaved towards Alex. After all, to the innocent eye, we must have appeared harsh and intolerant. But then I remembered that he avoided Alex whenever possible and I could only guess that, though he couldn't rationalise our behaviour, he instinctively understood.

With Alex absent, the day passed peaceably for the rest of us. At five o'clock, we went to collect her and waited a few moments before entering the Kids' Club. With an ear to the door, we instantly recognised the sound of her giggles. We went in to find her on sparkling form, holding court with three of the young Spanish assistants.

'She very laavly,' one of them gushed, as I signed her out. Our daughter dropped her eyes coyly and smiled.

The following day, we checked out without regret and boarded our flight home at seven o'clock that evening. Alex, apparently quite recovered from my attack on her, asked to sit next to me. I gave her one hundred and ten per cent of my attention, and any more I could squeeze out. Half an hour before we landed, she fell asleep in my lap.

The sense of liberation I felt when we finally walked through the front door of our house was exquisite. No less than it must be to step into a meadow after a week trapped in a mine shaft. I would never again call our home a hell hole.

At midnight, as we collapsed into bed, Rob and I agreed that if things did not improve by Christmas we would seek help, and this time we would not take no for an answer.

It took me a long time to forgive myself for my hideous loss of control with Alex, and even then, I knew I'd never be able fully to justify it. I consoled myself a little with the fact that she understood. She might not have deserved or liked it, but it had been the reaction she wanted. When I exploded in anger, I also lost control. The result for Alex hadn't been all bad.

Chapter Eighteen

*T*he dynamics at home changed overnight. We were now convinced that Alex was a very seriously damaged child who'd somehow learnt to mask that fact. We had our own theories as to how she'd managed to create this veneer, the most obvious being that she'd been born a gifted actress. To family and teachers this was of course a truly risible suggestion, one that we'd surely latched onto because, well, because we just weren't ourselves any more. But we held to our belief, not only because we sensed it was true, but because it was completely feasible – if Jodie Foster could do it, so could Alex.

As to *why* she'd chosen to hide her true self, again we had our theories, all but two of them textbook stuff. The first of the non-textbook theories was that Alex had learnt very early on that to expose her true emotions was not only futile, but also risky. We believed she had learned long ago to keep her mouth shut.

The second of our own theories, and the one that sat least comfortably with us, was that Alex had grasped the *power* of secrecy. She'd long ago realised how much control it brought her, and the frustration it caused to those around her, as they sought urgently to understand her. At three and a half, Alex had not yet been able to communicate verbally. Her speech development was delayed. We felt that, consequently, she had latched on to the extra attention her muteness brought her and sensed the impotence of those trying to unravel her state of mind.

Our newly cemented knowledge was not the primary cause for the shift in dynamics. That came from Rob and me who, for the first time in two years, stood united. A week with Alex had opened Rob's eyes, and because we were now like-minded, we felt stronger and more resolute. We were two heads working on the same puzzle.

Gone was the unspoken conflict between us which had sapped our strength and confused our perception of the real battle to be fought. We were holding hands again and, as happier people, we were less vulnerable to Alex's attempts to hurt or anger us.

Before we knew it, we were back in control of ourselves and our wellbeing, and although we still suffered daily frustrations at Alex's continued behaviour pattern, we were able to manage them. The anger, the hair-pulling and the pleading were gone. Calm descended over our corner of the Close. Daniel started bringing his friends round again and family and friends began to relax around us.

Alex picked up on this changed atmosphere immediately. Suddenly toilets were blocked with reams of toilet paper; too many toys needed fixing; her walk – a particularly prickly issue – grew more bizarre by the day until she was hop-trot-skipping everywhere we went; her footfall on the stairs grew ever louder, stopping just short of sounding stroppy; excessive mud was brought into the house and very obviously smeared on the carpet; her eating and drinking got progressively louder, even slower, and more clumsy until it was farcical; she would stand closer to us than ever and her staring was now blatant. And that was just for starters.

At this point, I would like to say we never once rose to the bait, but that would be untrue. In most instances we kept calm, especially when we knew we could 'mop-up' afterwards. However, some experiences were simply too excruciating. They were the 'drip, drip, drip' scenarios, as we called them; those we couldn't escape: the odd walking – how I hated that – the car journeys, and the crowding. In those cases, we didn't lose control altogether, but managed to confine our reactions to weary pleading rather than volcanic eruptions.

All in all we were doing well, with life at home manageable. And still we waited for Alex to trust in us.

I got home from work to find a message on the answerphone. It was from a Mrs Levitt whose daughter, Leah, was in the same class as Alex. She had left her number and asked me to return her call as soon as possible. She sounded terse and uneasy.

I rang the number and Mrs Levitt answered immediately. She wasted no time before explaining the reason for her call: she'd witnessed Alex elbowing Leah's recently broken wrist, and when she'd recounted the incident to Mrs Wilmot, the class teacher, Mrs Wilmot had not been unduly concerned. She hadn't even felt it necessary to reprimand Alex, and told Mrs Levitt that Alex had not understood the implications of elbowing her daughter's wrist and that she'd certainly not done it deliberately.

I was now grimacing down the phone. Leah's mum went on to say that she'd been left with no option but to keep Leah at home until her wrist had fully healed.

She waited for me to speak. I imagine she was challenging me to defend my daughter, but I couldn't. I was furious with Alex, and with Mrs Wilmot. I apologised profusely to Mrs Levitt, agreed that she'd been right to feel aggrieved, and gave her my assurance that I would put things right with Mrs Wilmot later that afternoon.

She thanked me, slightly derailed by my response, and put down the phone.

I waited in the playground, alone and pumped up with anger. When Mrs Wilmot emerged with her line of children, I walked right up to her and asked tersely if I could have a word. Her eyes widened at my clipped tone – I'd never so much as booed at a goose when Daniel had been her student. She asked me to wait in her classroom.

When the last of her children had been handed safely to their parents, and Alex had been coaxed into the library under instructions to wait there until I returned, I confronted Mrs Wilmot.

Why, I asked, had she not felt it necessary to reprimand Alex for elbowing Leah's wrist?

It took a moment for Mrs Wilmot to register the question and catch up.

'She didn't understand, Mrs Allen,' she said.

I'd learnt from Leah's mum that Mrs Wilmot had specifically asked her pupils not to touch Leah's arm which was in a sling. 'What *exactly* about "do not touch Leah's arm" do you think Alex didn't understand?' I asked. My tone was entreating rather than aggressive; it was instilled in me not to antagonise.

Mrs Wilmot crossed and uncrossed her feet. She was struggling to respond and I knew I'd hit the mark. We stared mutely at each other for a second or two.

'I know I sound slightly deranged, even unfair,' I continued, 'but I think Alex knew exactly what she was doing.'

Mrs Wilmot found her tongue. 'I don't agree.'

We were two mild-mannered people who'd never had cause to clash.

'Why?'

'Alex is not that sort of child.'

I tried a different tack. 'Yet on paper she should be the most troubled of the lot. She's been neglected, physically and emotionally abused, abandoned, she's "lost" her real mum, been forced to uproot and move more times than we've had hot dinners, and still she's not the kind of child to cause any trouble? I don't get it.'

Mrs Wilmot considered my words, but ultimately shook her head.

'Alex has got learning difficulties. We have to consider that fact, especially in situations like this morning.'

I choked back my frustration. Mrs Wilmot wasn't out to prove me wrong; she was merely speaking from her heart, and I left empty. However, as I sat in the kitchen later that evening, reflecting on the implications of what Alex had done, I knew we couldn't let things lie. The time had come for serious action.

The following Saturday, after offloading the children onto Dad, Rob and I sat down at the computer and typed a 'report' on Alex. It was an appeal to our family and the school to open their eyes and see that Alex was not the child she portrayed herself to be. We pleaded for their understanding that it was vital to Alex's wellbeing, and indeed our own, that we all work as a team.

The report took fourteen solid hours to type, starting from the beginning and working its way through to the present day. We included our own thoughts and an array of examples to back them up. By the time we'd finished, our eyes were gritty and we were emotionally drained, but we felt good.

When we reread our words the following day, we felt even more hopeful. The report was, we believed, honest, accurate, succinct and, most importantly, sympathetic to Alex.

On Monday, all family members received a copy, as did the school. Two weeks later we had still received no feedback.

A month after that, it was as if the report had never been written. Nonetheless, ironically, it proved to be our most valuable possession. Whenever we doubted ourselves, which Alex's abiding facial canvas of confusion, fright and timidity inevitably forced us to do, we re-read the report and those doubts were instantly dispelled.

A week after Rob left for Australia in late October, Daniel found slug pellets inside our rabbit's hutch. I confronted Alex, who only a week ago had been told the pellets were very poisonous to rabbits. Looking remorseful but confused, she said she'd forgotten. Her face and tone were so compelling, I almost believed her. Only when I remembered that she'd helped to lift the rabbit-run off the lawn so we could lay the pellets did I convince myself she was lying. I sent her straight to her bedroom for the remainder of the afternoon and told her she was banned from ever going near the hutch again. After a subdued tea, I sent her back to her bedroom.

At seven-thirty that evening, I was midway down the stairs with an armful of dirty washing when I froze, my ear cocked towards Alex's bedroom. 'You don't love me,' she sang. I waited. And waited. I didn't know what move to make next. I did know she was playing for my attention, but this time with words I'd never heard her speak. The message was too significant to just ignore, so I waited.

'You don't love me,' she sang again, her tone almost challenging. A small smile settled on my lips.

'Oh, yes, I do-oo. Oh, yes, I do-oo,' I chanted back, moving back up the stairs until I was right outside her door.

'No-o you do-on't. No-o you do-on't.'

'Do!' I continued.

'Don't!'

I pushed open her door, the slug pellets now history.

'Do! Do! Do!' I said, leaping towards her bed with mock clawed fingers.

She shrieked, giggled and dived under her duvet, and I tickled her ruthlessly. When eventually I stopped, she didn't emerge. So I just sat with my arm loosely slung across her duvet-encased form. An unusual silence filled the semi-dark room which neither of us, it would appear, wanted to break. Slowly, Alex disentangled herself and came to rest her head on the pillow beside me. My heartbeat increased. With every bone in my body, I could sense something strange and fragile moving between us. The silence continued. She took a piece of my hair and began stroking out the curls. I kept my swirling emotions hidden and my eyes soft but turned to the ceiling. She found an absent rhythm in her stroking and my eyes began to close. The minutes passed, and when the stroking ebbed away, I opened them again to find Alex asleep. Easing myself off the bed, I walked trance-like downstairs, sensing the huge significance of this moment.

Two hours later, I heard the first of Alex's cries. Not the cries of a nightmare or of a sleepy, disorientated, sick child, but those of a heartbroken little girl.

I launched myself upstairs and into her room. She was curled into a foetus-like ball with her head facing the wall. I picked her up and she instantly wrapped her arms tightly round my neck. Then I carried her downstairs and into our front room. 'It's OK,' I said, rubbing her back while attempting to lower both of us onto the sofa. 'I love you.'

'I love you too,' she said, stroking my back in turn.

And there we sat, rocking together, stroking each other's backs, and making genuine affirmations of love. The sense of unity and connection was overwhelming – and my own tears were now staining the back of her pyjama top.

Beneath the usual mountain of smiles and affection, I knew now that I'd not been imagining a disconnection between us. For suddenly we *were* connected. Like sliding away a glass partition, I could at last touch and hold her. Had she finally accepted me? Us, her new life? And if so, was that the reason for her tears? Had she, at last, allowed herself to feel the sadness of the life she was leaving behind?

Later, I carried her upstairs and into our bed, and fully clothed, I climbed in beside her and switched off the light.

I lay wide-eyed in the darkness, too emotional to sleep.

*

I rose from sleep with memories of the night before sprinkling contentedly across my mind. Turning my head slowly to meet Alex's gaze from the pillow beside me, I smiled languidly at her.

'Morning,' I said.

She returned the smile. 'Morning.'

'How are you feeling?'

'Fine.'

'I love you,' I said.

'I love you.'

'How would you like the morning off school – just you and me together?' The magnitude of this moment was too great to let go just yet and, besides, I actually *wanted* more time with her.

'I would,' she said, softly.

I rang Gabby who agreed to take my shift at work, dropped Daniel off at school, and full of expectations for the hours ahead, I asked Alex what she wanted to do.

'Play,' she said.

However, within minutes I could sense that whatever we'd shared in the night was beginning to slip away. After an hour it was almost as if last night had never happened. When I finally allowed myself to accept it, I was left reeling with confusion and disappointment – Alex was behind glass again. We played hairdressers, Lotto, Snap, and even a game of 'catch' on our tiny lawn; and although in the eyes of an observer we would have painted a picture of a happy and bonded unit, my eyes were now seeing a big, fat fabrication of affection, evident now in contrast with the fragile but genuine display of the night before.

My stomach churned uneasily. Was it possible she'd been faking a hundred per cent of her affection for us from day one? The question was too awful, too huge, to contemplate.

Alex gave me her usual wet kiss on the lips when I dropped her at school later. Today, I doubly recoiled from it.

Then I shook the unthinkable from my head. No one could be that cold.

When she came home from school, Alex hovered and flitted and shrieked and laughed and otherwise smiled innocuously, and I consoled myself with the fact that last night had been a breakthrough of some kind. I'd not imagined it and, judging by the escalation of Alex's unsettled behaviour towards bedtime, I knew that what had taken place at the same time yesterday had been a significant moment for her too.

Chapter Nineteen

*T*he backward shift in dynamics seemed to have crept up on us from nowhere. One day we'd not shouted in months, the next we'd been shouting for weeks.

It wasn't difficult to figure out what had triggered the turn-around: it was a simple matter of time. Time which refused to bring about any change in Alex's demeanour and no let-up in her behaviour. We had been knocking at her door until our knuckles were bloody and raw, confident that it would eventually open, but we no longer had the strength to keep knocking. We had buckled a bit, and then buckled a bit more, until we found ourselves where we were now – in an angry heap on the floor, unable to get ourselves back on our feet.

I couldn't concentrate on the crossword. Crosswords were no fun any more. Nothing was much fun any more. I put down the pen and climbed the stairs to Alex's bedroom.

A well-meaning friend of ours had once suggested that we stop explaining to Alex how her negative behaviour impacted on us. If she was as bright and manipulative as we thought, we were giving her too much rope to hang us with. Initially, I'd baulked at this, saying it was important for Alex to understand the implications of her behaviour, that she needed to feel we were an open book with nothing hidden. Bur our friend was right: the more we exposed ourselves and our thoughts, the more our daughter used the knowledge against us in her fight for control. This was why, when we resolved not to react to Alex's behaviour any more, we didn't forewarn her. Even when I'd picked up on her initial disquiet at the alarming change in mood, I resisted explaining.

However, the dynamics had changed again since then and here I was, sitting next to her on the bed, having all but apologised for screaming, and talking to her about her life, her feelings and her future. Once again, she responded by gazing at me with appropriate expressions in her eyes: sad when I sympathised, timid when I suggested she might be anxious, and hopeful when I told her things were going to get better. Ostensibly I was helping her, but in reality I was pleading with her to help us, and she knew it.

Our only saving grace was that Rob and I were still united – more so, in fact, than ever.

I stood with Alex in the fruit and vegetable aisle of our local supermarket. Two days ago, she had been awarded her first certificate, for swimming twenty-five metres unaided. I'd been overjoyed, and even more so when her teacher had commented that she was a natural swimmer.

'What would you like for lunch?' I asked. 'Anything you want. This is your treat.'

'Mmmm . . . um . . .'

She had flicked my switch. I didn't bother to suppress my sigh and the air started to crackle between us.

'Um . . . er . . .' she went on, her face now a mask of concentration and confusion. Time stretched. She scanned the aisle up and down, glanced at me, scanned the aisle again and then finally fixed me a meek look.

'Um . . . tomatoes.'

'Tomatoes. O-Kaay . . . anything else?'

She repeated the process.

'Um . . . carrots.'

'Anything else?'

'Um . . . um . . .'

She was waiting for me to prompt her with suggestions of burgers or pizzas, but we'd recently begun to suspect that part of the control/secrecy thing was getting us to speak for her. We did not believe – despite having read the theory in several textbooks – that Alex was frightened to say what she wanted in case we deliberately denied it to her later on.

'Um . . . no.'

I smiled wryly. 'Carrots and tomatoes it is then!'

It was only as I prepared her boiled carrots and sliced tomatoes that the reality of what I was about to serve hit me.

Rob was warned as soon as he and Daniel returned from his football match, but it took a moment for Daniel to register once we'd sat down at the table.

'Why is Alex having that?' he asked.

'Alex?' I said, challenging her to answer.

Alex's cheeks flushed an angry crimson. 'Um . . . I wanted to,' she said, her voice soft but flat.

Daniel shook his head, baffled for a moment, then accepted it as par for the course and tucked into his macaroni cheese.

For the next few minutes, Rob and I watched with both disbelief and amusement as Alex forked her bizarre lunch into her mouth. Each mouthful was stiff, but controlled and defiant, and for once she did not play with her food, stumble with her knife and fork, or linger for minutes between each mouthful. She'd been forced to play a different game.

We almost got away with it, but with just a few mouthfuls to go, the doorbell rang. Alex stopped eating immediately. Oh shit! Rob and I traded the same look. *Tell them to come back later*, I prayed.

I heard Rob open the door and I held my breath.

'Tess!' Rob exclaimed, loud enough to warn me. 'Erm . . . we're in the middle of lunch . . .' His voice trailed off. 'Come in.'

My stomach sank. My first instinct was to gather up all the plates and fling them in the sink. My next thought was for the message that would send to Alex. I took another deep breath.

'Tess, hi! Would you like a coffee?'

She clocked the situation before Rob had pulled up a chair.

'It was what she asked for,' I said weakly, as she gave a barely concealed shake of her head in disgust.

'Jesus Christ, Mel, what is the matter with you? I'm trying to understand, really I am – but you're not making this easy for me,' Tess jumped in as soon as we'd climbed the stairs and shut the bedroom door behind us.

I was perched on the edge of the bed, my head in my hands, a hotchpotch of emotions rendering me speechless. Tess was crouched at my feet, trying to find my eyes. She had lots to say.

'Alex needs to feel a part of your family. She needs to feel loved, not humiliated. I mean, Mel, tomatoes and carrots? That's just cruel.'

My head shot up and I glared at her, angry and hurt.

She quickly changed tack. 'Have you talked to your doctor about how you're feeling? That you're finding it difficult to cope? That maybe you need some time out to, you know, sort yourself out?'

This tack was even less palatable.

'Thanks for the confidence, but it's all right. I'm not having a nervous breakdown just yet. No, what you witnessed downstairs was just another little battle for control that we refused to yield to. And until you're prepared to even consider that Alex might not be the beguiling, innocent, butter-wouldn't-melt little angel that you want her to be, then you're just going to have to stew in it.'

'Mel,' she began again, almost imploring.

'No. I've got nothing more to say. Now please, if you don't mind, I'd like you to leave.'

As I closed the door on my concerned but equally indignant sister, I was too pent-up with fiery emotion – quite literally choking on it – to face another human being. So I climbed back up the stairs, picked up a pen and began carving out my bitter and despairing thoughts onto an unsuspecting pad of paper. I hated Tess and the rest of the disbelieving world but, most of all right now, I hated Alex for the divide she was creating between us and them.

Who is this child we call our daughter? Why is she so hateful? Is it possible for a person to become possessed? I want to love her. But how? I don't know her . . .

I didn't know for whom I was writing but it felt good – even the hateful stuff. In fact, it felt fabulous for all that I knew she didn't deserve my venom. I was hanging off the back of a runaway train with the wind in my hair, screaming with all the power of my lungs, knowing nobody could hear. So on I went, my emotive out-pouring mellowing gradually as, exhausted, the train climbed an incline towards the line's end, to a more rational search for answers.

That I came up with nothing new proved only one thing: it was just a matter of time.

Chapter Twenty

*T*wo years, three months and one day after Alex's placement with us, Rob and I collapsed in front of the TV to watch a movie after another 'normal' day. *Good Will Hunting* had just started on satellite.

For the first half an hour, we watched almost impassively as the story gradually unfolded. I'd almost decided to record the remainder of the film and go to bed, when the Robin Williams character, a psychologist, was introduced to his client, a rather remote but highly intelligent school janitor who, to the frustration of those trying to unlock his potential, refuses to yield to their efforts. During the first couple of therapy sessions, the psychologist fails to glean any emotional insight into his young client, who responds glibly, but otherwise offers nothing. Rob and I were suddenly sitting upright, all attention.

In the third session, however, the psychologist changed tack. He sat back in his chair, glanced at the clock purposefully, folded his arms and simply waited for the young man to speak. By now bells were ringing in every corner of my mind and when I turned to Rob he was looking at me. We exchanged a look of tacit knowing. When the client finally relented, we felt the psychologist's relief as if it were our own. By the end of the film, Rob and I were resolute – the janitor, who in so many ways reminded us of an older version of Alex, had relented. So could Alex.

The next day was Saturday. If it took all weekend, so be it. Alex needed to talk. Our instincts had been screaming for months that Alex's refusal to disclose an ounce of herself was almost spellbound rather than defiant or fear-driven – as though all it needed was for her to speak the first word and the spell would be broken. There would be nothing to hold her back after that.

We had no idea at this point how horribly mistaken we were.

Day One

'Have a lovely day in London,' I said, giving Daniel a kiss on his forehead. 'I can't wait to hear all about it.'

I kissed Rob, whispering in his ear, 'Make sure he has fun.'

Hand in hand, Alex and I waved them off.

'Right then!' I exclaimed, leading Alex into the kitchen. I gestured at her to sit on a chair, after which I stroked her hair. 'Don't worry, it'll be your turn next time. Right now, though, there's something important I want to say to you.'

I sat down opposite her, and taking both her small hands in mine, looked into her eyes.

'Dad and I were talking a lot last night and do you know what we realised?' I asked. She shook her head. 'We realised that we don't actually know the real Alex very well.' I smiled warmly into her *Alex* eyes. 'Not the Alex who must feel sad or afraid sometimes – or the Alex who must wonder why all this bad stuff has happened in her life, and who must get truly angry at how unfair life can be. We don't know the *real* Alex, who we think is hiding just in case bad stuff happens again.' I squeezed her hands. 'That's the Alex we want to see, so that we can understand her better and know what she wants.'

Her eyes didn't waver. She'd heard all of this before in different dressings.

'As you know, we are still having to guess what it is you want and don't want, or even how you're feeling,' I reminded her. 'Well, we don't want to have to guess any more, just in case our guesses are wrong. We want you to be happy, not sad or angry. We want you to feel safe, not trapped with a bunch of stupid dumb-heads who don't understand you and keep getting things wrong.'

Alex's mouth at last twitched in a small smile.

'So that's why we need *you* to talk. Not us, but you. We understand it's going to be hard, and that you might feel scared, but I'm here to listen for as long as I need to be until you are ready.'

Her eyes grew momentarily dark. She didn't like this at all; and she wasn't going to surrender without a fight. I leant down to pick up some boxes of colouring pens and paper and placed them on the table.

'I've also brought down your puzzles and some books. Is there anything else you'd like to do, whilst we're here? The Play-Doh?'

She shook her head.

'What about the Barbie stuff?'

'Um, no.'

'OK. Well, I'm going to do some colouring then,' I said. With my resolve almost as strong as the beating of my heart, I picked up a pen and began drawing.

When Rob and Daniel arrived home late that afternoon, Alex was giggling over my doctored rendition of 'Baa Baa Black Sheep'.

'How's it been?' Rob asked as soon as the two of us were alone.

'Nothing!' I said. 'Apart from a break to go the park, we've sat here for eight straight hours and she's not budged. I swear she hasn't even got bored.'

'Do you think she understands what we're doing?'

'Oh, yes,' I said confidently.

Day Two

Rob and Daniel left at eleven to go swimming and Alex and I retreated back into the kitchen. As soon as her excitable jabbering began, I told her I wasn't interested in jabber, we could do that another day. Today, I wanted to hear about Alex. Her eyes grew dim before she dropped her gaze humbly. We began doing jigsaw puzzles.

Six hours later, we'd completed all eight of them twice and I'd coloured in at least ten pictures.

'What are we going to do now?' Rob whispered at the end of that afternoon, as Alex settled down in front of a video.

'I don't know,' I said, 'but I told her I was prepared to wait until Christmas if necessary. I can't back down now. I'm going to sit with her tomorrow after school.'

'And if she still doesn't talk?'

'Then I'll sit with her the next day and the next and the next, for as long as it takes.'

'What about Daniel?'

'We're doing this for Daniel,' I snapped, a little too harshly. I was feeling the strain of the last six hours, but I was determined not to back down. Any lingering doubts we might have that Alex didn't understand what we were doing had evaporated. She'd so evidently dug her heels in. She'd never respect us if we backed down.

'Tomorrow, though, there'll be no books or jigsaws. Tomorrow it's about talking.'

Day Three

We were ten minutes into our third session and we could hear Daniel and the others playing outside.

'What do I have to tell you?' Alex asked, taking me by surprise with her unusually focused question. For the first time in three days, I could sense a wavering of her resolve. She didn't want to be here any more. I fixed her an equable look.

'Anything you want, love, as long as it's how you really feel,' I said. 'Maybe you could start by talking about the things that make you happy or sad or, if that's too difficult, maybe just what your favourite food is?'

She shifted in her seat but said nothing. 'You see,' I went on. 'For example, I think you like chocolate, but it's only a guess. Do you?'

She nodded, and I instantly regretted my question. I'd fallen right back into the trap of prompting her. 'OK. Well, when you're ready, I'd love to know a bit more about what you like. And don't like.' I broke the stare and began reading my book.

Day Four

Lilly turned up unexpectedly on her way home from work. I led her into the kitchen, insinuating that Alex and I were doing homework together. After reluctantly telling Alex she could go and play, Lilly and I sat down with a cup of coffee. She asked me how things were going at home and I lied as truthfully as I could. I told her they were going well. I told her that we felt we'd reached a crucial milestone in our relationship with Alex, and that hopefully things were on the up.

'I'm so pleased. She's such a sweet little thing,' she said, as though she was telling it to someone else. In a bizarre way, it didn't matter how many times I expressed our frustrations and concerns, one dose of Alex's sweetness was enough to wipe those words from her memory.

'Biscuit?' I asked.

Day Five brought nothing, and neither did Day Six – but that was a short stint because Alex had swimming lessons.

Day Seven
Nothing.

'How many hours is it now?' Rob asked me that evening.

'About twenty-five,' I said. Twenty-seven hours and fifteen minutes to be precise.

'How has she stayed sane?'

'Don't ask me!'

Rob sighed. 'Do you think we made the right decision?'

The thought had already crossed my mind a hundred times. 'Probably not,' I said, 'but if nothing else, at least this confirms that secrecy is a massive issue with her.'

'How much longer are we going to give her?' Rob asked.

'As long as it takes,' I replied. 'If we back down now, we'll have lost for ever.'

'Do you want me to take over tomorrow?'

I shook my head. 'Alex would conceive that as defeat. You just look after Daniel.'

Day Eight
It was Saturday again – a great long ten-hour yawn of a day. Surely there was no way her resolve could last that long, not now she knew we weren't backing down? Alex approached the kitchen table tentatively and then stood stiffly by her chair. I gestured at her to sit down.

'I don't want to,' she said quietly. My heart quickened.

'Alex it is important that you talk,' I said, and then reiterated all the reasons once more. While I spoke, she stared longingly out of the window, from which the playful noises of Daniel and the others were filtering in. 'Sorry,' I said, meaning it.

I watched the battle inside her move her eyes from the window to the floor to me to the window and back to the floor. For the first time I could see a hint of panic in her demeanour. I pretended to read my book and held my breath.

'I'm ready to talk.'

Lifting my head slowly from the book, I gave her an encouraging nod. 'OK,' I said simply.

She anchored me with a timid stare. 'I, um . . . I'm angry,' she said.

'I know you are,' I said, with a sympathetic sigh, and waited for her to elaborate. When she didn't, I said, 'But we need to know more. We can't help you with your anger unless you tell us—' I swallowed the rest of the sentence to stop myself prompting her again. Although her words had been more meaningful than revealing what she liked on her toast, they were not anything we didn't already know. Or put another way, they weren't words we hadn't already put in her mouth at one time or another.

She sensed my thoughts and her panic resumed. So did the battle she was waging within. There were moments when she looked like she might talk, but always something stopped her.

'Alex, nothing bad is going to happen to you if you talk. I promise,' I said. 'Maybe, a long time ago, you weren't allowed to talk. Maybe talking got you into trouble. But not here, not any more.'

She opened her mouth, shut it again, breathed rapidly, opened her mouth, held her breath and with a sense of defeat, shut it again. *What was going on? It couldn't be that hard, could it?* I thought feverishly. Then I could sense the moment slipping from my grasp. I thought hard and then another idea came to me.

'Do you remember your red boots with the zips? The ones you loved that we had to give to the poor people?'

She nodded, wanting me to help.

'They were just the right colour, the right height and they had those twinkly stars on the side,' I continued. 'But they got too tight and started hurting your feet. We had to get you new ones, except we couldn't find any the same, could we? We looked everywhere. In every shop in every town and in the end we had to buy you black and silver boots instead. Remember?'

'Yes.'

'At first you didn't like them,' I said, recalling how she used to resent having to wear them. 'But your feet didn't hurt any more, and slowly you forgot that you didn't like them. I guess now they're your favourite shoes because you wear them all the time.'

She smiled.

'Well, that's a bit like what's happening now,' I continued. 'You want to keep your life the same, even though it doesn't fit any more. You don't want the new one. We do understand that. Your old one feels safe to you because you know it so well.' I found her hands across the table. 'But Alex, that life is still hurting you, and the older you get, and the bigger you get, the more it's going to hurt. That's why we're trying to help you with it now.' I paused. 'Talking about yourself and telling your secrets will give you that new life. It might feel scary at first, even sad, but just like those boots, it won't hurt you like your old life did. Before you know it—' I stopped myself from saying it. She would find that out for herself.

I paused to let the concept sink in and scrutinised her face for signs that she'd grasped my analogy. For some moments the conflict seemed to intensify as she genuinely battled to allow that spell to be broken, but then her eyes grew still. Eerily so. A hardness came over them and I knew that her secrecy had won the first round.

'I'll wait,' I said gently. Biting back my disappointment, I began colouring again.

Day Nine

I cancelled my lunch with Sophie and friends. Alex had gotten so close to breaking that spell yesterday, I was confident it would happen today. However, just in case the moment needed an added incentive, I decided to write my Christmas cards. The message I was sending was loud and clear. I was here for the day, but not to be distracted unless she had something 'important' to say.

Alex's response was equally determined. She spent the morning talking to herself under her breath – a trait she had that drove us insane – playing with nothing more than a ball of fluff on the table and a piece of string that came from her toy-box, and swinging endlessly on her chair, often precariously close to toppling backwards. After the first time of telling her to be careful, I ignored all subsequent attempts to get my attention away from the cards.

As the hours passed, I could feel my angry despair grow. Her mutterings grew louder until I could hear what was being said: You don't love me; you're horrible; Daniel's so lucky; I'm never going to get out of the kitchen; I'm going to tell Tess what you're doing; I wish I had a different mum and dad; etc., etc.

Hope lifted me once more. Still keeping my eyes on the cards, I responded: I do love you; I know you think I'm horrible; Daniel *is* lucky and you'll feel lucky one day; you *are* going to get out of the kitchen — as soon as you've been brave enough to start talking. At her comment about telling Tess, I just smiled. I couldn't think of a response to that.

However, by three o'clock the deadlock remained intact. Several times I felt she got close to breaking it, but something always held her back. Her control and determination were immense. Could we face another week of this, considering we might as well write off the next five days, in our drive to get her to talk? They were two- or three-hourly sessions and yet barely long enough to generate a yawn.

But what choice did we have? The longer the stand-off, the bigger price we'd be paying for backing down. She'd feel she was unbreakable. I shuddered at the thought, and at the implications that that would have for both her and us. For starters, she would not feel safe enough to hand over control to two people weaker than she.

I decided to keep going.

When the children had gone to bed, I scanned a photo of Alex onto our computer and wrote *I'm Alex — I'm Fab* across her T-shirt. I printed off two copies of it, one of which I cut up into twenty-four neat squares. Then I downloaded a cartoon picture of a cute-looking, smiley-faced girl with blonde hair and printed that off too. On the back of this I glued the twenty-four squares in a haphazard order, creating a jumbled collage.

I went to bed that night hopeful that these images might at least explain to Alex why it was so important for her to talk.

Day Ten

I placed the picture of the cartoon girl in front of Alex. 'Who do you think this is?' I asked gently.

'Um, I don't know,' she said, genuinely puzzled.

'Go on,' I urged playfully. 'Who do we know who's cute like her and always smiling and laughing?'

Alex's mouth twitched. 'Me,' she said softly.

'Right,' I said. I then placed the card with the photo of Alex beside it. 'And who's this?'

Her smile faltered. 'Me,' she said stone-like, leaving me stunned at how quickly she'd picked up the underlying message in these two cards.

'But they can't both be you,' I continued, undeterred. 'There's only one *real* Alex.'

I'd planned to let this part of the script hang long enough for her to digest what I was saying, but she'd already cottoned on. I skipped to the next part.

'Can I tell you what we think has happened? We think that a long time ago the real Alex was so jumbled up by her mum and Kelvin' – I paused, turning the cartoon over to reveal the jumble of squares that made up her photo – 'that she had to make a new one.' I turned the card back over.

Alex glanced only briefly at the jumbled image before snatching her gaze away. Her eyes on mine were now uncomfortable.

'The problem is, love, that no matter how hard you try to pretend you're fine, that jumbled Alex is still inside you. It's still making you angry and sad and frightened because it got broken. The only way we can fix that is if you help us to put the pieces back together properly, and we can't help you if we can't see the pieces.'

She began furiously kneading a piece of foil chocolate wrapper into the table. I knew I'd hit some sort of mark.

'We understand you don't want to let go of this, Alex,' I said, pointing at the cartoon image, 'but until you do, the true Alex, the happy Alex that came out of her mum's tummy, can't be made happy again.' I then spent the next few minutes attempting to explain why the cartoon persona would never last the distance. But she'd shut down.

'I'm here when you're ready,' I said, putting the Alex jigsaw paraphernalia back in its bag. She leant over the chair, picked up a stray felt-tip pen lid, and began rolling it on the table.

Day Eleven

Daniel came in to the kitchen at four-thirty. 'Can I play cards with you?'

'Later, love. Why don't you go and play with the others outside?'

'I don't want to,' he said.

I felt a spike of irritation towards my son and was instantly ashamed. I smiled sympathetically and gestured at an empty chair. He responded with relief more than anything. It took me only a second to make my next decision. I told Alex that she could get down and that we'd 'talk' again tomorrow. Her eyes flashed me a dark look and for a second she didn't move. The irony in the fact that she now didn't want to get down did not escape me. 'Come on,' I said, and she followed me stiffly into the other room, where I turned on the TV for her. Back in the kitchen, I closed the door because I knew she'd be flitting and making noises until tea-time.

Before playing our first round of Trumps, I came to another decision. I then promised Daniel that the kitchen stint with Alex would be over by Sunday at the latest. If she hadn't talked by then, I would ring our doctor on Monday and ask for help. I'd not noticed the strain lines on Daniel's face until now when they fell away. I also felt relieved.

Later, when I announced my decision to Rob, he exhaled long and hard. 'Good,' he said, his one word conveying a dozen emotions.

Day Twelve

I finished my Christmas cards.

Day Thirteen

Alex and I only had an hour together before swimming. The mood was one of mutual acceptance that there'd be no talking today, so the atmosphere round the table was light. Five minutes before the end of the session, the phone rang. It was Gabby, wanting some help with the computer on the reception desk. I talked her through the problem, and after I replaced the receiver, Alex rolled her eyes theatrically. 'Computers,' she said. 'Stupid cerplunkers!' And I laughed and laughed.

Day Fourteen

Alex didn't talk, but she was more subdued. The next day was Saturday and this morning we made sure that Alex overheard Rob's plans to take Daniel to the seaside.

Day Fifteen

I lingered a few extra minutes in bed, mentally preparing myself for the day ahead. I sensed Alex might break the deadlock today, but I couldn't be sure. She'd lasted this long, so it was just as feasible she could last another two full days.

The sense that she might talk intensified over breakfast. Her eyes were strangely unsettled throughout.

We waved goodbye to Rob and Daniel and retreated back into the kitchen. We sat down and the smile she gave me was weak, almost nervous. The smile I returned was sympathetic, but I kept otherwise silent. I picked up my book and made a show of reading.

The next few minutes were torturous. The air around Alex seemed slowly to freeze. Her silence was palpable. *Please, please, please* I uttered silently in my head. *Please let her talk.*

Just when I thought I might die from lack of air, she spoke, smashing the frozen silence.

'I feel like a volcano.'

I put the book down and met her genuinely anguished eyes. This was no half-hearted admission, for I'd never used the word 'volcano'. Feeling suddenly unprepared, I searched my mind for the best response.

'It must feel horrible,' I said, using Tess's therapeutic tone of voice.

She nodded, and a sudden wrack of broken sobbing exploded from within her. I propelled myself off my seat and round the table, where I pulled her into my arms.

'Jesus,' I muttered, despite her presence. I pulled her tight into me and rocked her shaking body. 'Right. Enough,' I said, as much to myself as to her. 'It's all right. No more now.' We rocked until her tears dried up. I pushed her shoulders away from my chest so that I could find her eyes. 'Tomorrow, I'm going to find someone who can help you. OK?' I said. She nodded desolately and I pulled her back into my arms.

There was no applause. No victory salute. Just a strange and foul mist that began to fill my soul.

It took me a few seconds to realise that the mist was nothing stranger than a sense of self-disgust. The whole exercise now felt cheap and almost childish. Had it been worth it? No! For I'd just discovered that her secrecy had nothing to do with defiance. There had been no spell to break.

I knew now that we could not be trusted to help Alex. This was way too big for us to handle alone.

Chapter Twenty-One

As soon as I'd dropped the children at school, I rang our local surgery and booked an appointment to see Dr Norris.

The following day I walked into her consulting room, broke down in tears and told her we needed help.

She agreed to make a referral to CAMHS, Child & Family Services.

New Year's Eve, 1999. The damp December mist was shot through with festive lights, and Rob and I perched together on our front garden wall, bundled up in winter woollies and watching the Millennium night revellers enjoying themselves. The smell of charred sausages, fireworks and mulled wine hung in the fog that carried party songs from mobile discos and open windows near and far. We feigned good cheer, clinked many a glass and caught up on street gossip, but in spirit we were not really there.

It was going to be so different, I thought now, as I wistfully recalled when the residents of Mallard Close had first suggested a street party. I'd been another person that day, nearly two years ago. I'd been on cloud nine over Alex's arrival, brimming with hope and confidence for our new lives together, and set with preformed notions of how wonderful this celebration was going to be. Those distant days represented a period when the neighbours weren't afraid to knock on our door for fear of stumbling across another scene from a Roald Dahl movie; when they didn't cast furtive sympathetic glances at our children. They represented a time when the people didn't smile nervously at me as they passed me on the street; when family didn't hold their breath every time they asked how things were going. Two years ago, everyone had faith in what we had to say. In those days, we had faith in ourselves.

We were in bed by a quarter past midnight on the morning of the new millennium.

The phone call from CAMHS came in early January, 2000. The lady introduced herself as Wendy Bozier; a therapist from Child and Family Services.

She was softly spoken but earnest, and asked me to give a brief outline of the problems we were having with our daughter.

Rather shamefully, my first words were to remind her that she was our 'adopted' daughter. I then launched into a summary of Alex's history and her time with us. I explained that, although she came across as a sweet, compliant and loving little girl, she was, we believed, a frightened, unhappy and very angry little girl, who was as manipulative and as clever as she was funny and charming.

'The letter from your GP says she's got a developmental disorder,' Wendy Bozier said at this point.

Reluctantly, I confirmed this, but was quick to add that we felt the disorder was not the overriding cause of her profound learning lags, and that it was emotional defiance which presented itself as learning difficulty. I could almost hear her frown down the phone as she asked me for the school's thoughts on this. In a weak, almost apologetic voice, I told her the school didn't agree with our perception of Alex. She chuckled, and said that children often 'played-out' differently outside the home. She said this was very normal.

I didn't contradict her. Ours was not an easy case to grasp in one phone call, so at this point I told her about the notes/report we'd written, and asked if we might give her a copy. She agreed this would be a good idea, and went one better by suggesting we meet up next Monday at two o'clock. We said goodbye and hung up.

She sounded nice.

Clutching my Top Shop bag, with its stock of notes and reports in neat, coloured binders, I pressed one of the six doorbells on the panel beside the main entrance to Friesden House – a drab council building in the middle of town.

Stamping my feet against the icy cold, I was poised to ring again when a voice requested my name and then told me to come to the second floor. I had to press another buzzer before I was allowed into the offices. I gave my name to a large, buxom lady in the tiny reception, and was directed the waiting room opposite. Before entering, I glanced down the length of the long colourless corridor. All the doors flanking the corridor were closed and the place was eerily quiet.

In the waiting room, I occupied my time scouring the leaflets and posters promoting facts and help-line numbers for Depression, Suicide, Drug & Alcohol Abuse, Anorexia, Bulimia, Self-Mutilation, etc., which were tacked across the four walls. For the umpteenth time that morning, I wondered bleakly how I'd got to be here. The silence was broken by the ringing patter of heeled shoes marching down the corridor towards us. The door swung open and the wearer of the shoes appeared.

'Mrs Allen?'

I shot up, dropping my bag in my haste, apologised, and pulled my rucked jumper back over my bottom. 'Yes, hi, that's me!'

'I'm Wendy Bozier,' she said, offering me a bright smile and her tiny hand.

She was a striking woman, Scandinavian-looking with her shoulder-length blonde hair and pale blue eyes, and wearing a straight pencil skirt. I hastily reassembled my belongings and followed her down the corridor to her room.

Once inside, Wendy closed the door firmly behind us and directed me to a chair. While she searched for her notes, I looked around me. The room was small, functional, but characterless – an old doll's house tucked neatly in a corner next to a small plastic sandpit on legs was the only clue to its purpose.

Having located her notes, Wendy sat her pert backside on the chair opposite me, crossed one leg neatly over the other and flashed me a perfect smile – the kind of smile lovers might exchange across a dinner table when no words are needed. In our case, she was waiting for me to speak.

'Unfortunately, Rob's in Manchester with a client,' I said, hoping she wouldn't judge him by his absence, 'but I've brought a copy of our notes.' I reached into my plastic bag and handed her a folder with the copies we'd made for her.

Wendy's pristine smile prevailed. 'Thank you,' she said, placing them on the desk. 'I'll read them later.'

My eyes lingered for a moment on the file: I'd hoped she would read them first. I regrouped my thoughts.

'OK,' I said, 'where do you want me to start? She was placed with us just after her fifth birthday. At first, we couldn't believe our luck. She was the most affectionate, happy-go-lucky little girl I'd ever met. She settled straight away – there were no tantrums, no tears, nothing. Everybody adored her.' I took a breath. 'The only downside was that she was hyperactive, needed loads of attention, and had a developmental disorder – there's some information in that folder.' I pointed to it and gave her a brief explanation of ARND.

'At first it wasn't too much of an issue. We had bags of energy then, but as time went on and the weeks dragged into months, we realised she was learning nothing. And I mean *nothing*.' Wendy acknowledged my conviction with an attentive nod. 'We were literally having to do everything for her,' I said, and gave her as many examples as I thought she needed to fully grasp the situation. 'It was only after I began researching ARND that I began to realise things weren't quite adding up. For a start, there are children who are far worse affected but who could do more for themselves than Alex. And when Alex is struggling, she doesn't look frustrated or out of her depth, she just seems to have this baffled, almost frightened air about her.'

'Frightened?'

'I know what you're thinking,' I said hastily, 'but we don't believe it's some kind of emotional brain-freeze, or whatever you might call it. Not any more. We think she uses that look to mask a refusal to do something.'

Even as the words left my mouth, I knew how far-fetched that sounded. Wendy managed to keep her expression even.

'So you're saying she's putting it on?'

'Yes. At least some of the time. The rest of the time it's a constant juggling act between the developmental delay and the possibility that she's . . .' I paused, 'faking it.'

'But the school disagrees?'

'Yes. In fact, as far as they're concerned, we're the parents from hell for even suggesting it. Like everyone else, they adore her. Apart from the constant one-on-one she needs, she's a model student,' I said, fingering quotation marks around the word 'model'.

Wendy took a moment to file some thoughts away and then changed course. 'Tell me about the anger.'

My expression turned grave. 'I've never met a child so angry. Any little thing will trigger it off. Often, telling her to put her shoes on because we're going out is enough to, well, put that look in her eyes.'

Wendy's frown was asking me to elaborate.

'Her eyes grow dark, that's the only way we can describe it,' I said. A silence followed as I read Wendy's thoughts. 'I know, I'm not sounding particularly persuasive, but actually it's her ability to control her emotions that worries us the most. And it's not just her emotions she hides, it's everything. I know this sounds implausible, but we don't know a thing about her. She looks thrilled when we buy her new clothes, yet for all we know, she hates them. We don't know what amuses her or frightens her. We don't know what soothes or irritates her. We don't know – well – what makes her tick.'

There'd been a shift in Wendy's attentiveness, indicating she was beginning to understand. So I took her back to the beginning and for the next half an hour I described the contradictions in Alex's behaviour from day one. I told her about the physical affection she gave so readily, but that felt so empty. I told her about the soft, meek voice that so contradicted the penetrating bottomless stare of her eyes; the boundless compliance that never fulfilled itself; the coyness that moved so effortlessly between self-effacing timidity and self-possessed charm; and the paradox that she could play such acutely effective mind games yet appear so obtuse the rest of the time. I described the mind games and the attention seeking and the control they had over us. I told her about Scooter, about the slug pellets and the elbowing of Leah's wrist. I described the hell that was our holiday; the unyielding lack of interest she had in the world around her, and the utter helplessness we felt to change things. I would have talked for hours more had I not been conscious of the time.

I sat back in my chair, breathing hard and eager for her thoughts. 'Do you talk to Alex about her feelings?'

I sighed audibly. 'Till the cows come home,' I replied. 'When you meet her, you'll see how futile an exercise that is.'

She gave an uneasy laugh. 'Well, let's certainly hope not!' she exclaimed, and I apologised. She continued, 'Alex may not look like she's listening or understands, but remember, everything she's hearing is going in on one level or—'

At the vehement shaking of my head, her words trailed away.

'No! That's just it. She *does* look like she's listening,' I burst out through a sudden wave of gut-wrenching despair, 'but there's just no connection there. Her eyes look connected but her soul isn't. She's untouchable, almost as if she's shut down. Honestly, if it weren't for her anger, I'd say she was a machine.' I felt my throat tighten for the first time. 'And it's destroying us, day by day, minute by minute' – a tear fell down my cheek and I wiped it away – 'and we can't do anything to stop it.'

Wendy handed me a box of tissues. She looked deeply concerned. 'Are you all right, Mrs Allen?'

'Yes, sorry,' I sniffed. 'Can you help us?'

She paused. 'I can't promise anything. From the sound of it, Alex is a very complex child. She clearly has an extremely vulnerable inner core which she's trying to protect. Shutting down, as you put it, is her way of protecting it. Pretending to the world that she's fine is also her way of protecting it. She may need more than my sessions can offer her, but I'd like to give it a try.'

I felt the burden of the world had been lifted off my shoulders. 'Thank you.'

'No guarantees,' she reminded me.

Strangely, I found her final comment reassuring. Clearly, she'd grasped the severity of Alex's emotional state.

We chatted on more generally until the hour was up. Wendy asked about Rob and Daniel and a bit about our lives. I engaged in the conversation, but as much as she was attempting to learn about us – the backbone of Alex's environment – I was doing my own evaluation of her. Her mannerisms, her soft tone of voice, and her attentive, empathetic expressions were typical of her profession, and I hoped she was thick-skinned enough to withstand Alex's secrecy. But, I reminded myself, she was a child therapist; people like her surely knew that all children were shaped by their early experiences. I was confident she wouldn't be fooled by Alex into thinking that she was OK. Before I left the office, we agreed that she'd see Alex alone for three sessions, after which she'd hold a review session with Rob and me.

It was only as I exited the building into the sunshine that I felt the full impact of the meeting and became aware of its significance: Alex would finally get the help she needed.

A week later, I collected Alex from school and drove her to Friesden House. She'd had to be taken out of class for the appointment and was unusually quiet in the car; and by the time I pressed the first buzzer she was visibly unsettled. This was unexpected but reassuring – when we'd first talked to Alex about Wendy, she'd appeared unbothered. Her lack of concern at the time had been far more disquieting than the anxiety that percolated through her right now.

'It's all right, you're going be fine,' I said. 'Wendy is very nice and she's here to help you. She's helped lots of children like you and understands all about why you feel the way you do. She won't make you do or say anything you don't want to. OK?'

She didn't look at me and we climbed the stairs in silence. Once in the waiting room, Alex sat beside me, rigid as a board. At eleven o'clock on the dot I heard Wendy's shoes clicking down the long corridor. When she came in to the waiting room Alex didn't look up, choosing instead to stare at the floor. Wendy knelt down in front of Alex and found her eyes.

'Hi. My name's Wendy. It's good to meet you.'

Alex refused to lift her head and I was suddenly acutely aware that, of all the pictures I'd painted of Alex, this wasn't one of them. 'She's a bit nervous,' I said, like a script I'd been forced to write unprepared.

'Of course you are,' Wendy said gently. 'All the children who come here feel the same on their first day, but you'll see there's nothing to be afraid of.' When Alex still hadn't looked up, Wendy suggested I accompany them to her 'special' room.

I took my clearly reluctant daughter by the hand and led her to Wendy's office. Once inside, Wendy opened the wardrobe. 'Do you like colouring?' she asked. Alex nodded. 'Good, because I've got colouring pens and paper and scissors,' she said, trying to enthuse her. 'And look! Can you see what I've found?' Alex peered tentatively into the wardrobe. She found Wendy pointing enthusiastically to a tea set and Alex finally thawed with a coy smile. 'I thought you'd like that,' Wendy said, sounding pleased with herself.

I left them, moments later, to their tea party. Alex's eyes followed me out of the door and I felt her lingering apprehension in the pit of my stomach. For a good five minutes I stood at the end of the corridor, waiting, expecting, listening for something other than the sound of my own breathing. It was going to be a long hour, I realised, and settled on going out to distract myself with some retail therapy.

When I arrived back, with ten minutes to spare, the first sound that hit my ears was that of Alex's giggling emanating from Wendy's office. My first reaction was one of relief; my second, one of anticlimax. However, as I sat in the waiting room I reminded myself that this was only the first session. It was important that they bonded.

Wendy and Alex entered a few minutes later, both flushed by their time together. Wendy gave me a reassuring wink. 'See you next week,' she said and left.

'Well, that's good!' I said, injecting some energy into my voice. There was a spring in Alex's step as we left the building but instinct told me there'd be no changes in her this week.

Daniel shuffled into the kitchen, wrapped up in his duvet.

'How are you feeling this morning, love?' Rob asked him.

'Better,' he croaked.

As I was pouring out a tumbler of orange juice for him, he spoke again. 'What's that on Alex's face?'

I turned round to look, and frowned. 'Ooh,' I said, 'you look a little red. Don't tell me you're coming down with this bug as well.' I walked over and placed the flat of my hand against her forehead. It was hot, but that wasn't all. I ran my fingers across a rash on her face.

'Rob,' I said, trying to keep my voice even. 'What do you think of this?'

Rob did the same as me. 'Get a glass, Mel,' he said.

Fifteen minutes later, Dr Slater who lived five doors down from us had pumped Alex full of antibiotics and she was being stretchered into an ambulance.

'It's gonna be fine,' Rob reassured me as I climbed into the back of the ambulance. He and Daniel would follow in the car.

Brushing away my tears, I held Alex's hand under the blanket as the young paramedic attended to a machine that would monitor her vitals until we reached the hospital.

'I'm sorry,' I said, and her mouth twitched in a soft smile. *How long had she been ill?* With a shameful sense of foreboding, my mind re-ran the events of the last couple of days. She'd been quieter than usual, I realised now, but we'd been so wrapped up in Daniel's virus that I hadn't really registered it. And then an even more mortifying thought struck me. If Daniel hadn't noticed the rash, would we have packed her sick body off to school? My God! Had things got that bad? I cursed in self-disgust.

I smiled gently down at Alex again. It's the staring, I acknowledged silently as she continued to hold my gaze. Even now, in this ambulance, sick with meningitis. I wanted to tear my eyes away, but I also wanted her to live. Come on, I willed the ambulance driver. If she died now, I'd never forgive myself. Never.

It was with huge relief that we reached the hospital. Alex was immediately rushed through a side door of the A & E Department and into a resuscitation room where five medics were waiting in their gowns. For the next ten minutes I was a silent onlooker as the three men and two women descended on Alex's ears, eyes, mouth, nose, chest, arms, legs and stomach – probing and gauging with instruments I'd only ever seen on TV. With my heart almost pounding out of its cage, I scrutinised each of their faces above their masks, searching, waiting for the sickening confirmation that Alex might die – and that it was all my fault.

'How long has she had the rash?' the tallest doctor asked, giving me only the briefest of glances as he probed a purple cluster of spots on one corner of Alex's mouth.

'I don't know,' I breathed heavily. 'We didn't notice them until this morning.' This was a nightmare!

'So the rash wasn't there last night?' he asked, the seconds ticking on.

All eyes were on me now. What was I going to say? 'No,' I said. *Well it wasn't, was it?*

'Thank you,' he said, and they turned their attention once more to Alex.

I retreated with my tremors into the corner of the room and waited. Suddenly the questions were rolling in thick and fast.

'How long has she been ill?'

Guess. 'A couple of days.'

'Any vomiting?'

Easy. 'No.'

'Coughing?'

'No.'

'Headaches?'

Shit! 'Um . . . she didn't say.'

'Aversion to bright lights?'

'No, at least not that we noticed.'

'Her throat is extremely inflamed. When did your daughter first complain about it?'

My mouth dried up as the full horror of this moment scalded my insides. *Why hadn't she told me?* 'She didn't, I mean she hasn't complained at all.'

Owing to the urgent action Alex's rash demanded, their astonishment was thankfully short-lived. When I next looked up, it was Alex they were addressing.

It was the first time she'd spoken in an hour, and in a tiny voice, she answered their questions.

How long had her throat been sore? 'A little while,' she replied.

Was her head sore? 'Um, a little bit,' she replied.

Did she feel sick? 'Um, a little bit,' she replied.

Was her neck hurting? 'Um . . .' she faltered, looking quickly at me. My eyes urged her to answer. 'Um . . . I don't know,' she offered.

And then they were asking her to sit up. 'Can you touch this with your chin?' a young medic asked, holding a pen just below Alex's chin.

The room held its breath, and after a moment's confusion in

which the medic illustrated his request, Alex lowered her head and connected her chin with the pen. The medics' palpable collective relief was superseded only by their frowns. They were fairly confident it wasn't meningitis, they said, but they wanted to keep an eye on her for the next couple of days, nevertheless.

I stood in my corner, smiling gratefully, as though I'd just been given parole. 'Can I stay with her?' I asked.

'Of course. She'll be in the isolation room which is large enough for a fold-out bed.'

As the medics began packing away their gear, I asked the tallest one what may have caused the rash.

He shook his head, baffled himself. 'It's certainly strange,' he said. 'We sometimes see rashes like this on patients whose excessive vomiting or violent coughing has caused the tiny blood vessels beneath the skin to burst and create the rash. But you say your daughter's not been vomiting? Or coughing?'

'Definitely not.'

'Then I'm afraid I can't answer. Unfortunately, as Alex was given antibiotics before she arrived, any test we do to eliminate meningitis will give a false reading. It may be that we never find out what caused it.'

Rob and Daniel had just arrived as we were filing out of the door. 'It's good news,' I mouthed at them both. Rob sighed with relief. The looks we exchanged spoke volumes.

For me, the following three days played out like a warped tale from somewhere akin to hell, relieved only by visiting hour, when I would escape to the stinky, shabby haven of the hospital cafeteria and its stock of chocolate and relative normality.

Thanks to large doses of penicillin that were being pumped into Alex via a vein in her right hand, I had not been allowed the 'devoted mother tortured by shame and willing to die for the daughter she'd nearly lost' number for long, before it became business as usual. I was quickly trapped, in full glass-fronted view of the nursing station, reading books to Alex she had no interest in; enduring endless box games she couldn't play; sitting through children's videos neither of us wanted to watch, and otherwise looking stiffly on as she beguiled doctors and nurses alike. During rare moments when we were unwatched, the room fell quiet, thick and edgy.

And then it was over. On the fourth day, we were given the option of going home on condition that Alex came in once a day for her injection of antibiotics. I grabbed it. The nurses fawned and fussed over Alex as they bade their fond farewells. As soon as we'd rounded the first corner, Alex wriggled her hand free of mine.

I drove straight from work to Friesden House to meet Rob for our first review session with Wendy Bozier.

'What are we going to say to her?' I asked.

'That we've seen no difference?' Rob suggested drily.

'We can't say that.'

'Why not? It's true.'

Nevertheless, we weren't about to enter the session stamping our feet and demanding an explanation. Not because we weren't disappointed – we were – but it was still early days. Added to this, Wendy was always so confident about how well things were going. I could sense by now that she wasn't the kind of person one contradicted.

We agreed to wait and hear what she had to say.

Wendy greeted us with her customary beam which was beginning to irritate me. I introduced Rob, and the three of us made our way to her office.

'So, how do you feel it's going?' she asked.

'Yeah, fine,' I said, and Rob added, 'She likes coming here.'

Wendy's smile grew. 'Good, because I believe I can see a big change in the shy, anxious little girl who first stepped into my office.'

She wasn't supposed to say that!

'I know!' she said, sparing our wilted smiles from dropping to a soggy mess on the floor. 'It's early days yet and I'm *not* forgetting the superficial element you've talked about. But it's important that Alex and I establish a bond; that she learns to trust me.' Her smile did little to disguise the obvious satisfaction she was feeling.

For the next quarter of an hour, she summarised the progress they were making in the sessions: Alex's willingness to work with her; her increasing confidence to tackle the more difficult emotions within her; the play therapy Wendy was using to unearth Alex's feelings of guilt, fear and sadness, all of which she'd seen glimpses of.

We asked her to elaborate. My interpretation of her subsequent rather hazy illustrations of this unearthing was more of a girl acting on the prompts of her therapist. However, Wendy hadn't known Alex long enough to grasp that just yet.

Just when I thought we might be going home empty-handed, she produced three drawings, all of which she felt were significant.

The first was of Scooter. This was significant because Alex loved Scooter, she said. She hoped we'd be encouraged by that.

'But it's these two that fascinated me most,' she said, handing us the second drawing. It looked like a bird with a beak at either end. 'This is a bee,' she said. 'Look at the sting on it. It's almost as large as the bee itself. I believe it's how Alex sees herself,' she said, her tone thick with concern.

Then, with the flourish of one who's left the best till last, she revealed the final drawing: a more complex picture, created in colour. Filling almost the entire page, it depicted a dark, looming figure wearing a long cloak. The sword it was carrying had blood dripping from it.

She certainly now had our attention. 'Interesting, don't you think?' she said, watching us intently.

It wasn't just the content I found alarming, it was the fact that Alex could draw with such clarity.

'Did Alex say what it meant?'

'It's an angry wizard who's been fighting.'

'Do you think she sees herself as that wizard?' I asked, tearing my eyes from the drawing.

Wendy paused. 'No, I believe it's more a manifestation of her fear.'

'Fear?'

'Yes. I've shown the picture to my supervisor, Sheila Hawson. She agrees with me. We believe that Alex has a quite profound fear of men.'

There was a stunned silence, then Rob raised a disbelieving eyebrow. 'A fear of men?' he asked.

'Yes.'

I found my voice. 'I don't think so. At least, not that we're aware of,' I said tactfully. 'She's as comfortable around men as she is women.'

Wendy considered this for a moment. 'I talked to Alex about it and she said she's been scared of men since living briefly with a man called Kelvin.'

Rob and I nodded attentively. Kelvin was Michelle's schizophrenic ex and the only boyfriend known to have lived with her and Alex. Kelvin had hurt Alex both physically and emotionally, and Michelle had been forced to end the relationship or risk losing her daughter.

It made perfect sense that Kelvin's legacy would have left Alex with a fear of men. Yet . . .

Rob and I frowned at each other. Why hadn't we picked up on this fear? Images of Alex, comfortable and relaxed with Rob, my dad, my brothers, etc., were at odds with what Wendy was telling us. Nevertheless, we knew how adept Alex was at disguising her emotions so, yes, it was possible. We remained transfixed by the drawing. Whatever the meaning behind it, it was clearly significant, and I was grateful to Wendy for the progress she'd made.

The remainder of the session was taken up with her thoughts on future sessions. She asked us if we'd sanction her plans to record them – the tapes would serve as a back-up for her supervisor who, she reiterated, was keen to follow progress. We were happy to agree to this.

As the weeks went by and the sessions rolled on, Alex remained unchanged. And though we scrutinised her for signs of specific anxieties around men, we found none. Hope was dwindling and we were back on the downward slide, but the slide was growing steeper.

As I dragged myself up the final couple of steps to the door of Child and Family Services, the temptation to turn round and flee the building with Alex still in it was so powerful it frightened me.

Thankfully, the waiting room was empty and I took my usual spot in the corner by the window. Then I leant my head against the wall and tried to conjure up pleasant images of the forthcoming work jolly to the theatre. However, the intrusive sound of Alex's infectious laughter drifting relentlessly down the corridor kept disrupting my efforts to stay calm and relaxed: the previous week I'd left the offices so tightly coiled that I'd driven through a red light and almost run over a pedestrian.

I gave up. It was easier to stew.

Had Wendy Bozier not heard a thing we'd told her? Had she not read our notes? Why did she insist on talking to Alex as though she were a baby? Was it any wonder we'd seen no change in Alex these past three months? I gave an involuntary shudder. How I resented Wendy's little rufflings of Alex's hair, the unintentional but patronising way she spoke to me, and most of all the way she addressed Alex as her 'little scrumptious'!

The most alarming product of her sessions, though, was Alex's new voice. Until recently, Alex had possessed only three – her coy voice, her frightened voice and her full-volume screech. Now she could add a fourth to her repertoire – a honey-sweet, almost self-effacing voice. It was incredibly potent when used on adults, although we continued to question why people didn't find it the least bit strange, even cloying.

Sophie had once reassured me that Alex wouldn't be able to ingratiate herself with people through her bumbling ways for ever – she'd get too old for that. Sitting here now, I had an uneasy feeling that she had found a new, age-appropriate voice that was equally effective, and for reasons I'd soon appreciate, that was scary.

I jumped from my stew as I heard Wendy's footsteps. Just smile, I told myself.

'Are you going to tell Mummy what you've been playing in the sandpit today?' Wendy said, addressing Alex like a two-year-old, but Alex had forgotten, so Wendy reminded her: she'd been playing 'families' in the sandpit. 'Do you think Mummy and Daddy might want to play with the sandpit next time they come?'

And that was the moment my lights went out. Black.

I mumbled something polite and appropriate, took Alex's hand, and on detached legs walked her out of the building.

As afternoon moved into evening, I could feel a deep foreboding germinating in my gut and spreading gradually through the veins in my body, until it was pumping fear into my heart. A very real fear that we were running out of options. And then what?

I sought desperately to switch the light back on, but found not even a glimmer. Wendy had been our last hope, and with no confidence in her I was overwhelmed by despair. Rob and Daniel anxiously noticed my trance-like state. I told them it was a headache and that I'd be fine tomorrow.

I couldn't sleep; the sense of foreboding would not leave me. An hour after we'd gone to bed, I tiptoed out of our room and into the study. I closed the door and switched on the light. Then I pulled down a dusty box-file and began rifling through the various Government-issued booklets on adoption. I found what I was looking for at the very bottom. A mud-red glossy brochure – *Learning from Disruption*.

I would read this purely out of interest, I convinced myself. I sat down, cross-legged, and turned to the introduction.

Chapter Twenty-Two

'Disruption' was the one word that no one in adoption liked to hear – a prissy understatement for the breakdown of an adoption. Terminal, and only applicable to those sadly inept adopters who didn't have what it takes.

I speed-read the introduction before turning to chapter one, page three, entitled 'The Children'.

Staring at me from the page was a picture of Amy. I felt a flutter in my stomach as I recognised the expression instantly. Steely, controlled and staring. Her short write-up was headed Distorted Attachment and Role Confusion. I read on. Slowly at first, but then as each word, each sentence, began to drop with a clang of familiarity into my brain, my heart rate quickened:

> She showed a worrying ability to switch her challenging behaviour on and off . . . Outside the home she was sweet and charming . . . Carol & Dave became increasingly demoralised about their ability to help Amy . . . She had learnt quite sophisticated ways of covering up her neediness . . . Carol felt the full force of Amy's infantile rage while she effectively blocked her attempts to respond to her needs . . .

I could barely believe what I was reading. I mean, I could, but I just couldn't believe that there might be another child like Alex out there. I moved eagerly to the next child featured, Michael:

> He was described as indiscriminate in his relationships . . . Here, but not here . . . Rarely expressing any emotion and never crying . . . severe attachment problems . . .

By now, I was reading so fast and feverishly that my mind was struggling to keep up. I moved from feature to feature, drinking in the words like a dehydrated woman in an oasis:

> Control was a crucial issue . . . presenting with many subtle and manipulative behaviours . . . She brought to her placement significant problems around attachment and control . . . attachment . . . control issues . . . Struggling to attach . . . the child's ambivalence . . . completely unattached . . . attachment . . . control . . . superficial . . .

Attachment . . . attachment . . . attachment . . .

And then, suddenly, there it was on page twenty-one: *the passive, overly-compliant child can be just as wearing to deal with as the openly defiant one – if not more so.*

I exhaled in shock. Had I just read the words 'passive' and 'over-compliant'?

At that moment, I knew we were going to succeed – if there was one more child like Alex in this world, we were going to succeed. I crept back into our room, bent down and gave Rob a kiss on the cheek. 'Everything is going to be all right,' I whispered. He stirred, mumbled in his sleep, and fell still again. I returned to the study, too wired to sleep.

I picked up the booklet and re-read the first few features, more slowly this time. I didn't need to read any more. I put it down and stared into the distance. How was it possible we'd missed it? It wasn't as if we'd been unprepared. I could remember the lecture we'd attended about attachment-disordered children four years ago. What was it they'd said? *Always be cautious of the child who embraces you too well – who settles too quickly.* I shook my head in disbelief at our own heedless complacency. We'd been too eager for Alex to be the one; too sure we could overcome any problems she presented.

Why had it taken until now to remember those words of advice? The answer I found was that the lecture had never thrown a passive, compliant child into the equation. The image we'd come away with that day was of an overtly aggressive and destructive child.

Suddenly, I wanted to know more. I switched on the computer, and while waiting for it to boot up, I crept downstairs and made myself a cup of tea. It was now nearly two o'clock in the morning.

I clicked on the internet browser icon and debated my search words. I settled on ATTACHMENT, DISORDER, CHILDREN and ADOPTION, then clicked on the find button. Within seconds I was agape: Google had found literally thousands of sites. My search for the truth had well and truly begun.

For the next few hours, I lost myself in the world of Severe Attachment Disorder, or RAD – Reactive Attachment Disorder. There is ongoing debate over the appropriate term used to describe this condition. Some call it Severe Attachment Disorder or Difficulty; others call it Reactive Attachment Disorder. As someone whose life has been affected by the condition, I believe the term 'Reactive' is more congruous than 'Severe', so I will refer to it as RAD.

Attachment forms the building blocks of society. It is the thing that makes humans what they are – interactive beings who depend on each other for survival. It underpins every codependent relationship. The most significant of all attachments is that of a new-born infant with his or her mother/carer: the infant is wholly dependent on the mother for survival.

Imagine attachment as a string between infant and mother. The infant's cry for food, warmth, touch, reacts like a tug on the string. Alerted, the carer responds to the cry by fulfilling the infant's needs and, in doing so, has returned the tug on the string. This child feels secure and in control: it reacted, its carer responded. The infant has learned trust – it feels a sense of worth and it feels bonded.

Now imagine the infant born into an environment where its carer is unable to respond due to mental health problems or drug-induced oblivion. His or her cries for food, warmth and wellbeing are ignored. This infant's string is useless, therefore it has no sense of attachment, no sense of belonging to anyone, nor anyone to it. But most frighteningly, this infant has no control over its carer or its environment. Its fundamental instinct is that it will die.

The emotional consequences of this profound neglect are many. They include:

- Fear – of being out of control and left to die
- Rage – resulting from unfulfilled needs and general misery and discomfort
- Shame – born from abandonment and a sense of worthlessness

By the time this infant is removed from its environment of neglect, it is a broken soul, harbouring a terrible cocktail of emotions including a profound fear of attachment. To him or her, attachment signifies loss of control. Losing control signifies death. This infant must never allow itself to attach again.

Some of the other consequences of neglect include:

- lack of conscience – neglected children are not taught right from wrong until it is too late
- lack of cause and effect thinking – neglected children are not taught consequences. Their unpredictable life is a lottery of consequences
- lack of self-esteem – rejection destroys self-esteem
- lack of compassion or empathy for others
- developmental delay due to lack of stimulation

There is mounting evidence to suggest that stress caused by neglect and abuse can significantly affect the development of a baby's brain. This is supported by recent research on Romanian orphans – victims of extreme and sustained neglect – who were found to have a 'virtual black hole' where the orbitofrontal area of the prefrontal cortex should have been.

This area of the brain (known also as the social brain) is responsible for managing our emotions and is responsible for the development of self-control, empathy and sociability (a sense of connection with others). It is the final part of the brain to develop and, most crucially, develops almost entirely post-natally. As such, its development directly reflects the baby's early experiences and the amount of emotional stimulation the baby receives – or, more specifically, how the baby is loved and cared for.

A baby is born with billions of neurons, most of which are unconnected, or in other words, have yet to be 'wired'. Stimulation is paramount to making these connections and therefore developing the brain. Love and attention is crucial to positive 'wiring'.

Another key element in the development of this part of the brain is hormones, one of which is cortisol, the stress hormone. As a baby is born unable to regulate its own stress levels, it is dependent upon the carer to manage its stress, i.e. respond to its needs and so soothe its distress.

The brain of a baby who is loved and well cared for becomes conditioned to produce the body's optimum amount of the stress hormone cortisol. However, the baby who is unloved, neglected and/or abused suffers prolonged periods of acute distress, flooding the brain with cortisol. This flooding adversely affects the brain's receptors, affecting the long-term production of the hormone, i.e. the brain becomes conditioned (potentially for the lifetime of that child) to either underproduce cortisol (linked to aggression and emotional detachment) or to overproduce cortisol (linked to depression and anxiety).

We did not have full access to Alex's files. However, the reports we had been given in the early days made shocking reading and wholly justified the comment from Social Services that Alex's formative years with her birth mother had been as lonely, unpredictable and frightening as it could get.

Michelle was an alcoholic and drug addict who sustained her habit by prostitution. Abused as a child, she was brought up in care. She had no contact with her family and had just one friend, Rose, a fellow alcoholic thirty years her senior, who lived in the flat beneath hers and who kept an eye on Alex when Michelle was 'working'.

When the local authority was first alerted to the situation, one social worker commented she'd never seen a place as squalid as Michelle's flat. The stench of decaying matter – food, soiled nappies, damp, rot-infested towels etc. – had made her gag. The temperature was barely above freezing and mould clung to everything. Acting on an anonymous tip-off they had been forced to break down the door. Inside they discovered Michelle unconscious on the floor, her drug-taking paraphernalia around her. Her eighteen-month-old baby was lying in her own faeces, awake but silent in a cot in another room. She was grossly underweight, malnourished, and suffering a nappy rash so severe that parts of her groin area were oozing.

Alex spent the next two weeks in hospital, after which she was placed in a foster home, where she continued to recover physically. In the meantime her mother was treated for her addiction.

Off the drink and drugs, Michelle was a sweet, well-meaning twenty-two-year-old whose remorse over Alex was genuine. So, after several months and a vow that she'd never touch drink or drugs again, Alex was returned to her care.

Social Services monitored their situation closely and were pleased with the level of care Michelle was giving her daughter – and even more pleased when Kelvin, Michelle's new boyfriend, moved in. He presented as an earnest young man who clearly doted on Michelle and who helped out with Alex. Over the next few months, the fortnightly visits from Social Services dwindled away.

But Kelvin held a secret that he shared with no one, not even Michelle. He heard voices in his head – voices which told him to punish Alex, now a damaged child who was difficult to manage and who took up too much of Michelle's time. Time she should have been giving him.

Alex was suddenly plunged into a different nightmare. Terrified of Kelvin, she rarely left her bedroom and was too scared to speak out of turn for fear of interrupting something she shouldn't have. Michelle, unaware of Kelvin's voices and the ferocity of the punishment they demanded he mete out to Alex, was just grateful her daughter's terrible tantrums had stopped.

However, the nursery school was growing concerned. Alex was withdrawing into herself. Once a feisty, demanding child, never frightened to express her volatile emotions, she now looked pale and haunted. The fire in her eyes was dimming by the day to reveal a deep pool of trauma. Two weeks before her third birthday, the nursery called in Social Services.

The situation was investigated. Alex was found to have a few more bruises than was 'normal', but no broken bones or scarring. Kelvin admitted to inflicting the bruising but said he only hit her when she was naughty. Social Services cautioned him against physical punishment and advised Michelle that if her boyfriend continued to hurt Alex, he would not be allowed to live with them. Michelle understood.

However, as soon as the three of them were alone again, the beatings resumed. Michelle, now aware of what was going on, pleaded with Kelvin to stop, but he was powerless to resist the demands of his voices. With pressure from all sides, Kelvin was finding it increasingly difficult to hide his schizophrenic tendencies and, during a particularly agitated exchange with Michelle when she threatened to leave him, he exposed his secret. Michelle tried to contain the situation, but Kelvin's behaviour was growing increasingly disturbed and two weeks later she was forced to have him evicted.

Alone, depressed, and having to manage a damaged child, Michelle turned once more to drink and drugs. Twice more Alex was taken into care and twice returned on Michelle's assurance she was clean again. Then one day she took an overdose, coming to in hospital to learn that she and Alex had narrowly escaped being burned to death during an attempt by Alex to feed herself.

Alex was made a ward of court and freed for adoption.

Chapter Twenty-Three

When I next looked up, the sun had begun to rise over the park beyond our window. I stretched long and hard and kneaded my aching eyes. It was five-thirty in the morning and Alex would soon be awake. It wasn't worth going to bed now, so I switched off the computer, made another cup of tea, and curled up on the sofa with Scooter, a blanket, and my thoughts.

The full weight of comprehension had now set in and new emotions had formed.

I smiled sadly to myself, aware of the irony that this morning it was I who wanted to wake Alex. We had paid a heavy price for nearly three painful years of misunderstanding; the cost to Alex had been even higher. This 'machine' that had come to destroy us was no more than a human being whose perfect blueprint had been smashed at birth, taking with it her innate capacity to trust and to bond. Her sense of alienation from the world around her was not influenced by emotion: her place in our society had been severed as clinically as a string severed by a pair of scissors. For most of us this is inconceivable, until one remembers that the foundations of society are built on relationships.

Alex would have fared better on this earth had she fallen from a space ship; she'd have been treated with the respect and consideration she deserved. Her fear, her anger and her loss would not have been questioned or dismissed, or her social morals been met with such outrage.

She knew right from wrong, but it was not instinctive. Moral sense is not something with which a human being is born, it is taught to us in order for us to serve our purpose in society. Morals cannot be learnt effectively in an environment dominated by anger or fear. I recalled my talk with Alex about robbers. She knew the robbers were wrong to rob a bank, but she didn't 'feel' it; she'd learnt anger long before she'd learnt right from wrong.

Of all the personality traits in damaged children that I'd read about through the night, the one that most alerted me was the element of superficiality. Alex had not arrived on the doorstep of the Radfords with two heads and webbed fingers. No, she looked like a normal person. They'd taken her in as one of them and she'd had no choice but to learn how to be one of them. She watched and learnt and quickly discovered how to stay in control and safe in a world which was alien to her. Until now, I'd bitterly resented her superficiality, which I'd branded as dishonest and manipulative. How wrong I'd been!

My last thought before nodding off was the memory of her tears the night she'd fallen asleep stroking my hair.

I was roused by Daniel, fully dressed and wearing a puzzled look. I pulled him into my arms and ruffled his hair. I would explain things to him later.

Alex was hovering by the door, entirely oblivious of the profound place she occupied in my heart right now. 'Come here,' I said gently, beckoning her into my arms. I didn't care that she might not want to be there. I had something to say to her.

'I'm sorry we didn't understand.'

She could hear the lump in my throat and I knew she didn't know what I meant. But again, I didn't care. I held her just long enough not to frighten her and then let go. She hesitated a fraction and disappeared into the kitchen.

Rob, who'd been showering, found me upstairs dressing for work. 'Morning!' he chirped. 'Sleep well?'

I smiled and shut the door. Five minutes later, I'd explained as much as our limited time would allow. Everything else would have to wait.

Five of the phone calls I took at work that morning were from Rob. He was on the internet and learning about RAD.

We ordered Chicken Satay and Beef Chow Mein later that evening, but before it was delivered I fell asleep.

We spent the rest of the week preparing for a new beginning.

Our first task was to order the recommended reading from the Post-Adoption Centre. The only book not currently in stock, owing to high demand, was called *When Love is not Enough* by Nancy Thomas, a specialist in therapeutic parenting. We ordered it from Amazon.

Our second task should have been to talk with Alex, but we decided to wait until we'd read the books.

Our third task was to talk to Daniel. We told him – promised him – that now we understood why Alex was the way she was things were going to get better. We explained about attachment disorders and gave him a copy of some of the poems and writings we'd found on the internet written by children with RAD. We explained that the change in Alex's behaviour would take time and we asked him to be patient. He said that he would and that he felt sorry for her.

Then it was time to tell those who needed to know about her condition. We started with Wendy. One thing we'd learnt about RAD was that conventional therapy did not work. Conventional therapy was based on trust and respect between the therapist and her client. It required emotional honesty and the ability to articulate feelings. Children with RAD did not trust. They respected no one, not even themselves, and were emotionally dishonest. The trauma inflicted upon them usually occurred long before their conscious memory was formed, and they were therefore unable to understand why they felt the way they did.

We chose one of many websites which explained this and printed off the relevant information. Rob and I shared a brief moment of doubt as we re-read it, but we dismissed it. If Wendy didn't like the idea, she'd have to say so. We folded it into an envelope with her name on it. The following day I rang her with a brief explanation and we agreed that I'd meet her alone the following Monday.

Our thoughts then turned to my family and the school. We printed each of them a copy of the most clear and informative web pages. When we next got the chance, we'd speak to them more comprehensively.

The final and most difficult task was to ring Rob's family. It was already May, and if we were going to follow Nancy Thomas's therapeutic parenting techniques, a trip to Australia in the foreseeable future was out of the question.

My stomach was in knots as I waited for Wendy. Here I was, about to enter her office armed with a folder and a head full of thoughts. To ask her to forget everything she'd ever been taught, i.e. her life's work as a successful therapist. Not only that, but to ignore her own instincts – and in Alex's case, what she believed her own eyes were telling her – and instead listen to me, an adoptive mother with nothing but a diploma in shorthand and typing.

Yeah, right!

Conventional psychological thinking had been drummed into me from a very young age. It was as instinctive in me as it was in her. That I could even entertain the idea that there existed a human being unconditionally resistant to the fundamentals of conventional therapy was only because I'd lived with one.

My conviction swelled. I straightened my back and slapped the top of my thighs. I'd lived with one, she hadn't. She could either embrace the idea – although 'embrace' might be asking a little too much – or she could refer us on. Either way we couldn't lose.

'And that's it. That's everything we know about RAD,' I announced, with the air of someone who'd pleaded their case and was now awaiting the verdict.

A silent beat and then a blanket smile. 'You have been busy.'

Ouch! When she didn't immediately follow this with anything, I instinctively took the plunge. 'We'd quite understand if you wanted to refer her to someone else.'

There followed an awkward moment or two as I held my breath.

'What do *you* want?' she asked, putting a pointed stress on the word 'you'.

Her question derailed me completely. Wendy's tone was edgy.

'I don't know. Whatever's best for Alex, I suppose.' I smiled nervously. 'Obviously, if you feel you can help her, we'd like to stick with you. I was only suggesting you refer her on because everything we've read recommends specialist attachment therapy.'

Her face softened. 'Attachment is a wide issue, Melanie, and one we're all trained to recognise. I've worked successfully with several attachment-disordered children.'

'Have you?' I asked, both surprised and relieved. 'Well that's great – because Alex likes you a lot,' I added, grabbing the chance to make amends; one message that rang loud in all the reading we'd done was that the therapist and the parents had to work as a united team.

However, doubt still lingered. I didn't believe she fully understood the difference between Attachment Disordered and Reactive Attachment Disordered. I wanted her to read our notes and, in particular, a book we'd just finished that was pertinent to the therapeutic intervention in RAD. If she declined, which was possible, then we would ask to be referred on. It was also more than possible she would read the book and disagree with its radical ideas. Again, that was understandable, and we'd have to find someone who did agree. To this end, I reached into my bag and pulled out the book. I knew I wasn't brave enough to demand she read it, so I embarked on a long-winded, roundabout way of persuading her.

I'd barely covered three sentences when Wendy surprised me with a tactful 'Would you like me to read it?'

Any bad thoughts I'd ever had about her went whooshing out of the window. 'Thanks,' I said gratefully. 'And, by the way, I'm not suggesting we use the holding technique on Alex.'

Wendy looked straight at me. 'Good,' she said simply.

I'd not heard of the technique until that week. It involves containing the child in a cradle-like hold across the therapist's lap, allowing the child a safe environment in which to express its emotions. I had vague recollections of a child in America dying in the hands of her holding therapist, although that wasn't my reason for discarding it. In fact, Rob and I agreed that, properly applied, the holding technique was undoubtedly a most effective way of building trust between the therapist and the child. No, my reason was, quite simply, that I didn't feel we'd need to use it.

This was not a case of smug complacency – an attitude I'd once been prone to, as I now knew to my cost. My confidence had come

courtesy of Nancy L. Thomas, whose book had arrived that morning and which, thanks to the guile of the girls in the office who'd
crafted me several extended coffee breaks, I was already halfway
through reading.

Wendy and I agreed that the sessions would resume with Alex
next week and that we'd hold a review in a few weeks' time.

I left Wendy's office, eager to continue reading *When Love is not
Enough*, and almost indifferent to her role in Alex's healing.

'You're looking at Mrs Pizzazz,' I said, stabbing a pointed finger at
my chest with a satisfied grin.

'It suits you.'

We clinked glasses, left the bar area and found ourselves a table
in the farthest recess of Soprano's Wine Bar.

'So go on, tell me,' she urged.

'OK. Well, two weeks ago . . .'

Sophie sat rapt for the next half an hour as I educated her on
RAD. I spoke with the same wonder and excitement as a palaeon-
tologist who'd unearthed a missing link between sea and land
animals, and when I'd finished she squeezed my arm and said, 'I am
sooooo pleased. Where do you go from here?'

'That's where Nancy Thomas comes into it,' I said, referring to
her book. 'It's brilliant. It's aimed solely at the parents and gets you
right inside the head of an RAD child. It cuts through the namby-
pamby PC approach, explains that every bitter, hateful thought
you've ever had about your child is more than understandable. And
it's given us hope.'

'Can I read it?'

I gave an uncertain grimace. 'If you want to, but you might find
her techniques a bit, well, harsh – to say the least. Most of what she
advises goes totally against the grain of conventional parenting.'

'Why?'

It took a moment to formulate my thoughts.

'OK . . . Imagine you're five years old. You've been dumped, abandoned – whatever you want to call it – on your fifth doorstep and
you've nowhere else to go. You don't speak their language – emotionally, that is – because you've come from a place where rules were

immaterial, so you're totally self-governing. You have no concept of respect and no intrinsic sense of right and wrong. Every other person in your life, bar none, has let you down and, to compound it all, your insides are churning relentlessly with rage, fear and loss, none of which you can rationalise but all of which you've lived and breathed every single day of your life.

'Then just when your new carers, if they haven't jumped under a train by now, are still clinging to the hope that you might yet be fixable with some extra-super-understanding, patience and love, throw into the equation that you *can't* love. Loving someone requires you to attach, which you can't because you're autonomous. And the overriding reason for your autonomy is because the last time you were dependent on anyone, you could have died. Yes, died. We used to think that Alex's fears were of getting hurt again. Well, "hurt" doesn't come into it when you're a newborn baby denied food and warmth.'

Sophie was shaking her head, anguished as she tried to make sense of all this.

'Rob came up with an analogy that kind of sums it up,' I went on. 'We've got a friend who won't get into a lift. If he has to travel any-where, he'll make a phone call first to ascertain whether or not the stairs are in use. And why? Because he once spent two hours stuck in the lift at work.

'Now, imagine the child who once got stuck in a place long enough to touch death. A place of dependency on someone else to keep them alive with food, touch and warmth. It's irrelevant that their needs may have been met sporadically, or even steadily later on, because by then it's a lottery. The fear was already there. You could no more persuade Alex to relinquish her control and become dependent on us than you could get our friend into a lift.'

'So what are you going to do?'

'Apparently, we're going to put Alex in that lift whether she likes it or not. We're going to take her back to infancy, strip her of her control, make her dependent on us for everything, and bit by bit re-grow her. Only this time, into a trusting and responsible social being, who feels in control without having to take control.

'The way I understand it is that Alex cannot responsibly control her disruptive behaviour, which makes her not actually responsible for this behaviour. So, when she tries to disrupt a conversation for example, we have to say to her, "That's fine — I understand you can't help what you're doing, so I'm going to relieve you of your responsibility to sit quietly until I'm finished. When I'm on the phone or Dad and I are talking, you must leave the room. We'll call you back in when we're finished." Then, when she's able to control her disruptive behaviour, she will earn back the privilege — in the sense that she's responsible enough to handle something — to share the room with us when we're on the phone or talking. Yeah?'

Sophie nodded, slowly. 'That doesn't sound too harsh.'

'Can I remind you of that next time you come round and discover Alex is not allowed to initiate any hugs or kisses, and that she's spending most of her days helping me with the housework?'

'Aah. Why?'

'I'll lend you the book.'

As we were leaving Soprano's, Sophie asked, 'So what's the pizzazz bit?'

'The sort of attitude that says no matter what you throw at me I'm still going to love you, so tough!'

Chapter Twenty-Four

*I*n an ideal world, Nancy Thomas's therapeutic parenting techniques are put into practice as soon as the RAD child steps through your doorway for the first time. If that isn't possible, as was our case, it begins as soon as the book has been read, digested and understood.

However, after the euphoria of having had our daughter identified and explained to us in every page and paragraph of Nancy Thomas's book, it began to dawn on us that ours was far from the ideal world.

We'd already made several blind, diluted and unsuccessful attempts at it. Alex had her eyes wide open, knew the procedure, and it hadn't worked. We were going to have to pull very, very hard before we had her in our grasp.

In real terms, pulling hard equated to time. It was going to take us double the time to achieve the goal.

But we were determined that achieve it we would!

The night after I'd been out with Sophie, as soon as Alex and Daniel had gone to bed I sat down to plan.

I began with the easy stuff.

Alex needed a 'thinking within' spot – a place she would be asked to sit, following any disruptive behaviour. A place to think about the consequences of her actions and regroup. I chose the dining room table and a chair facing away from the rest of the house.

Then I dug out our old 'action plan' and set about modifying it. The exercise brought home just how tough this was going to be. I remembered how quickly we'd given up on it last time and why. I took a deep determined breath and continued planning.

Knowing that Alex would attempt to control our breakfast, I made sure we were at the table half an hour earlier than usual. Sure enough, she began to stare. Following what I hoped would have been Nancy Thomas's advice, I took Alex's hand, led her to the sofa in the other room and, with soft and loving eyes, calmly explained that because she was finding it difficult not to disrupt breakfast, I was relieving her of that 'responsibility'. I told her I'd let her know when we were finished and then she could eat hers. I left her rigid on the sofa.

Had I done that right? With a heart still hammering, I joined the rest of my family.

When we'd finished, I called Alex in. Then I placed a tiny portion of cereal in front her. Her cheeks flushed but she kept her eyes firmly fixed to the plate. When ten minutes later the plate was still half full, I quietly took it away.

Alex left the house wearing neon-yellow socks. Following the therapeutic parenting concept, I ignored the fact. The school would haul her up on her non-regulation socks and if they didn't like the cereal on her chin, they could wipe that off themselves. But her laborious clambering into the car brought my first moment of indecision. Nancy Thomas's advice would probably have been to meet her with soft eyes and suggest that until she found it 'easier' to climb in, we would walk, but we had no time for that today – it was impossible to walk both Daniel and Alex to school since he'd moved up to the junior school across the other side of town. Tomorrow, I'd see if Rob could share the morning school run until she'd earned back the privilege. I was thinking like Nancy Thomas already!

The jabbering began as soon I reversed out of the drive. I stopped the car, turned round, and met her with soft eyes. I said that until she was able to talk so that I was able to understand her *and* concentrate on driving, she was relieved of her responsibility to talk in the car. Daniel shot me a curious look and the car plunged into silence.

Alex wound down the window. I stopped the car again, turned around and, by now straining with the effort, once more met her with soft eyes and relieved her of her responsibility for the electric windows. She took the news with her usual look of dull compliance.

Then she began kneading her feet through the back of my chair. I stopped the car, turned around, met her with soft eyes and . . . faltered. Nancy Thomas would probably have met her child with compassion, saying that as long as he/she wasn't currently able to let her drive them safely to school, she suggested they walk. Instead I asked her to stop kneading the chair.

First big no-no. *Never ask anything of the child,* I could hear Nancy Thomas saying.

I was pleased to get to Daniel's school; Alex was radiating ice from every pore in her body. I gave Daniel a kiss, wished him a good day and we continued our journey.

By the time we reached the car park, I was growing concerned that Alex's muscles might have seized up. However, she hopped from the car and waited patiently for me to lock up. In recent months, we'd reached a deadlock with the walking issue – she walked dutifully by my side, but with as many bizarre little trots as were needed to infuriate me. I cursed myself for not having prepared for this and wondered what I should do and say next. *Until you're responsible for walking – safely? . . . nicely?* No. The book was not about good or bad behaviour – RAD children weren't in control of their behaviour. I just couldn't think! And then it dawned on me that from tomorrow we'd be walking everywhere and I had to think of an appropriate response. All I could come up with was a buggy! The ludicrousness of that made me smile.

At her first furtive skip hop, I sighed inwardly. Sticking to the therapeutic parenting concept was proving harder than I'd thought.

Alex faced her first chore later that afternoon. Daniel had wanted me to test him on some spellings, and when I next found Alex she'd cocooned her Dotty inside half a roll of sellotape. Following the same gentle ritual, I relieved her of the responsibility of using sellotape until such a time as she was able. I did the same with Dotty Dalmatian (which I told her we'd keep until she'd earned the 'privilege' of having it back) and, as a consequence of using up the sellotape, I told her she'd have to earn the money to pay for a new roll.

She reacted with just the smallest of flickers, but I could tell I'd surprised her. I prepared a bucket of hot soapy water, gave her the mop and left her to the floor.

Ten minutes later, I returned. 'That looks lovely,' I said, clocking that she'd missed half the floor. 'I really like this bit. When you've cleaned that bit too, it'll look even better,' I said. Her eyes grew dark and I left with my smile still warm.

I was sure I was doing everything right, so why had the day felt so disturbing?

'Where's that lovely neck hiding?' I said playfully, peering into the bathroom. 'Not here. Oh well it must be in—' I crept into the front room '—here!'

'Aaah!' Alex shrieked from behind the door and dived behind the curtains.

'Gimme your neck. I want to kiss it!' I began advancing on the-atrical tiptoe towards her.

'No! No! No!' she cried, giggling. She scrambled out and I gave chase. I grabbed her in a bear hug just before she could dive behind the sofa.

'Just here,' I said, finding my target and planting a quick-fire kiss on the side of her neck, 'And here.' *Kiss.* 'And here.' *Kiss.* 'And just here!' *Kiss . . . Kiss . . . Kiss.*

Alex was writhing and giggling hysterically. 'Get off! No, don't!'

And then it was her turn. 'Remember, no licking,' I said with an exaggerated grimace. I wiped at my soggy cheek as she expelled a raspberry on the other side.

'Love you too!' I said, and she ran out of the room.

I fell to the floor exhausted and smiled. I was under no illusion that she yet liked to be kissed, but the kissing game, inspired by my interpretation of Nancy Thomas's RAD parenting principles, was visibly easier on her emotions than the conventional affection we'd been giving her for the past few years.

We'd lost our TV remote control. On and off for three days, we hunted through every crevice of the house. I kept a gimlet eye on Alex's helpful search; if she'd hidden it, which we suspected she had, she was doing her usual fine job of hiding the fact. Although there was still a chance that it had been mistak-enly dropped in the bin or put in a drawer, we didn't think so. It was no coincidence that the remote had gone missing in the week we'd begun to limit Alex's TV viewing – another piece of advice from the book.

On the fourth day, I found it under her mattress. She reacted with a frightened face, but empty eyes. For the first time since we'd begun the new regime a week ago, Alex got the chance to try out her 'sitting within' spot. Without a word, she sat herself down at the table and stared at the blank wall ahead of her.

Five minutes later I gave her the chore of emptying the cutlery from the dishwasher, explaining gently that she would have to pay back the time we'd spent looking for the remote control.

When she'd finished, I found her waiting dutifully by the empty basket. It didn't surprise me when I opened the drawer to find a jumbled mess of north- and south-facing implements. I took the same line as I did with all her unfinished chores – I congratulated her, saying how much better it would look when she'd finished. I should have walked away, but the habit of showing her how it should be done was too ingrained. The last time she'd emptied the cutlery was a few months ago. It was just possible that, as a child with developmental delay, she was still confused, but my gut reaction told me otherwise – she'd not yet managed a chore successfully but . . .

I rearranged the first two layers of knives, forks and spoons, and then I ruffled her hair and said I'd be back soon.

My amazement when I opened the drawer ten minutes later was genuine. 'Wow!' I exclaimed. 'You can be my helper again.' I'd never seen the cutlery tray looking so neat. She accepted my compliment humbly and left. I stood rooted to the spot, my mind trying to make sense of it. Was it possible that the therapeutic parenting techniques were beginning to work?

When I was preparing tea a little while later, I pulled the top few layers of cutlery from the drawer to lay the table and discovered one knife, one fork and one spoon misplaced with perfect precision. Why had I not seen this turnaround coming?

I didn't know whether to feel disappointed or relieved. But more immediately, how should I respond? Alex was expecting me to discover the 'mistake' shortly.

'Daniel?' I shouted up the stairs, for the whole house to hear. 'Please can you help me lay the table?'

As part of Alex's Special Needs status, we had been invited to a handover meeting on 12 June between Hollybrook School and Oak Manor Junior – the school where Alex would be starting next term.

It turned out to be the most bizarre of any such meetings.

Hollybrook School vs The Allens. Conflicting thoughts – just the wrong way round. All very polite because neither party wanted a scene and because respect still lingered from Daniel's days at Hollybrook.

At the end of the meeting Oak Manor Junior looked none the wiser. Did Alex have emotional problems or not? What *were* her learning difficulties? And what on earth was this RAD stuff all about? With a polite smile, we bade each other farewell until September, when we would meet again.

Later that evening, I was on the phone recounting the meeting to Sophie.

'Why is she not going to the same school as Daniel?' she asked.

'Truthfully? Well, before Alex started at Hollybrook, I loved that school. I loved the teachers, I loved the mums and I think they liked me. I don't think I could cope if the same thing happened at Daniel's school,' I said. 'At Oak Manor, I know no one, so I've got nothing to lose.'

'You can't go outside until I've kissed you,' I pronounced playfully from the sink. She screeched, shot out of the kitchen and crouched, panting, at the foot of our front door. I was about to give my usual chase, when something about her expression stalled me. Despite her smile, her crinkled eyes looked dull. I felt a twinge of alarm, but lifted my waning smile and forced myself to move.

'Coming to get you,' I said as I came towards her.

She giggled and shot her two small arms out rigid in front of her, just in time for her raised palms to connect with my shins.

'Stop!' she commanded. This time, I did. I grabbed one of the stair banisters.

'Oh, go on, please,' I said, changing the dynamics of the game completely, but trying to read her face.

'No!' she barked, harmlessly.

'Just one little kiss?' I implored, hating the pucker on my lips.

She giggled, but again her eyes dulled over. 'All right, but you must stay there.'

Alex stood up, offered me the crown of her head and I kissed it. Then she blew me a jovial raspberry and left.

I sat on the stair to reflect.

As the days ticked on, and as our therapeutic parenting captured every move Alex made, she seemed to be withdrawing rather than fighting back. Our faith began to waver.

That summer Alex received her second school report. She could almost count to ten and knew most of the letters of her alphabet.

Dad had been a lifelong member of the Natural History Museum and the yearly excursion with his children had since become a tradition with his grandchildren.

The July day arrived, warm, blue and sunny, and spirits in the house were unusually high: Rob's and mine because of the impending break from Alex; Daniel's because he looked forward to the outing every year; and Alex because she could escape Nancy Thomas.

Minutes before Dad was due to turn up, I gave Daniel and Alex their customary two pounds to spend at the museum shop.

'Thanks,' Daniel said, and disappeared upstairs to get his backpack.

Alex said nothing. I looked at her; she looked at me. I raised my eyebrows as if to say 'what do you say?' Still nothing. Eventually, I held out the palm of my hand. Her face looked momentarily perplexed, but she was kidding no one. With a flash of darkness, she handed me back the two coins. 'When you're ready,' I said calmly, and left her standing there.

Five minutes passed and I'd not seen or heard her. I attempted a furtive glance from the kitchen into the sitting room, only to find her positioned exactly as I'd left her, looking my way. I pulled back, humiliated at having been caught looking at her.

I heard Dad's car pull up. *Bugger! Think!* There was nothing more I wanted than to wave Alex goodbye for the rest of the day but—

The doorbell rang. I opened the door and beckoned Dad inside. 'Can you give me a minute?' I said.

'Daniel!' I called upstairs, 'Grandpa's here!'

A few seconds later, I was looking expectantly into Alex's timid eyes, poised to remind her of what she had 'forgotten' to say, but I resisted.

Confirmation that I was right to resist came when, on hearing Daniel and Dad's enthusiastic greeting at the front door, Alex's gaze took on an anxious urgency. I said nothing. Her body began to twitch. Still I said nothing. As the moments passed my resolve held, but only by a thread. *Come on, say it!* I silently urged. *What are you waiting for?*

'She's not coming,' I apologised to Dad a couple of minutes later. I couldn't meet his eye.

For the first time ever, Alex took herself to her bedroom. If this was a good sign, it was no consolation. Alex was unhappy and I was confused. Rob retreated outside to clean the car and the house fell silent for the next half hour. It was with mixed feelings that I reacted to Alex starting to chatter to herself again. She came downstairs shortly afterwards as I was swallowing the last dregs of my coffee.

As I looked up, I felt a twist in my stomach. Alarm quickly turned to fear as I caught sight of her mottled cheeks. I launched myself off the sofa and over to where she stood, mouse-like. I ran my fingers across the rash on her cheeks and felt her forehead. It was cool.

'Are you feeling OK?'

She nodded.

'Rob?' I yelped through the patio doors, but he didn't hear. I told Alex to sit down and then ran to the garage.

'She's got that rash, again,' I said.

'What?' Rob wiped his oily hands across his overalls and we raced back into the house.

'Are you sure nothing hurts?' Rob asked Alex, peering down her throat. She managed to nod.

A minute later, Rob and I stood in our bedroom about to phone the doctor. Rob lifted the receiver.

'Wait,' I said suddenly. My head was clearing. 'I don't think she's ill, I think this is anger.'

Rob looked quizzical.

It was intuition on my part and I wasn't conscious of where it had come from. I took a moment to formulate my thoughts. 'That doctor at the hospital told us a rash like this can be caused by pressure on the face, remember? Well, I reckon this is suppressed rage or unexpressed pain – like she must have been feeling that day she was rushed to hospital – being squeezed through her face.'

Silence fell as we considered the possibility.

'So what do we do now?' Rob asked.

'We leave it a couple of hours, and if she develops a temperature, we ring Dr Norris,' I replied, and we went down to Alex.

Rob slid our *Aladdin* video into the player, pressed start and joined us on the sofa. For the next hour and a half we held our breath, every fifteen minutes or so lifting the palm of our hands to Alex's forehead. When the closing credits began to roll, I went upstairs and curled myself into a ball on our bed.

I'd expected to feel relief, not this dull disabled feeling that had been building for the past couple of hours. If I looked deeper, though, I would have to say this feeling had begun before then, when the hold I thought I had on Alex's problems began to slip from my grasp. That Alex's silence, her secrecy, had once seen her blue-lighted to hospital, was suddenly too much for me to handle. Lying on the bed I felt myself fall.

Think!

Far from bringing results, our use of Nancy Thomas's advice was confusing us. Alex didn't need a chair to calm down in – she was shutting down all by herself. A week ago, I'd re-read the book. There was nothing in there that talked about a detached child who did *not* scream or shout at the consequences she gave them. Her children fought back: they *wanted* or *didn't want!* Alex just switched herself off like a computer at the plug. Correction, the computer was still running; it was the monitor screen she had switched off.

There would be people who'd tell us this was early days; that we'd known it would take us longer than most. There would be others who'd say we *should* have put Alex in the buggy that morning, but they didn't know Alex. She'd have borne the humiliation and blacked out the screen.

Why?

I tumbled to the bottom of my fall and my brain blanked out.

'*Why* Alex?' I said. Rob and Alex spun round to meet my imploring face.

I sat on my haunches and looked pleadingly into Alex's eyes. 'Why?'

She looked slightly dazed.

'I know you wanted to go with Grandpa,' I said, recalling the image of her anxious urgency, 'so why?'

Alex registered. She met my question with meek bemusement, but her eyes were already beginning to disengage.

'No,' I said, 'come back.'

Alex twitched in fright. 'Um . . . um . . .'

'Why wouldn't you say "thank you"?' I implored.

'Um . . . I don't know.'

'You *do* know'

'Mmmm . . .'

I shook her knees and she flinched, but I was desperate.

'Is keeping quiet more important than having fun?'

A flash of anxiety crossed her face. Rob and I kept absolutely still.

'Is it?'

Anxiety flashed again.

'You won't die if you tell us,' I said gently, before I could stop myself.

Another flash. And another and another. And silence.

'Alex. *Please* tell us. We want to help.'

No response, and her eyes began to switch off. I gripped her knees. 'Alex!'

'Um,' she squeaked.

'What is it?'

'I don't know.'

'You do!' My voice was now so high, it was breaking. 'Tell me!'

'I *can't.*'

My heart missed a beat.

'You can.'

She shook her head.

'Alex!'

'*It* won't let me!' Alex exploded and then dropped her head.

Stunned silence.

Tick . . . Tick . . . Tick . . .

'What won't let you?' I said, breathing hard.

Alex looked as though she was going to be sick. 'Um . . . I don't know.'

'Try . . .' I wanted to take her hand, nurse it out, but her RAD made that impossible.

'Um . . . it's . . .'

The cogs in my mind were working furiously.

'What is the "it" Alex?'

Silence.

'Can you see it?'

She shook her head, almost defeated.

'It's all right,' Rob soothed her.

I had to be careful. 'Can you hear it?'

A beat of silence, then, 'Yes.' Her voice was a whisper.

'Can *we* hear it?'

'No.'

'So where do you hear it?'

A beat. 'In my head.'

Rob and I traded a look; my heart was hammering blood round my veins.

'What does it say?'

But she was shutting down again. I moved quickly. 'Can you describe it?' Silence. 'What does it say?' Silence. 'Do you talk to it?' Silence. 'Can we talk to it?'

'No.'

'Do you have to do what it says?'

Alex's light went out.

Chapter Twenty-Five

Did hearing a voice in her head make Alex schizophrenic? And if so, what had triggered it? Might she have inherited it? We knew nothing of Michelle's family, but we *did* know that the troubled and abusive Kelvin had suffered with the condition. Perhaps Alex's secret voice was a product of his illness that she'd 'learnt' from him . . . Whatever it was, the one thing we were confident of was that this voice was all-dominant.

After putting the children to bed, we retrieved Alex's old files and found the relevant section on Kelvin, written by Michelle's social worker: *Kelvin explained to me that the (secret) voices were extremely jealous of Alex and made him do the opposite to what Alex wanted or needed.*

Everything was beginning to make sense, and as Rob and I talked deep into the night we recalled a never-ending list of behavioural examples that tallied, and we now registered each episode with new clarity and understanding:

- We expected Alex to say thank you for the pocket money. The Voice wouldn't let her, even if it meant forfeiting a trip to the museum.
- We wanted Alex to amuse herself. The Voice wouldn't allow it so she fell asleep.
- The school wanted her to count to ten, work by herself, etc. The Voice stopped her.
- Daniel wanted her to learn to bowl. The Voice prevented her from learning.
- We wanted her to dress herself one way. The Voice ordered her to do it another way.

And so on and. Oh, how we all wanted and expected things, and how powerless she was to comply. Comply? She always complied!

Except she actually didn't – ever. She merely appeared to be complying, and now we understood why. Because, like Kelvin's, her voice was a secret that demanded secrecy of Alex. If she'd stamped her feet and screamed 'no' every time she was asked to do something that either the RAD or the voice wouldn't allow, she'd be revealing her thoughts and her emotions. We were prepared to wager our life's savings on the fact that total secrecy was what the voice demanded of her. Why else did she never reveal her thoughts and emotions?

It wasn't just her anger she kept hidden, as we'd learnt over the past two and a half years – she seemingly wanted nothing. Why? We concluded now that it was either because to reveal what she wanted would be to disobey the voice, or because revealing what she wanted was something we expected of her. Either way, she was impotent to say what she liked or wanted, as the incident with the tomato and carrot lunch had demonstrated.

As we talked on, the essence of Alex's RAD and of the voice grew increasingly cloudy as the two merged. How much of her inability to comply was due to anger and control, how much was due to the demands of the voice, and how much to a combination of the two? The part her developmental delay played in this was irrelevant right now. As we continued to piece the jigsaw together, we were forced to confront the fact that this voice was also a very convenient ally in Alex's battle for control. By the end of the night, we realised that we were way out of our depth and needed help. More importantly, Alex needed help, big time.

What sort of help was needed and from where? We talked the question round and round and eventually decided that the voice, whatever its origins, dictated her disturbed behaviour, and concluded that the voice had to be dealt with before anything else.

As we heaved our exhausted bodies off the sofa to go to bed, Rob pointed out the grim task ahead of us: to convince CAMHS that Wendy's 'scrumptious' was totally detached, that she had a voice in her head, and that she was a gifted actress. As improbable as these things might seem, we had found nothing to contradict them.

With our thoughts back on CAMHS and Wendy Bozier, it was

only now I remembered she still had our book on RAD and I had no idea if she'd even read it.

'A voice in her head?' Wendy repeated disbelievingly.

'Yes. She couldn't – or wouldn't – describe what "it" was but she said it was in her head.'

'Anything else?'

'No. When we try and talk to her about it, she just says, "it won't let me". We don't know what to do next.' My tone was polite but detached. She was not on our team, but we still needed her help.

The disdain in Wendy's barely concealed exasperation was palpable. She gave me a look of studied concern and suggested that we might be delving too deeply. Then she moved back into conventional territory, talking about a little girl who wanted to love, who wanted to trust, who wanted to fit in, but who was too frightened to do so, and suggested that the voice was a tangible way of expressing this.

I silenced her with a 'No!' so fierce it surprised even me, and went on. 'Whatever the voice represents, it's too powerful. We would guess she has no more control over it than we do,' I said firmly. 'Again, we're prepared to stand corrected, but either way, Alex needs help with it.'

It was clear from my expression and tone that we were not expecting this 'help' to come from Wendy. We'd already made the mistake of not referring her for Attachment Therapy. We weren't going to repeat that mistake.

'I'll speak to Sheila Hawson,' she said in a flat tone I'd not heard her use before. At that moment, I sensed the irreparable break in our relationship. Had I been in a position to, I would have thanked her politely, wished her well for the future and left, knowing I'd never again have to writhe under her obvious disdain again. However, that luxury wasn't afforded us. This was the system from which all referrals had to be made and it didn't allow us to refer Alex ourselves.

My only salvation was that, owing to the summer holidays, I'd not have to deliver Alex to this office for another five weeks. By then, hopefully, we would have a confirmed appointment with Sheila Hawson.

Letting the voice out of the bag changed nothing. Unlike the confession of a forbidden love, Alex's revelation had not been the
unburdening of a secret, for her secret demanded secrecy. She was
still unable to reveal her thoughts or feelings. We could no more
reason with her controlling voice than we could persuade Alex to
relinquish her own control. Alex was a controller being controlled.

When we'd finally accepted that we were not going to fix this
overnight, we were faced with the dilemma of how to survive until
Alex got treatment. We had only two options: to continue with the
therapeutic parenting or to abandon it.

The decision wasn't difficult. Although the therapeutic parenting
was powerless to stop the voice, we decided to stick with it. Firstly,
we believed that Alex would despise us if we dropped it now and,
secondly, life under the guidance of Nancy Thomas still gave us
some semblance of control.

And so life moved on. Alex remained untouchable; we adapted.
We were living in limbo.

Sheila Hawson, Chief Child Psychologist at CAMHS, was a slight
lady in her early forties, with a short dark bob and dark, penetrating
eyes. She greeted Rob and me with a firm handshake and, thankfully,
without quite the same air of studied warmth we were used to
encountering.

With professional attentiveness she absorbed our story, our conviction and our desperation. She didn't dismiss a thought and her
expression at no time suggested she was sceptical, which gave me
hope. When we'd finished, she took a moment to formulate her
thoughts, and while she did so, Wendy kept her eyes firmly pinned
to the floor where they'd been for the past half an hour.

'A psychotic disorder, which is what you seem to be suggesting,'
she said finally, 'is very rare in children of Alex's age.'

She explained that mental health disorders generally fell into one
of two brackets: neurotic disorders or psychotic disorders. Neurotic
disorders were conditions such as anxiety and depression; psychotic
disorders were more severe and involved the distortion of a person's
perception of reality, often accompanied by delusions or hallucinations. She cited schizophrenia and manic depression as examples.

'Whichever category Alex's problem falls into,' Rob said, 'we don't believe she has any control over it. Which is why' – he took a deep breath and steeled himself – 'we think she might need medication or something.'

That roused Wendy, whose eyes shot to Sheila and were met by an answering look. When Sheila spoke again, her demeanour had noticeably stiffened.

'Mr and Mrs Allen,' she said, 'we medicate children *only* as a very last resort and *only* after a very thorough assessment,' she said.

I jumped on the latter. We'd known the chance of her agreeing to medication straight away had been minuscule. 'Who would carry out this assessment?' I asked.

'Probably Solomon's Hospital. They have a juvenile psychiatric ward there.'

Our eyes pleaded with her until she relented. There was a condition, however – she insisted on carrying out her own assessment of Alex before making the referral.

We left Friesden House hugely encouraged and undeterred. Whatever Sheila's assessment revealed, Alex was going to Solomon's. We'd chain ourselves to the hospital gates, if necessary.

Now all we had to do was wait for the phone call to arrange a date.

We decided to spend the rest of August hiding out in Mallard Close. Invitations to picnics were turned down and the Brighton weekend with my family was politely excused, and the excuses gratefully accepted. A summer holiday away was out of the question. In short, we were avoiding people like the plague.

Daniel spent the five weeks outdoors playing with the gang of neighbourhood children. Alex spent most of it indoors with me. Our only respite came courtesy of Dad, who was happy to take Alex off our hands once a week. Or to put it more truthfully, who was terrified I might be suffering a breakdown.

September came and, with it, Alex's first term at Oak Manor school. At the end of her first week, I was standing on my own under the imposing tree that had given its name to the school, waiting for my daughter to file out of her classroom. She was the last to emerge, accompanied by her teacher, Mrs Coley, who wore a beaming smile. Aside from a brief word of reassurance at the end of Alex's first day, I'd not yet had any feedback.

I braced myself for the spiel I now knew off by heart, listened, and smiled until I thought my face would crack.

And just when I thought there were no more positives left to speak of, Mrs Coley looked affectionately down at Alex for a further time and added, 'Alex had us all laughing today. She came in after morning break with so many paper towels stuffed up her jumper, she looked like a scarecrow.'

My smile withered. She held up a hand. 'Don't worry! I've told her the towels are expensive – she won't do it again. But, oh, you should have seen her. She's a regular little comedienne.'

Like an ape, I followed her smile, nodding her enthusiasm, and when I could, I snatched a brief look at Alex. She wouldn't meet my eye.

How dense did Mrs Coley think Alex was?!

As soon as we'd climbed into the car, I turned to Alex and asked her why she'd done it. It took a while, but eventually it transpired that she'd earlier asked Mrs Coley if she could get a paper towel from the toilets to blow her nose and had been angry because Mrs Coley had told her to wait the five minutes until the end of class.

Later that evening, I perched myself on Alex's bed and we locked eyes.

'Dad and I have decided that, until you're ready to show people how you're really feeling, we don't want to pretend with you,' I said. 'Next time something like that happens, I'm not going to laugh with them. Understand?'

'Yes,' she said dully and with empty eyes.

'I don't care how mean people think we are. It's more important to us that you get better.'

I didn't add that faking it with her made *us* look stupid and we needed her respect.

When Sheila didn't ring back with an appointment date, we rang her. It was now thirty-one days since our meeting and every day had felt like a week.

She apologised. She'd been busy. Did I have my diary? Yes, I did. In the end, she couldn't fit us in for another three weeks when, she said, it was fortunate she'd had a cancellation.

She obviously couldn't wait to get off the phone but there was so much more I needed to say. We were desperate, I explained. She understood and she'd do all she could to hurry things along.

Had she remembered, I asked, that Alex might fake her demeanour during her assessment? If that was the case, she'd quickly discern it, she said. She had years of experience working with children like Alex. I swallowed my misgivings, crossed my fingers, and suggested she might like a copy of our notes. By all means, she said, but her tone was saying 'now please get off the phone.'

I slipped in a final reminder of the urgency of our needs and thanked her for listening.

When Mrs Coley asked me proudly if I wanted to hear Alex's much improved reading, I curdled. *No I don't.* 'That would be nice, yes please,' I said.

With Alex looking decidedly flushed and twitchy beside her, I watched as her teacher shuffled a deck of flash cards.

She gave Alex an encouraging grin and held up the first card: in large bold type, the word read *AT.*

Alex shuffled, smiled nervously and cleared her throat. 'Um, A . . . A . . .' she sounded. And again 'A'. We waited, 'T . . .' and waited, 'A . . . T . . .'

Mrs Coley had her mouth wide open, straining the shape of the sound 'A', and looking like she might burst with the effort.

Alex frowned, looked, frowned, looked: 'A . . . T . . . T . . . AT.'

'Well done!' Mrs Coley exclaimed in a puff of expelled air. She beamed blindly into my wooden smile and pulled out the next card. We all looked at the word *IT.*

Alex managed eventually to sound it out, but it took no less effort.

The whole affair repelled me, and the indignity I felt at being subjected to this farce had me grinding my teeth and clawing at my forehead.

The wretched woman pulled out the third card: *LOOK.*

'Now, we had a few problems with this one, didn't we Alex?' she said, as though talking to a dumb animal. I closed my eyes, unable to watch. 'This is the "oooo" sound, remember? L – OOOOO – K. L – OOOOO – K.' The air stopped moving as Mrs Coley held her breath, willing her, willing her . . .

'L . . .' Alex paused, her forehead creased with the effort of recalling the next sound.

I opened one corner of my eye. Alex's brows were creased in concentration and effort. What was the sound she'd just made?

'L—'

'We'll go back to that one,' Mrs Coley said hastily but sympathetically, and pulled out the next card: *IS*.

Alex took an exaggerated breath. 'I . . . I . . .' she frowned, 'I—'

I'd had enough. 'Actually, I don't want to hear any more,' I said evenly. 'Perhaps when she can read them, I'll come back.'

My voice seemed to belong to someone else, and Mrs Coley looked like I'd just thrown a bucket of water over her head. I wanted to cry.

The silence as Alex got her coat and bag together was thick and knotty. Mrs Coley had her head resolutely down, gathering up the cards.

I stopped at the door and turned round. 'I know what you must think of me – you're not alone,' I said wearily, 'but whether you believe it or not, we're doing this for Alex.'

She didn't look up.

The full impact of my actions hit me as we got in the car.

'Do you like it when Mrs Coley talks to you like you're a baby?' I spat, venting my anguish at Alex.

She stared at me. 'Um, no.'

I fired up the engine and revved hard. *I bet you love it!*

Three days later, Rob found me pacing the floor in a fury, following another session with Wendy.

'What happened?'

'*This* is what happened!' I said, and dropped a bundle of white envelopes onto the coffee table. 'Go on, read them,' I challenged. 'One for every member of our family and all, apparently, having been dictated by Alex and typed by Wendy during the last two sessions.'

Rob pulled the first one out and read it aloud. 'Dear Grandpa, I hope you are having a nice time in Devon and I hope your cold is feeling better now. Love from Alex . . .' His tone dribbled away to one of dull disbelief.

'Go on,' I said, urging him to read the rest.

'Dear Matt and Lilly, I hope you are having a nice time with your new dog. Thank you for letting me ride in your car.' He pulled out the next one. 'Dear Tess, I hope you have a nice time going shopping with me.' And the next one. By now Rob had an eyebrow cocked in sheer disbelief, and shook his head as he read, 'Dear Tim, I hope you like your new house. I hope that I can come and see it soon.'

Then he picked up the fifth letter and any trace of wry amusement fell from his expression as it hardened. The letter was to Rob's mum in Australia: 'Dear Grandma Allen, I hope you had a nice birthday. I am sorry I could not be at it. Love from Alex.'

'Horrible, isn't it?' I said in the ensuing silence.

'Whose idea was this?'

'Alex's, apparently.'

'So first she's cleaning Wendy's office, now she's dictating weird love letters to her.'

'She's also had her helping her with homework, apparently.'

'So she's got Wendy firmly round her little finger,' said Rob.

I agreed. 'Do you know what Wendy said as Alex coyly handed them to me? She said, "Alex is worried you might think they're fake." She wanted me to deny it, but I just turned to Alex and said, "Well, are they?" You should have seen Wendy's face. I'm surprised she didn't ring Child Protection, there and then!'

'What did Alex say?'

'She batted those huge nervous eyes of hers and said, "Um-um-um yes." In other words, No, but I'm so scared of you, I'll say whatever you want me to say. You should have seen her skipping back to the car – she was as high as a kite,' I told him.

We could only marvel at Alex's audacity.

That evening, I wrote Wendy a letter outlining our thoughts on why we believed the letters to be fake and saying we felt it best we didn't discuss the sessions in front of Alex. She never replied and, thereafter, she and I exchanged only the minimum of words, which was fine by me.

Life in limbo ticked on. As we waited for the appointment with Sheila, the deadlock tightened. The therapeutic parenting was growing more wooden by the day. Things at home had reached such an impasse that we'd been forced to say to Alex that, unless she could join in without being disruptive, she would have to sit some place else – in front of the TV or in her bedroom.

She reacted with the same numb acceptance as she did to all the things denied to her by her detachment and the voice. When her noises and chanting grew too loud, we turned up the radio.

When I dared to confront what had become of our lives, I could find no words to describe the nightmare. We were characters in some kind of sick horror film – Rob, Daniel and I living downstairs; Alex upstairs, though not, as in a film, locked away in the attic. Day after day, we sought other solutions, but always found ourselves at the same dead end. The RAD was untouchable because of the voice and the voice fuelled the RAD. We continued with our 'talks' because we thought we might yet be able to touch the soul inside Alex – the soul I'd seen the night she woke up crying: the soul we'd witnessed screaming and spitting in rage. But we were talking to the voice, not to Alex, and we both knew it.

However, there was one bright spot to emerge from this darkness. It had begun to seep into our bizarre existence at the end of the summer holidays, and came courtesy of Alex's acute wit – the only force substantial enough to defy the voice. We were like two people from opposing teams, stuck in the same piece of quicksand and finding humour in our shared misery.

It had begun one evening as I'd been putting Alex to bed.

'Your voice must have some super-horrible names for us,' I said, plonking my bottom on her bed.

There was a shift in her smile, but she said nothing.

'Go on,' I prodded her playfully, 'I bet it has.'

Pause. Then the temptation was too much. 'It calls you the Chumps.'

'The Chumps, huh? Not the Munsters or The Addams Family,' I said. 'What about me? What does it call me?'

There was a glint in Alex's eye, mischievous and genuine. 'It calls you snake-licker.'

I clasped my mouth in mortification. 'Well! Now that one's more like it,' I exclaimed. 'Anything else?' But I thrust the palm of my hand towards her. 'No. Actually, I think it's better I don't know.'

It had only been when I was going downstairs, feeling a ton lighter, that I realised just how potent and honest the names were.

The droll honesty that continued thereafter wasn't enough to rescue us, but it came to represent the nearest thing we had to a bond.

CAMHS regional head office shared the same bland sterility as Friesden House, except it was larger and the waiting room housed a fish tank. Alex, however, was uninterested in the fish. She was unsettled.

Our names were called within minutes and we were directed to a small room not dissimilar to Wendy's office.

Sheila rose to her feet, gave me a cursory greeting, indicated a chair for me in a corner, and then bestowed a smile on Alex.

'Hello Alex,' she said with deliberate care. 'My name is Sheila Hawson. Have a seat,' she said, pointing to a chair across the table from her. Alex smiled nervously and sat down. Sheila reseated herself then fixed her with an earnest look. 'Has Mummy explained why you're here?'

Alex glanced across at me before fixing Sheila a jittery, befuddled look. Sheila looked at me, but I held my expectant stare on Alex. The silence hung taut but my resolve held – I was not going to speak for her.

Fortunately, it seemed Sheila wasn't about to prompt her either, and when the silence grew too prolonged, Alex had no option but to speak.

'Um . . . yes.'

'Good,' Sheila said with a serious smile. 'So you know there's nothing to be afraid of, I'm only here to listen.'

Alex nodded, though now her face was grave too, almost as though mirroring Sheila's.

'Right,' Sheila said gently, 'why don't we start by talking a bit about you. Mummy tells me you like music, is that right?'

So the session began. Slowly, agonisingly slowly, Alex went through the motions of answering her questions. I marvelled. Alex was managing to look both confused and despondent, and as the questions rolled on, I was trying to make sense of her demeanour. Surely it wasn't possible she'd finally been able to defy her voice and reveal all? But I dismissed the idea. The answers to Sheila's questions were as vapid as always.

'Do you like your new school?'

'Um . . . yes,' she said, her eyes downcast.

'What about your teacher? Is she nice?'

'Mmm, yes.'

'Is there anything else you like about your school?'

'The building.'

I stifled a smile.

'Oh, that's good. Anything else?'

'Er, I don't know.'

'What about playtime?'

Hesitation, then, 'I don't know?'

Sheila gave a small frown and fixed Alex a concerned look.

'Who do you play with in the playground?'

Alex lifted her head, 'Um . . . um . . .' and then hung her head miserably again.

What *was* she doing?

Sheila's voice dropped to almost a whisper. 'Do you have some friends you like to play with?'

'Um . . . no.'

Liar! My widened eyes shot to Sheila, imploring her to read my shock. Instead, she returned a tiny but firm shake of her head, silencing me.

Concern stuck softly to Sheila's voice. 'So what do you do in the playground?'

Alex lifted her head. 'I go to the Ark.'

A scoff rose in my throat and I had to cough to suppress it. My daughter didn't look at me.

'The Ark?' Sheila asked.

'Um . . . Noah's Ark.'

'Tell me about the Noah's Ark.'

'Er – it is for quiet play.'

'Do the other children like the Noah's Ark?'

'I don't know.'

'What do you do when you're in Noah's Ark?'

Alex couldn't tell what she did, so Sheila rephrased her question: 'If I was a little mouse sitting in the ark, what would I see Alex doing?'

'Um . . . sitting.'

'Can you draw it for me?'

As Alex drew what was a vaguely discernible stick-figure, sitting alone on one of the two long benches, Sheila began nodding earnestly to herself. She looked deeply concerned.

Deeply concerned. Suddenly my irritation vanished and I stopped trying to meet her eyes. As long as Sheila was concerned, that was all that mattered.

The next quarter of an hour unfolded in a similar vein. She asked Alex about her feelings in general, predictably steering the discussion to her life with us, and in particular to the time Alex was spending alone in her bedroom. She felt lonely, Alex said. That was why she went to her bedroom.

With ten minutes to go, Sheila finally and carefully broached the subject of The Voice. Suddenly the air around Alex changed and I held my breath, as did Sheila, because Alex was taking her time answering. When she did answer, the moroseness had gone. All that was left was the bumbling timidity and a soft but flat voice. She told Sheila that, yes, she could hear it in her head; yes, it was there all the time; no, she didn't know what it was; and no, she couldn't draw it.

Then Sheila, who'd seemingly failed to notice the change in Alex's demeanour, braced herself and asked, 'Alex, what does this voice say?'

Alex twitched. 'Um . . . um . . .'

Silence.

Sheila was still and transfixed – the clock kept moving. Tick . . . tick . . . tick . . .

Finally, Alex lifted her eyes and said, 'It tells me to stare at Mum.'

It took me a moment to recover, and even longer to try to make sense of it, which I never did. Sheila had no more questions, she'd heard enough. She thanked Alex for allowing her to understand how she was feeling and said to me, 'I'll ring you on Monday.'

We'd never know for sure why Alex altered her demeanour, depending on who was probing. She was an actress – maybe she mirrored the attitude of whoever was talking to her. Or maybe she was cleverer than that and she knew precisely what each person wanted or needed to hear. One day, when all her records would be collated, the array of individual assessments made of Alex would read so disparately as to be risible.

Chapter Twenty-Six

The following day, I rang and made an appointment to see Mrs Harcombe, the head teacher at Alex's school. For our own peace of mind we wanted to make certain Alex didn't spend her lunchtimes in the Noah's Ark. I could have asked Mrs Coley directly, but our relationship, though polite, continued uneasy.

'Who told you that?' the head teacher asked me, shocked.

'Alex,' I said with a small grimace.

She frowned, gave a small laugh, and then as if to reassure me said, 'No. In fact, I don't think I've ever seen Alex playing in the Ark. She likes to be outside where all the action is.'

'Thanks,' I said. 'Can I ask just one more thing? Does Alex play with the other children?'

The Head laughed. 'Oh, yes. She doesn't have any one particular friend, but she's always in the thick of things.'

A few minutes later I left her office, buoyant and vindicated.

Monday came and went without the phone call. By Tuesday afternoon, I couldn't wait any longer. I sat down and dialled Sheila's number.

'Sorry, I didn't ring, it was a hectic day,' she said. 'Right, Alex. Yes, she's clearly unhappy at the moment and I do feel an assessment of some sort is needed.'

I punched the air with my fist. 'At Solomon's hospital?'

She paused and my heart sank again. 'Solomon's may not be the right place for her.'

'But you said—'

'I said I'd do my own initial assessment, and if I felt she needed a hospital assessment, I'd refer her,' she said, while I scratched painfully at my furrowed forehead. 'In my view, Alex is displaying classic symptoms of depression.'

Depression? Sheila would struggle to find anyone else in Alex's life to support that view! Instead, I asked, 'What about the voice?'

'At this stage, I feel the voice represents some inner conflict, rather than a psychotic process.'

'But—'

'I'm not saying it's not there, Mrs Allen, or that she doesn't feel it,' she said. 'What I am suggesting is that she's an unhappy little girl who is struggling to express those intolerable aspects of herself. This isn't unusual in children like her and as we treat her depression . . .'

I walked across to the patio doors and began thumping my head against the glass pane. Had she not listened to a word we'd said? What about the RAD? . . . Maybe she *was* depressed, but *just* depressed? No! No! No!

'Hello?'

'Yeah, I'm still here,' I said, raking a hand through my hair.

'Mrs Allen, we will do all we can to treat Alex.'

'Then *please* give her this hospital assessment. She is seriously disturbed – not just depressed,' I implored, 'and she's brilliant at hiding it.'

I could hear nothing at the other end. This was the moment I'd so hoped wouldn't come.

'Sheila, she—' I closed my eyes. '—she lied to you. That bit about her being in the Noah's Ark wasn't true.'

It took Sheila just a fraction of a second to scramble together a defence. 'Maybe she did, maybe she didn't—'

'She did! Ring the school – they'll tell you the same.'

She sighed. 'Whether she lied or not is irrelevant. What's important—'

'But it *is* relevant; it proves what we're saying.'

She made a brittle sound. 'Please Mrs Allen, I'm finding it difficult to talk to you while you keep interrupting.'

Her tone was tense, so I trod carefully and said, 'You're an astute person. If she can fake it with you, she can fake it with anyone.'

Sheila didn't respond, so I took the opportunity to give it one last stab. 'We're living with a child who's secretive beyond belief, who's got a voice in her head, who talks of death, who's filled with hate, who at eight years old can't even write her name and who can shut herself down like a computer. We do *not* believe her problems are just depression.'

There was a long pause and then a resigned sigh. 'I've got a friend who works at a similar hospital. I'll speak to him and call you back.'

I grinned madly. 'Thank you! Thank you so much!'

But the line was already dead.

'Let me ring her,' Rob offered two weeks later. We'd heard nothing from Sheila and I didn't trust myself to speak to her. In fact, once I'd heard Rob greet her on the phone, I fled to the kitchen and the shelter of my radio.

Five minutes later, he found me. His face wore the mark of a fraught altercation.

'OK,' he began, 'she's referring Alex to Orchid House – the ward her friend works on. She's set up a meeting for the fourteenth of February, but the earliest they'll be able to take her will be April.'

'That's six months away!' I erupted in despair.

He held up his hands to me in a plea to stay calm. 'I know, I know. That's exactly what I told her. So she's offered us a prescription for antidepressants for Alex until then.'

My mouth fell open. 'You're joking! You told her where to stick it, I hope.'

'I told her we'd take it.'

'You didn't!' I was incredulous.

'Mel, I didn't know what else to do. Besides, we both agreed she might be depressed. Maybe this will help.'

I rolled my eyes angrily. 'And what if it doesn't? What if it has some kind of adverse affect on her? Rob, her state of mind is so fragile it could send her off the rails, and then what?'

'Shit, Mel. I don't know. I just don't bloody know.' He slid his back down the kitchen cupboard, and slumped to the floor with his head between his knees. Neither of us spoke for a while, then he lifted his head slowly, looked me in the eye and said, 'I don't know how much more I can take of this.' His voice had been quiet and too grave. I turned away. His voice pleaded with me to turn round again. 'I want my family back,' he said. 'I want my life back.'

I was staring into the face of a stranger. Someone I'd barely noticed in the last year. Someone I'd forsaken in my blind crusade to fix Alex. He'd been a rock in his support, but now the rock was crumbling and suddenly I was scared. I walked over, knelt down and wrapped my arms round his shoulders. 'Please . . . I'm sorry. I want my life back too.' I buried my head in his neck. 'But just a few more months. She'll have this assessment and if they still think there's nothing wrong with her, then we'll have done all we could. We'll call it a day, I promise. Please?'

Silence. Then a sigh. And then a nod.

'I love you.'

'I love you too,' he said.

The prescription was never collected.

Over the coming weeks, as another Christmas loomed ever closer, our home grew progressively quieter – the air in it thicker than molasses. Daniel was now spending a record amount of time in neighbouring houses; his own front door represented the gateway to a tense netherworld, avoided by children and adults alike as though it displayed the cross of the plague.

We tried to create some sense of festive spirit for our son, but Alex's presence, invisible or not, pervaded every Christmas breath we took. Decorating the tree, writing out Santa's wish lists and making crackers were about as pleasurable as listening to your favourite song on a crackling radio.

Every day we invited Alex to join in, and every day she showed us she couldn't. And as she climbed the stairs time and time and time again, she took with her our peace of mind and our smiles.

Three days before Christmas, Rob and I were sitting by the gas fire, quietly wrapping presents when Daniel came in.

'Can we go to Grandpa's on Christmas Day?' he asked.

Rob and I swapped looks. 'Why?'

'I just want to,' he said.

For a moment neither of us spoke. Christmas morning at home had always been the highlight of his year, better even than his birthday.

'We'll ask him,' I said gently. My smile couldn't mask my sadness.

His spirits lifted a little, and he walked back out.

'That's it,' Rob declared. 'I'm ringing Sheila.'

I sprung to my feet before he could leave the room. 'Don't! She already hates us as it is.'

'Too bad. We can't go on like this for another four months. It's not fair on Daniel. Or Alex for that matter,' he said. 'If her problems had been physical and severe enough to confine her to a bedroom on Christmas Day, she'd have been rushed to A&E by now.'

It was just what I needed to hear, but I was anxious nevertheless. Sheila wasn't going to like this.

She didn't. The phone call was a disaster. I'd stood by Rob's side, snagging at my hair in frustration as I grasped each and every one of her comments, and fanning my other hand, urging Rob to keep his rising voice down.

'I appreciate there's a waiting list but we can't wait that long . . . No, I don't think you do understand . . . Please don't patronise me . . . No we don't have a choice. Nor does Alex, she has a voice in her head.'

And so it went on. Finally, when it became apparent that Rob might lose control, I grabbed the receiver.

'Sheila, it's Melanie. It's not you we're angry with,' I said, forcing a conciliatory tone. 'But you've got to understand, and I mean *really* understand, we can't wait another four months.'

'I understand you're finding Alex's behaviour difficult to deal with, but—'

'No, Sheila. Looking after Alex is *not* the difficult bit. Getting help for her is.'

She took the blow during a pregnant pause. Then she spoke. 'Mrs Allen, I find that tone offensive. It's very difficult for me to reason with you when you're so angry. Maybe you should find someone else to help you.'

My eyes sprung open. 'Sorry?'

'I'm clearly unable to give you what you want. I suggest you find someone who can.'

There it was: her return blow. I handed the receiver back to Rob, utter desolation sending me crashing to the floor in a ball.

Rob grabbed the phone and walked it into the garden.

I lay there in pieces, unable to move. Then slowly rage began to seep into my bones. How dare she take this personally? This wasn't her hell – it was ours! We'd not been rude, we'd not been aggressive. In fact, we'd made no attack on her whatsoever. Rob returned with the phone still connected. His colour was high and his eyes livid. He cupped the mouthpiece of the phone and said, 'She's offering us respite for Alex over the Christmas period.'

I sat up. 'Where?'

'At our local hospital.'

'You've got to be kidding me,' I said.

'What do I tell her?' he said, pointing at the phone.

My mind was racing. We would never forgive ourselves for letting Alex spend Christmas in a general hospital ward – yet if we turned it down, we'd be showing Sheila we weren't that desperate.

'Tell her we'll take it.'

But the next day, when the hospital administrator rang, we'd come to our senses and we turned the offer down. Not just for Alex, but our relationship with our family was now so fragile that it would not survive a blow like that.

Instead, we phoned Dad and asked if he'd have us for Christmas. He made the day bearable.

Six days later, we received a letter from Sheila. In it, she informed us that an all-parties meeting had been set up for the middle of January. Invited were ourselves, Oak Manor School, Wendy, herself, and Social Services. I frowned. Why had Social Services been invited?

But I stopped pondering the question because attached was a copy of a letter she'd written to a Dr R Parks at Orchid House. She'd marked it as urgent.

For the next few minutes the room was quiet as we read the letter, at the end of which I shook my head despairingly.

Her referral was based entirely on meeting our request – the request of two evidently desperate and misguided parents. Nowhere did she even insinuate that she, or Wendy, felt the referral to be necessary.

'So much for urgent,' Rob said.

Later that evening, I wrote to Sheila thanking her politely for the referral and for arranging the all-parties meeting.

Sheila rang a couple of weeks later to say that she'd managed to move the initial meeting with Dr Robert Parks forward by two weeks. However, she warned us that this would not guarantee a quicker hospital assessment. We kept our fingers crossed.

It was now the fifteenth of January 2001, and Rob and I had agreed that we would remain detached and calm during the review meeting. We'd said our piece a hundred times. There would be no one in the room who wasn't dreading the moment we opened our mouths. So, unless Wendy and the school were, miraculously, to present something new to the meeting, it was an hour of our lives to endure rather than in which to participate.

Nevertheless, sitting in the waiting room of Child and Family Services, I was riddled with nerves. For the next hour, we would be sharing the same air as Wendy, Sheila and Mrs Coley, and Social Services would be watching.

Rob reached out, took my hand and gave it a squeeze. 'Remember: detached and calm.'

'Detached and calm,' I chanted several times until I was sure I'd not forget it.

Sheila and Wendy appeared in the waiting room together to escort us to the meeting. Our greetings were deceptively polite – we were getting good at this – and they led us to a large room where Mrs Coley and Alex's head teacher, Mrs Harcombe, were waiting. We exchanged similar greetings.

As we were seating ourselves, a pale, clean-cut young man arrived. He introduced himself as Greg Taylor from Social Services.

Sheila opened the meeting by announcing that she would be presiding and that Wendy would take the minutes.

'Maybe we could start with you, Mrs Coley,' she said, smiling at Alex's teacher.

Detached and Calm . . .

Mrs Coley let out a self-conscious puff of air, suggesting she was a novice at meetings such as this. With only the briefest of uncomfortable glances in our direction, she made her speech. It spoke of a sweet, well-behaved little girl with significant learning difficulties. Judging by the look Wendy and Sheila shared, they were satisfied with her report.

Detached and Calm . . .

But then Mrs Coley made the well-meaning mistake of pulling a file from her bag and saying directly to Rob and me, 'I've brought some examples of Alex's work, which I believe shows the progress she's made.'

Detached and . . . Gone! 'No thanks.'

The room froze like ice. Only Sheila could find her voice. 'I think I speak for all of us when I say I don't understand why you're so resistant to Alex's achievements. Children like Alex need encouragement, *not* rejection.'

It was like a slap in the face and there was nothing detached or calm about my retort. 'Do you think we don't know that? What sort of monsters do you think we are?' I gestured angrily at Alex's work sheets. 'This isn't progress, it's – it's a farce! Those are the drawings of a three-year-old. Her work is that of a four-year-old. You say she can almost count to ten now? She could count to ten at the age of *four!* Forget progress – she's going backwards! And you want us to get excited about it?'

Silence.

'She's right,' Rob said. 'And until someone gets to the bottom of it, all these meetings, all the hours of effort you're putting into Alex, *are not* helping her.'

People looked down, shuffled uncomfortably in their seats, glanced up, shared concerned looks then looked helplessly towards Sheila.

'Mrs Coley, is there anything else you'd like to add?' Sheila asked.

Mrs Coley gave an agitated shake of her head. She was embarrassed.

Apparently determined to soldier on, Sheila then asked for Wendy's thoughts.

Wendy's report was short, typically earnest, but offered not even a whisper of insight into Alex.

Evidently, I wasn't the only one who thought so. 'So what *have* you learnt?' Mrs Harcombe asked. My gaze bounced off the floor and landed on her face with immense gratitude.

Wendy stiffened. 'These sessions are – er – very much about the here and now. They're led by Alex, and ... er ... offer her a safe place just to ... er ... *be*.'

'I see,' Mrs Harcombe said dubiously.

'Would it be possible to have a report?' Rob asked.

Wendy wheeled round. 'Melanie told me you didn't want to know about our sessions,' she said.

'What?' I said, wide-eyed.

Wendy continued to address Rob. 'Melanie told me she didn't want to discuss the sessions.'

'Why would I ever say—?' I paused, remembered, and glared hard at her. 'Are you referring to that letter I wrote last September?'

Wendy shifted in her chair and I gave an indignant gasp.

'I said I didn't want to discuss the sessions in front of Alex. That's hardly the same thing!'

She began shuffling papers and I looked furiously at everyone else in the room for support. All eyes were on Sheila.

'There's obviously been a misunderstanding,' Sheila said.

'Don't patronise me!' I spat, all trace of civility gone now.

Sheila's smile was sad. 'I am not patronising you.'

'Actually, you are,' Mrs Harcombe said.

It was so kind. And I burst into tears.

A few seconds later, Sheila and Wendy, two well-respected women in their field, had brought the meeting to a most unexpected close. They'd walked out.

Greg was the first to speak. 'Would you like a glass of water, Mrs Allen?' he asked nervously. It was the first time he'd opened his mouth since introducing himself.

I lifted my head off my knees. 'It's fine, thanks,' I said and wiped my eyes. 'Sorry,' I apologised to everyone in the room.

Their faces were etched with concern.

'Are you all right?' Mrs Harcombe asked both Rob and me.

We nodded. 'You must think we're awful,' I said, bleakly.

'Of course not,' Mrs Harcombe said. 'You're Alex's parents – you know her better than anyone. Unfortunately, we can only comment on what we see.'

You and everyone else, I thought to myself.

When Mrs Coley and Mrs Harcombe rose to leave, our farewells were warmer than our greeting had been half an hour earlier. A vestige of harmony had been restored from the most bizarre of experiences.

'Welcome to Alex's world,' Rob said drily, and Greg looked down at his feet. 'So what happens now?'

Five minutes later, we'd learnt that we now had an official social worker and that he'd be carrying out a core assessment of all our needs.

We didn't question or argue. That Sheila had felt it necessary to bring a social worker into our lives was neither here nor there. Our family had just one need: to see Alex treated in a hospital specialising in disturbed children.

We exchanged phone numbers and addresses and agreed a date for a home visit.

Chapter Twenty-Seven

A s the day of our meeting with Dr Parks loomed, we agonised over what to say to Alex. We considered the impassioned, imploring tack: *This is your last chance for help. We need you to tell them what you've told us. It is so very important you're honest with him, etc.* That was tempting – really, really tempting.

We also considered telling her nothing, which, ironically, would probably have been the best option. However, Dr Parks would not have understood that. Turning up with Alex unprepared would have earned us a huge black mark.

In the end, we opted for a half-truth: that Sheila had been worried about how unhappy Alex was feeling (the distinction between her perception and ours we had left blank) and thought her friend, Dr Parks, was the best person to help. We didn't tell her about the hospital stay.

The big day had arrived. 'Our day in court.' Alex vs Her Parents. CAMHS vs Her Parents.

And, boy, were we going to have to pull out all the stops!

Short of giving Alex a truth drug, we could write off that part of the hearing.

Our only chance was to disprove the CAMHS judgement. Sheila was a friend of Dr Parks and she was also a colleague. We had a mountain to climb: not only had we to prove Alex's case, we had to prove our own. We had to show Dr Parks that we were level-headed, objective, equable people – the sort that didn't go off the rails. Detached and Composed was still the motto, only this time we couldn't stray from it. Dr Parks was our last chance.

We'd spent the previous week deep in our notes and our thoughts, writing our testimony. Finding proof of Alex's emotional state was not difficult. Her history and her lack of progress, beyond ARND, and her ongoing and excessive need for attention at school was part of that proof – not in itself necessarily conclusive, but when Dr Parks was presented with our own proof of Alex's RAD and of the voice, the evidence was incontrovertible.

Armed with our testimony and our motto, we were ready to go.

We were shown into the waiting room of CAMHS head office, and this time Alex made straight for the fish tank. We found some seats and sat down to wait.

'I feel sick,' I whispered to Rob, my leg pulsing up and down.

'We'll be fine.'

I glanced at the clock on the wall. Alex stared at me. I smiled. I peered into our carrier bag; our notes were still in there. I picked up a magazine, flicked absently through the first few pages, closed it again, glanced at the clock and then ordered myself to calm down. I replaced the magazine in its stand, sat back and closed my eyes.

Alex began dropping floor dust into the fish tank. Rob crossed the floor, took her hand, led her to his chair and gave her a comic to look at, which she did without a murmur.

At four o'clock exactly our name was called.

'Just remember,' Rob whispered.

'I know! I know!'

We were shown into a largish conference room. The large man who greeted us had a shock of red hair and freckles. I gauged him to be in his early fifties.

'Mr Allen and Mrs Allen. My name is Dr Parks. Nice to meet you, at last.' His handshake was vice-like, his smile wide, his voice large and confident.

'Alex?' he said. 'Nice to meet you too.' He held out his oversized mottled hand, which Alex shook with an achingly coy smile. Sheila sat quietly to one side.

Dr Parks then informed us that the meeting would be broken into three parts. Firstly, he'd like to speak to Rob and me alone, then he'd spend some time with Alex. Finally, there would be a round-up discussion in which he'd give his verdict – though 'verdict' was not the word he used.

Alex and Sheila left the room and Rob and I sat down. We watched nervously as Dr Parks pulled a chair closer, large enough to accommodate his frame, and eased himself into it. Then he stretched out his legs, crossed his feet, knitted his fingers behind his head, and reclined comfortably.

'OK, I'm all ears,' he said with a challenging grin.

'Right!' We grinned disconcertedly back and I grabbed for the file. 'Well, we've made some notes which we—'

'No notes. Just talk,' he said.

It took us a moment to scramble onto an even keel again, but we did. If he wanted talk, we'd talk.

For the next half an hour, Dr Parks remained largely silent, nodding or frowning occasionally. However, by the end of it, his air of professional attentiveness had shifted to one of intrigue.

When we left the room, we'd done all we could.

Dr Parks returned twenty minutes later with Sheila. The answer was 'no'.

'Why?' Rob asked. Such a small word.

'You're clearly very intelligent and well-meaning people. You've read all the books, done your research,' he said. 'But my belief, having met Alex, is that you're looking for stuff that isn't there. Your daughter has quite significant learning and comprehension difficulties and that's hard to accept as parents; no doubt even more difficult to manage. But as for your child "faking it", I can assure you that she isn't.' His expression softened. 'She doesn't even understand the concept.'

In my head, I choked, spluttered and coughed. My mouth, though, weakly asked him how he'd come to that conclusion.

Dr Parks told us that he'd made out to Alex that he himself didn't know what 'faking' meant and asked could Alex to explain it to him. Alex replied that she couldn't as she didn't understand what it meant either.

I stared dumbfounded. Then I spun round with a glare at Sheila. *Tell him about the Noah's Ark, damn it!* If that wasn't evidence of being able to fake something, nothing was! But her eyes were glued on her colleague.

The room hung in silence, and suddenly Rob and I were falling . . . falling . . .

'I'm aware this isn't what you wanted to hear,' he said, gently now. 'Adoption is never easy – take some time to yourselves, join a support group. Alex loves you very much.'

'Did she tell you that?'

'No, but she asked me not to take her away from you.'

Take her away from us?! There'd never, ever, been even a whisper of Alex leaving us.

Rob who'd not moved for a while then lifted his head sharply. '*That* is exactly what you'll be doing if we don't get this assessment,' he said. He let the notion register and then tried again.

'Earlier, you listened to what we had to say. We weren't lying – we gave you proof. You agreed that the numbers didn't stack up. The only thing that's changed since then is that you've met Alex and she's convinced you she's not faking it. But the numbers still don't stack up,' he said, before taking a few minutes to reiterate those numbers for him. He concluded: 'If Alex is that sweet, loving, compliant little girl with nothing more than learning difficulties, why aren't we patting ourselves on the back? Why aren't we lapping up the congratulations? If we're such intelligent, well-intentioned people, why are we choosing instead to shoot ourselves in the foot over and over again? Because, trust me, life would be a lot easier if we believed what the rest of you did.'

Dr Parks was listening again and he acknowledged this with a thoughtful nod.

'Please, at least give us the chance to prove we're right,' Rob said. We waited.

'And if this assessment proves you wrong?'

Did he say assessment?

'Then you have permission to hang us,' Rob said.

We held our breath.

'OK, but first I'd like you to visit the unit. The children she'll be living with for those six weeks are disturbed, to say the least. Their behaviour is typically extreme and antisocial. You need to be sure that Alex can cope with the trauma of it. Understood?' His tone was grave.

'Understood.'

'And one more thing. If we do go ahead, part of the assessment will involve you too. You'll need to spend some time at the hospital so that I can observe your relationship with Alex.'

'Fine,' we said, our smiles puckering a fraction – we'd deal with that later – 'and thank you.'

Dr Parks didn't smile – he looked almost bewildered – as though he couldn't quite believe he'd offered it to us.

As Dr Parks opened the door for us to leave, the door to the play-room opposite was quickly pulled shut. We found Alex alone, seated at a table surrounded by colouring pens and paper, trying hard to look like she'd been sitting there for the past ten minutes.

I felt only a tinge of uneasy disappointment when our social worker, Greg Taylor, rang to postpone our first home visit. We weren't pinning our hopes on his core assessment, but he'd let us down. Sophie told me I was being neurotic and way too sensitive.

'Maybe,' I brooded.

A week later, though, as we waved Greg goodbye at our front door, I felt more secure in his dedication to our plight. He'd stayed for two and a half hours, listened intently to our story, convinced us he'd understood the complexities of Alex and RAD, and committed himself to a full and thorough assessment of our needs.

He would call us in two weeks with an update.

Three weeks went by and we heard nothing from Greg. His core assessment update was now one week overdue. Although largely indifferent to the assessment, we were eager to hear Wendy's input. We were crossing our fingers that she had had nothing of any value to say and that our loudly proclaimed beliefs that the real Alex was a closed book would be vindicated.

I rang Greg and was told he was out of the office, so I left a message asking for him to ring back. After replacing the receiver, I found Alex in the front room watching another of her favourite high-impact, gory, alien monster cartoons on ITV.

'How do you hear what they're saying on the television?' I asked, moving automatically to the buttons below the screen. I turned the volume up to an audible level.

She didn't look up. 'Um, I don't know.'

The truth was she could hear it – her experienced ears were tuned to pick up everything – including the phone call I'd just made.

I settled into the sofa beside her and rested my hand lightly on her leg.

'Did you have a good day at school?'

'Yes.'

'Good.'

We were both in the same ball park now and this was as far as a genuine conversation could go.

After a few minutes, she closed the two-inch gap between us and laid her head against my upper arm. As always, I kept perfectly still.

Greg didn't return my call, so the day before our visit to Orchid House I tried him again. An hour later he returned my second call, apologising for not having contacted us earlier. He then informed me that the initial assessment had been completed and that the core assessment was under way.

I asked whether Wendy had submitted her report. She hadn't, but he had chased her up for it.

'If she's having problems compiling it,' I said drily, 'remind her she has the tape recordings.' And then I explained that eight months ago she had undertaken to tape her sessions with Alex. He thanked me politely for that information, wished us luck with our appointment at Orchid House, and said he'd call again soon.

The first of March, when we drove the seventy miles to Orchid House, was a bitterly cold day. The unit stood alone, tucked behind the main hospital and surrounded by a frosted lawn, which fell away to a dense border of woodland.

The unit itself was a cheerful affair – nothing like the sombre image I'd created in my mind of stark white rooms with padded walls. Nor could I hear the lamenting cries of patients; just the murmuring sounds of routine goings-on.

Dr Parks's demeanour as he showed us around was at complete odds with that of the man we'd met four weeks ago. Gone was the languid manner and easy smile. Today he looked overworked, and was stressed and uptight; our presence was no doubt an added irritation.

'I didn't realise it would be so small,' Rob said as we neared the end of the tour. The unit could only sleep eight children.

'Now you understand why the waiting list is so long,' he said.

We nodded, a little contrite, but no less resolved that Alex deserved a bed. 'Where are the children now?' I asked.

He explained they were having lessons in the classroom downstairs and it brought home the reality of the length of time Alex would be away. Not an unwelcome thought, I acknowledged rather shamefully to myself.

We'd reached the final door. Dr Parks rummaged around in his trouser pocket and pulled out a set of keys. He unlocked it to reveal a cold, musty-smelling bedsit.

'This is where you will be staying if you decide you want to go ahead with it,' he said.

I felt the shock like a punch to the forehead and for a minute I felt dizzy.

'Sorry?' I said, in a tiny voice.

Dr Parks had anticipated my reaction. 'I did warn you,' he said.

The colour had drained from Rob's face. 'That's impossible. We can't stay here. We've got Daniel to consider and jobs to go to and—'

Dr Parks absorbed Rob's panic. He reassured him that only his wife would be expected to stay, and only for two or three days a week. Any assessment of Rob could be done during hours to suit.

I was shaking my head in dull shock. 'But . . . I can't . . .' I said. I well knew I might have no choice, yet this was unthinkable. I couldn't leave Daniel for six weeks. And what about my job? It was the one aspect of my life that kept me sane and on my feet, but I'd have to resign. Suddenly, the enormity of what was being demanded hit me full in the face. 'Do you ask all your parents to stay?' I asked in a shaky voice.

'If necessary, yes.'

But this place stood empty and hadn't been lived in for weeks. 'Why us?' I asked, unable to disguise the hurt. 'I mean, Alex is being assessed for something that happened to her years ago. Long before we arrived in her life.'

There was a careful pause. 'Truthfully? The way you portray Alex, the way you speak about her, raises some uncomfortable questions about your ability to care for her properly. We need to assess this.'

My chest was suddenly too tight to breathe. I gasped. It was one thing to be considered misguided – it was quite another to be considered harmful. Now I understood why a social worker had been brought into our lives. I felt the trickling of fear.

'What are you talking about?' Rob said. 'We've never said a bad word about her.'

'You believe she's a fake – that hurts to hear.'

'No,' Rob said firmly. 'We've never said she's a fake. We're saying she fakes the way she is.'

'Same thing,' Dr Parks said.

We fell silent. Dr Parks waited, Rob and I, locked to each other by our eyes, scrambled together thoughts of what to do next. If we walked away from it now, we'd be walking away guilty as charged.

'If we decide to take this assessment, how soon would it be?' Rob asked.

He talked of bed shortages and priorities. 'Probably September time.'

'We'll ring you next week,' Rob said. I'd lost my voice.

We left the building, steadying each other.

Neither of us spoke until I'd steered the car out of the hospital gates.

'Are you OK?' Rob asked.

'I don't feel like talking,' I replied.

The truth was, I had no grasp of how I felt; just numb. We'd covered about half a mile when a car behind us sounded its horn. It startled me. I glanced at the speedometer. The dial was hovering just above the 20mph mark. I squeezed the accelerator and the car began to pick up speed. It was the spark I needed.

'If he thinks I'm going to stay in that hospital . . . Jesus Christ! We're not the problem. He is. Sheila is. Wendy is. And all the other—'

'Mel, watch out!' Rob screamed, veering the Volvo away from a row of parked cars. I brought the car under control and pulled into the curb. I reached shakily for the ignition keys and switched off the engine. 'Sorry,' I said and erupted into tears.

Rob stared despondently out of the side window. A young mother pushing her baby in a buggy gave us a cursory glance through the window. I dried my eyes.

'I am not prepared to be assessed with Alex,' I said resolutely. 'Dr Parks has made up his mind – Alex is backward. You can just imagine the scenario and the cameras rolling: Alex struggling with getting herself dressed; Alex stumbling over a question; me sitting there, arms crossed, staring at the floor; Dr Parks spluttering and indignant, rushing to her aid. I DON'T THINK SO! But what choice would I have? If I faked it with her – there, there Alex, let me help you – the whole assessment would be a farce. Alex will play me, either way.'

'So what now?'

'We tell them we're not prepared to do it!'

'You heard him, Mel. There's no assessment unless—'

'Exactly. We ring Greg tomorrow and tell him it's over. The adoption is over.'

The words which had flown unbidden from my mouth ricocheted round the car. Rob and I looked at each other for a few moments in silence, then he looked away. I couldn't trust myself to speak.

Rob broke the silence. 'Let's go home. I can't think straight right now.'

Once we'd reached the motorway, my mind began to roll. In one scene we were breaking the news to our family and friends, who struggled to hide their horror and their sadness for Alex. But maybe once they'd seen our smiles return . . . I shook off the idea. Our smiles would never return.

My imagination moved to another scene in which we were ringing Greg, asking that he collect Alex. And her suitcase. My stomach twisted painfully and the scene was cut.

In the next scene Rob, Daniel and I snuggled under a duvet, eating tortilla crisps and watching re-runs of *Star Trek*. We felt relaxed – undisturbed and unwatched. We played a game of Monopoly and then

ordered crispy fried duck like we used to. I felt a sudden ache of longing and then the image was gone, replaced by that of Alex making us
laugh with her wicked sense of humour; Alex dancing to Abba; Alex's
beautiful face, so innocent when she's asleep; and then Alex waking
herself up crying, stroking my hair . . .

We couldn't do it!

There was help for her out there somewhere. There had to be.

But then reality trickled slowly back. We'd been to the summit. It
got no better than Dr Parks and his psychiatric ward.

Chapter Twenty-Eight

'Rob!' I whispered, shaking him awake. 'Do you think they'd let us foster her, instead?'

'What?' he mumbled disorientated. It was two o'clock in the morning and the idea had just come to me.

I repeated the question as he leant across and switched on the bedside light.

'Think about it,' I said, feverish with excitement. 'By fostering Alex, we remove the pressure on both sides. Alex would be free from the expectations to attach; we're free from the expectations of trying to make her our daughter.'

Rob was now sitting upright and listening. 'Go on.'

'OK. Let me think . . . We want Alex to love us. We want her to conform, and when she doesn't we resent her. Why? Because she's our daughter, and daughters are supposed to love their parents. Asking Alex to attach to us as a daughter is like asking her to run before she can walk. If we take a step back, we've at least got some hope of teaching her to walk.'

'And what if she doesn't? She'll still be angry, and she'll still have the voice.'

'Yes, except we'll be better able to detach ourselves from it – at least until we find someone who can help us.'

'And just say that never happens.'

'Rob, she's not going to be able to hide her emotions from the rest of the world for ever, especially once we've detached ourselves.'

'What do you mean?'

'We're a threat to Alex's RAD and the voice. One doesn't want to be fixed; the other's a secret. Because she knows we talk to people about it, she's having to work extra hard to prove us wrong, to prove she's the perfect daughter. If we take that role away from her, there'll be less for her to prove. So when someone gets her angry, she'll have one less reason to hide it.'

He nodded but continued to look doubtful.

'Rob, what have we got to lose? They can only say no, and if they say yes we can always hand her back if it doesn't get any easier.' I shuffled under his arm. 'Know something else?' I continued, 'I would take her to Australia tomorrow if she were our foster child rather than our daughter.'

It was emotional blackmail, but it was also true. 'Go on,' I pleaded.

'Mel—'

'Or at least think about it.'

He switched off the light but, after an hour of tossing and turning, he switched it on again. We'd give it a try!

My last thought as I drifted into sleep was of Alex and me, side by side, bonded and in love and in front of the adoption judge for a second time.

We tried unsuccessfully for a week to contact Greg. He was out of the office each time and didn't return our phone calls.

At the start of the second week, I tried again. This time, they said he was in a meeting and I was promised a return call by the end of the day. It never came, so two days later, I tried a fifth time – and again at the end of the week. On both occasions he was unavailable and by now I was verging on distraught. I had no idea why he wasn't responding.

At the start of the third week, we wrote a letter to Greg asking that he call us, but by Thursday we'd heard nothing, so I rang again. This time I asked to speak to a duty officer and pleaded.

Greg called back half an hour later. He'd had an overload of work; he'd taken some much needed time off. He was apologetic. Only when he asked how our meeting had gone at Orchid House did I find my voice.

'We've decided not to take up the assessment,' I said and explained why. 'But there was another reason for contacting you. We'd like our adoption annulled. We'd like to foster Alex instead.' Again I explained why.

My speech took a while, and was met with silence. 'Hello?'

At last he spoke. 'Yeah, right, OK – er . . . sure, um . . . maybe I ought to come round and have a chat. Are you free tomorrow afternoon?'

He arrived promptly at four o'clock. Jude was looking after the children and I made us a cup of tea. After we'd sat down, I reiterated our thoughts. As I spoke, I felt more detached and in control than I'd ever been. We'd come to the end of the road and we had nothing to lose. Nevertheless, I still had to plead our case for fostering and if CAMHS were going to have an input, we wouldn't stand a chance.

So I did something only the deceitful and desperate might have considered – I ambushed Greg with the last three years' school reports – Alex's happiness spelt out on every page. Either Alex was faking it or she was indeed happy. Either way, Greg could choose. Then I hit him with the truthful stuff. Moving Alex yet again would strip her of her last vestige of faith in the system, and taking away her adoring extended family would be unthinkable.

I'd done enough. Greg agreed to look into it.

'Have you had a report from Wendy, yet?' I asked next.

'No, but I'm chasing it up with Sheila now.'

'Did you mention the tape recordings?'

'Apparently, they were never made,' he said, uncomfortable with delivering the news.

I gave an arid chuckle. 'Oh, why am I not surprised?'

He looked even more uncomfortable, as if he had more bad news.

'What?' I prompted.

There was a fraction of a pause. 'I think it's only fair to tell you that she believes Alex may be self-harming.'

'What?!' My head began to swim.

He nervously allowed me time to react.

'That's ludicrous! How – I mean, when could – how on earth did she deduce that?' I could barely splutter through my fury and exasperation.

'Apparently Alex was scratching her arm during their last two sessions. Although Alex said she didn't know why she was doing it,

Wendy felt the scratching symbolised some sort of inner turmoil created by her, um, home environment.'

My cheeks were inflamed and my insides were on fire. I could find only one explanation which made any sense: Wendy had urgently needed something for her report and her attempts to delve had conveniently precipitated the scratching. If, as she'd suggested, it had been a reflection of her home environment, she'd have been scratching long before now.

As soon as he'd left, I sat down at the computer and wrote a letter to Wendy, formally requesting a report for ourselves, her thoughts on Alex's self-harming and an explanation as to why she'd decided not to tape their sessions together. Ha!

A week later Wendy Bozier announced her resignation. She would leave in one month's time.

'Yippee!' I yelled, doing a dance of jubilation round our kitchen floor with the letter in my hand.

Rob looked more relieved than anything. 'Thank God for that.'

A few seconds later Rob interrupted the tail-end of my euphoria. 'Mel? She signs herself as "Senior Social Worker". I thought she was a child therapist?'

I stopped jigging instantly. 'Let's have a look . . .' I glanced at the bottom of the page and my chin dropped. Why would a social worker be assigned the role of therapist to a child with such a horrific history of abuse?

We rang Social Services. It was true, but it transpired she was also a qualified Play Therapist.

A *play* therapist . . . right!

An explosion of activity followed Greg's previous visit.

Five working days after my asking for a reversal on our adoption, he rang to say that a bed had become available at Orchid House.

After recovering from the shock, I reminded him that we didn't want the assessment.

'I've spoken to Sheila and Dr Parks and it won't be necessary for you to spend all that time on the unit,' he replied.

'How much time, then?'

'A few hours a week.'

I gave an incredulous gasp, but was quickly shaking my head again. 'We wanted this four weeks ago, *before* Dr Parks told us we were the problem. Four weeks ago, Dr Parks felt there was nothing wrong with Alex apart from her learning difficulties. What's changed his mind?' I asked. As the words tumbled from my mouth, I suddenly understood. Our adoption was about to disrupt and now everyone, it would seem, was back-pedalling to prevent it.

Greg didn't answer my question. 'Obviously, it's your decision, but personally I would suggest giving the assessment a second chance. After all, what can you lose by it?'

I grew silent. He was right. At best, Dr Parks and his team would discover Alex's emotional problems; at worst, Alex would come home six weeks later unchanged.

'If we say yes, when will it be?'

'The bed's available from Monday.'

Aaah! 'I'll call you back.'

I replaced the receiver and stood absolutely still, preparing myself. Oh my God! It was finally happening.

The next ten minutes passed by in a flurry of telephone calls. First to Rob, who was initially hesitant but then caught my infectious enthusiasm. I called Greg next and confirmed that we would go ahead. The third call was to Mrs Harcombe at Alex's school. She wished us good luck. Finally, I called to tell them at work that I'd be late in on Monday.

Then I had just five minutes to calm down before leaving to pick up the children. How was I going to explain this to Alex and how was she going to handle the news? Indeed, how would she handle the next six weeks? . . . I decided to wait until Sunday to tell her.

Between now and then, I had a mountain of preparation to do: I wanted everything clean and up to date before the assessment. Alex would be staying away Monday to Friday each week. Our routine was about to change completely.

I barely managed a wink of sleep that night – my head was too full and my heart refused to slow down. The following day, Rob took the children fishing while I worked my way through the dusting, polishing, hoovering, scrubbing and bleaching at a vigorous sprint. I was elbow-deep in cleaning the bathroom when the phone rang. Peeling off my Marigolds, I ran to the kitchen to answer it.

'Hello?' I said.

The lady introduced herself as Sarah from Orchid House. 'I've got some bad news, I'm afraid. We've had to give Alex's bed to another child. He's an emergency case. I'm sorry.'

The smile fell from my face. I breathed hard, stifling an impulse to discharge a despairing wail, then I asked her calmly when another bed might become available.

'It could be a few weeks, or it may be a few months.'

Her words after that became blurred. She said something about calling us as soon as a bed became free. I thanked her, replaced the receiver, and then I wailed. The unfairness of it all was too much.

The girls' surprise to see me at work at nine o'clock on Monday morning soon turned to outrage when they heard why. By nine-thirty, Megan had given me the number of her solicitor.

'Seems to me if you wait for Social Services to sort this fostering business out, you'll be waiting for ever.'

I spoke to the solicitor for a long time. He couldn't help personally as Family Law was not his speciality, but he suggested I rang an organisation like the Post-Adoption Centre for a list of solicitors who could. I thanked him, promised him a beer via Megan, and hung up.

I looked at the girls. 'Thanks.'

The lady at the Post-Adoption Centre had never come across a case of an annulled adoption. I waited whilst she asked her colleagues, but neither had they. It seemed an adoption certificate was more binding than a marriage certificate.

She could hear the anguish in my voice and invited me to tell our story.

'Has your daughter been assessed for an attachment disorder?' she interrupted midway through.

'No, but that's partly our fault. When we discovered this voice, we didn't pursue the RAD assessment. We felt that the voice was the dominant issue, and until she'd been treated for that attachment therapy was going to be ineffective.'

She pondered this a moment. 'It's very possible that the voice is related to her attachment disorder, but it may be that you're right. Either way, an attachment therapist will be best qualified to recognise whether or not the two are related.'

'Can you give me the name of a therapist?'

'I can, but from the sound of it, Alex's problems are quite complex. Your best bet would be to have her referred to one of the attachment centres. The treatment they offer will be more intensive.'

'An attachment centre?' I said. The words had triggered a spurt of excitement.

'Yes. Do you want me to send you details?'

'Yes please!' I said. My mind was now rolling again. 'Should we write to them or can we just ring to make an appointment?'

'It doesn't work quite like that,' she said. 'You'll need a referral from your local authority.'

My stomach sank. 'But they don't believe she's got RAD.'

'Only an attachment specialist can make that judgement.'

Her words were tonic to my ears. *Too right!*

A few minutes later I thanked her with more gratitude than my words could convey and put the phone down.

I wasn't able to contact Greg over the following few days. It was now early April and we'd received the details of Fountains Attachment Centre, less than a hundred miles from us. When I rang Fountains, they explained the procedure: Alex would be referred for an initial assessment. If the assessment revealed a Reactive Attachment Disorder, she would be admitted to the centre for treatment. She could be resident at Fountains for anything up to three months.

I rang Greg twice on Thursday. The first time he was in a meeting, the second time he was on a visit and wouldn't be in the office until Monday.

By Monday, I was ready to combust. I'd now rehearsed a hundred times the lines I'd use. I got put through to his office straight away.

'Hi, it's Melanie,' I said. 'I spoke to the Post-Adoption Centre—'

'Oh, hi Melanie,' he interrupted. 'How's Alex settled in at Orchid House?'

It took me a moment to catch up. 'They gave the bed to someone else,' I said dispassionately, 'but I've spoken to the Post-Adoption Centre and they've sent me details of an attachment centre where they treat children like Alex. We'd like to have her referred for an assessment.'

His end went quiet. 'So Alex's not at Orchid House?'

'No.'

'What happened?'

I explained.

'So you're waiting for another bed to become free?'

'No. We'd like Alex referred to this centre, instead.'

'But, Orchid House—'

'We don't want Alex assessed there. Dr Parks doesn't either; he never did. So we're asking if you could refer her to Fountains instead.'

Silence.

'Please.'

As I held my breath, I heard a muffled disturbance at the other end of the phone. 'Tell them I'll call back in a minute,' I could hear Greg instruct a colleague. Then he returned to me. 'Can you send me the details of this place?' he asked.

'I'll put them in the post today.'

He thanked me and we said goodbye.

By Friday Greg, who'd received the details, agreed to the referral.

Rob and I soared at the news.

It way now May, a month since I'd spoken to Greg.

'Shouldn't Greg have contacted us by now?' Rob asked. He was looking strained at the end of a particularly fraught weekend.

I nodded. 'I was going to leave it another week before chasing him up.'

'Why?'

That was a good question. Probably because this referral was all we had left. If it was bad news, I didn't think I could bear it.

'I'll ring him tomorrow.'

I did, and he was out on a visit. I left a message asking him to return our call. He didn't, and on Thursday I rang again. He was in a meeting. His colleague promised us a call by the end of the day. On Friday morning I left an anguished message with a duty officer.

At two-thirty in the afternoon, my stomach was in knots. When the phone rang, I sprinted to pick it up.

'Hi, Melanie. I gather you wanted to speak to me,' Greg said.

I gripped the receiver until my knuckles turned white and kept my voice even. 'Yes. We were wondering how the referral to Fountains is going.'

There was a fraction of a pause and then Greg said, 'Haven't they called you yet?'

My heart leapt. 'No.'

'I'm surprised. Give me ten minutes. I'll call you back after I've spoken to them.'

I replaced the receiver and paced the floor until it rang five minutes later.

'I've spoken to Fountains. They're sorry it's taking so long, but they're still in the process of getting information from Alex's school and from CAMHS.'

I panicked. 'Why do they need that?'

'Calm down Melanie,' he said. 'It's just a formality.'

I took a deep breath. It made sense. 'When will they contact us?'

'Once they've got everything they need.'

I frowned. This felt all wrong. 'OK,' I said.

Another month dragged by. Fountains evidently didn't believe we were an urgent case.

'Daniel! Can you hurry up and get yourself dressed. We've got to leave in five minutes.'

Daniel pulled a long face and slunk out of the kitchen. I followed him.

'What's the matter?' I asked, once inside his bedroom.

'Do I have to go to Tess's?'

'Why? Don't you want to?' I asked, concerned.

'No.' He stared hard at the floor.

'But you like going to Tess's . . . Think of all those ice-creams you're going to have,' I said, trying to whip up some enthusiasm.

'I'll go next time,' he said.

Light dawned. 'Daniel, is it because of Alex?'

He wavered before saying yes, and then the truth came out. 'She's so annoying when we're there. She's always making stupid faces at me behind Tess's back and she's always silly when we play games.'

I rolled my eyes slowly in jaded despair. Not just at Alex but at Tess too. How many more times did I need to ask her to be aware of Alex's behaviour? I firmed up. 'Get dressed,' I said, then explained that until Alex was 'better', they'd be taking it in turns to go to Tess's.

I found Alex waiting on the sofa, playing with a piece of string.

'You're not going to Tess's today,' I said gently and explained why.

'When it's your turn, think how much more fun you'll have without Daniel to think about,' I said, trying to soften the blow.

The blank stare she held was black.

An hour later, I was at the kitchen sink when I heard a single clicking sound behind me. I spun round to find Alex pointing Daniel's red metallic spud-gun at me. Apart from a quick flicker towards the floor, her eyes were locked to mine. I looked down. A two-inch nail lay on the floor inches from my feet. My heart began to pound and for a moment I was too stunned to speak. Then I bent down, picked up the nail and held out my hand for the gun. 'It works better with potatoes,' I said, my voice unsteady. She handed me the gun, turned and walked out.

On shaky legs, I found Rob by the garage washing our car. After a backward glance to make sure we were alone, I recounted the incident.

Rob paled. 'That's it Mel! I want her out of our house.'

'We can't do that.'

'We can. We've got Daniel to think about. I'd never forgive myself if—' He couldn't finish the sentence.

'I know, and we won't let it. But nor will I forgive myself if we gave up on Alex so close to getting help,' I said.

Rob balled his fists and squeezed them against his temple. Time was running out.

Tomorrow I would ring Fountains, tell them about the gun incident, and see if they could speed things up.

Tess arrived home with Daniel.

'Can I speak to Alex?' she asked coldly at the door.

'No, not now.'

Her mouth pursed. 'I have something for her.'

I held out my hand. 'I'll pass it on.'

Tess looked stupefied. Her anger was sizzling and for a moment
I thought she might refuse. She slapped the chocolate bar into my
hand. 'Please tell her I was sorry she couldn't come today.'

'I will,' I replied. Then I pulled an uncomfortable-looking Daniel
inside and closed the door.

I rang Fountains as soon as I got home from work. 'I'd like to speak
to the department that handles referrals,' I said.

'One moment please.'

As I waited to the sound of tinkling music, my hands grew ever
clammier.

'Can I help you?' It was a woman's voice.

'Yes. My name's Melanie Allen. Our daughter, Alex, is currently being referred to your centre for an assessment. I was
wondering if you could tell me what stage the referral is at.
Things at home are getting pretty desperate,' I added with an
apologetic laugh.

There was a pause. 'What did you say your daughter was called?'

'Alex. Alex Allen.'

There was another pause. 'I'm not familiar with her name. Would
you mind holding a minute?'

'Sure,' I said, my mouth suddenly dry. The wait seemed interminable.

'I'm afraid we have no referrals under that name. Are you sure it
was to this centre?'

'Yes,' I said.

I could hear her rifling through paperwork. 'Aah,' she exclaimed
suddenly, 'Yes, here's something . . . A Greg Taylor rang about a
month ago. Is that right?'

'Yes,' I said, through a wave of relief.

'Mmm . . . According to this note, he was going to call us back with contact details for your daughter's school and therapist.'

'You mean he *hasn't?*' I could barely find air.

'I'm afraid not,' she said.

I couldn't make my mouth move. My mind was spinning. 'Are you OK?' she asked me.

'Yes,' I whimpered. 'Thanks for letting me know.'

I said a hasty goodbye. I was shaking so violently it took me several attempts to replace the receiver. Then I sat helplessly on the floor. The pain I felt was unbearable and for a moment my mind seized up. Then, as I began to grasp the reality of what I'd heard, I wanted to cry, but couldn't. To cry required letting go. I was terrified of letting go.

Scooter came in and brushed himself against my thigh. My arm was a dead weight.

I could get no hold on what this meant for our future. The prospect was too frightening and too bleak. I disengaged from the fear, allowing my anger to seep in. But then that too became unmanageable. The fact that Greg had not referred Alex to Fountains was like trying to balance the final stacking block on an unstable tower. I just wanted to go to sleep.

Chapter Twenty-Nine

*F*or the next two days, I hid myself away. Rob took care of the children and our phone went unanswered.

Rob tried to speak to me and I told him I wasn't ready, but when Daniel exploded with undue frustration over an Airfix model that wouldn't come together, Rob wasn't prepared to wait any more. He burst into the bedroom where I was curled up in bed.

'Alex has got to go back,' he said, meeting my dulled eyes with steely resolve. I rolled away. 'Mel! Enough's enough.'

'We can't.'

'We can! We have no choice.'

'We can't! There's got to be more we can do.'

Rob's tone grew gentle. 'We've tried everything. You *know* we have. Alex is not going to change for us and by the time Social Services wake up, it'll be too late. We have to think of ourselves now. We have to think of Daniel,' he said. 'How much more pain are we prepared to inflict on his life? She may not be as strong as Daniel but she fired a gun. A *gun*, Mel.'

I lifted my hand to stop him before folding it round my head. Then I began to cry. Rob climbed onto the bed and enveloped my foetal-like form with his body. We lay like that for a long time – each with our own grief; each with our own thoughts of how we were going to tell Alex.

Then suddenly Rob rolled away, got off the bed and disappeared into the study. I heard the computer switch on and then some rapid typing. He came back a few minutes later and handed me a sheet of paper. I took a deep breath. This was the letter I never thought we'd have to write.

Dear Sir/Madam
Re: Alex Allen
We are writing to let you know that unless we have a confirmed
date for an Initial Assessment with Fountains Attachment Centre
by Friday 29th June we will be handing Alex back into your care
until such a time as she's been treated.

We are sorry it has come to this, but as you will appreciate, we
have exhausted all other options.
Yours faithfully
Rob and Melanie Allen.

Rob had given them one more chance. I actually broke into a smile
as I said thank you and sprang up, wrapping my arms round his
neck.

After ringing Social Services on Monday to confirm they'd
received the letter, we took a deep breath and held it.

That summer Alex received her third school report. She could
almost count to ten and knew most of the letters of her alphabet.

As the days dribbled by without so much as a phone call, so our last-
ditch hope began to recede. And when the twenty-ninth of June had
closed for the day, we knew it was over. We were ready. Mentally,
we'd said goodbye.

On the Monday, we drove to the headquarters of our Social
Services in muted mood. We were spent, but nervous nevertheless.
We wanted the moment over. Alex was all but gone, and we wanted
our lives back.

We arrived at the reception desk without an appointment.

'Please could you tell us the name of Greg Taylor's supervisor,'
Rob said.

'Can I have your names please?'

'Mr and Mrs Allen.'

She picked up the internal phone and made a quick call. His name
was Raymond Landers.

'We'd like to speak with him please.'

'I'm afraid he's in a meeting.'

'We'll wait.'

Two very long hours later, Mr Landers arrived in reception. He wore a nervous smile and bore a small file. We followed him through the security doors and into a conference room.

He began by expressing his sympathy for our difficult situation and asked if we'd received his letter.

'No,' we replied, indifferent.

He frowned, dug into his folder and pulled out the letter. He handed it to us across the table. It was dated 29th June – deadline day.

'It should arrive tomorrow then,' Rob quipped drily.

We read it. No mention of Fountains, just a request for us to ring and arrange a meeting with Greg to try to resolve matters.

'Do we gather from this that there is no date for an assessment at the attachment centre?'

'It's not that simple. Alex will need a referral before she can be assessed.'

'Actually, she got that referral two and a half months ago, but that's not important any more. What we want to know now is how you intend to move Alex back into care. We need to prepare her.'

Mr Landers looked utterly taken aback and unprepared. He'd evidently not been told of the referral nor had he taken our threat seriously.

It took him a while to respond. 'It's not as simple as that,' he said again.

'Believe me, it is,' Rob said calmly. 'We gave you the choice. Either get Alex in for an assessment or take her back into care until she's well enough to come home.'

When Mr Landers could find no response, Rob continued, 'Tell me, did you even speak to the centre?'

Nothing.

'We want Alex out by the end of the week,' Rob said. 'We'll be expecting a call, telling us where we need to take her.'

We returned home on autopilot. It was in that same trance-like state that I curled myself up in Alex's bed, with her Dotty Dalmatian pulled tight to my chest; the Dotty that still lay there day after day only because Alex was not empowered with the honesty to rip out its eyes and stamp on it until all the stuffing had been expelled from its body.

Someone smiled at me as I stood outside Alex's classroom door later that day, but I felt utterly remote from the airy atmosphere of the playground. Then Alex emerged and I waved a disjointed arm at her.

I asked her if she'd had a good day. She said yes. I said I was pleased.

I wanted tears in my eyes. I wanted to feel heartbroken. All I felt was a little bit sick.

Alex did her vintage walk back to the car, slithered in backwards, whispered to herself all the way to Daniel's school and was popping with suppressed giggles by the time we got home.

I was ready to have my peace back.

Alex could sense something different in the air. Today I wasn't ignoring her mind games, I simply wasn't reacting. I was cocooned within myself, waiting for Rob and for the treacherous moment we'd be breaking the news to Alex that she was moving on – yet again; that we'd lied about being her 'for ever' Mum and Dad.

By five o'clock, when Rob returned from work, Alex was sitting propped against her bedroom wall with her knees up and her eyes straight ahead. I think she knew.

'Alex, love, we've got something to tell you.'

The eyes she turned on us were dead.

'You're going to be staying somewhere else for a while, just until we've found someone to help you,' I said, looking deep into her fathomless eyes. 'I'm sorry.'

The one small word landed with a thud in my heart. I still had one, and the tears that finally came weren't for me. They were for the girl who'd never been loved – not by me, not by anyone. I was grateful for those tears, I wanted her to know she could make me cry.

'This isn't something we want, but we can't go on like this. Not you, nor us.' Then I talked about fighting to get her well again, and that we'd never give up. I talked about the family she'd always have, about waiting for her to come home again, 'when you can make me laugh again with your funny faces and your dancing'. It was all I could say, the tears were too thick.

Rob took over. 'I know it's going to be scary,' he said, hoarsely, 'but you'll see – it'll be OK. Hopefully, you won't be far away, and any time you want to see us or even just speak to us, give us a ring. We'll come and see you, OK?'

I was glued to Alex's face. She nodded, barely displaying a hint of emotion. I wanted so badly for her to cry, yet at the same time I hoped she wouldn't.

'This isn't your fault, Alex,' I said. 'It never will be. Not ever. Do you understand?'

There was a ripple of expression across the blank canvas of her face and I lunged forward and took her in my arms. 'You don't deserve any of this, and I'm sorry.' For a while, Rob and I rocked Alex's stiff body back and forth. When I finally pulled away, Alex was wiping a tear self-consciously from her face. 'Cry, Alex, if you want to,' I said.

She at last looked as though she might let go, but then the moment was gone. She was moving on, dragging her broken heart on a thread behind her.

Later, Rob, a cauldron of emotion, sought Alex out in her bedroom.

'Alex, do you *want* to go?'

Alex looked up, flat, as though defeated. 'I want to stay,' she said. 'But the Voice wants me to go.'

Had Rob been a violent man, he'd have punched a hole in the garage door, before folding into himself and weeping.

At eight o'clock, I peered silently into Alex's darkened room. She was asleep, her face unlined and still. I sighed, wondering if I'd ever understand what kept her going.

Then I crept downstairs to where Rob and Daniel were watching TV.

'Can we switch this off for a minute?' I asked. Daniel nodded, a trace of disquiet crossing his face. The atmosphere in the house had been strange and subdued.

I knelt down in front of him with a direct look.

'Daniel, Alex is not going to be living with us for a while.'

He looked startled. 'Why?'

'Because Dad and I feel it's for the best. She's not happy here,' I said gently. 'She needs help — not the sort we can give her, but proper help from people who can fix her and make her happy again. But until then, it's not fair on any of us to carry on like we are.'

'Does this mean we can go to Australia again?'

I squeezed his knees. 'It'll be the first thing we do.'

'Where will Alex go?'

'Probably to a foster home like Pat and Ken's. Remember?'

He nodded. 'Will we visit her?'

'Of course.'

An empty silence followed. He had no more questions and nothing more he wanted to say.

The following morning, Rob and I rang to say we wouldn't be going into work for the rest of the week. Admitting to Megan that we were handing Alex back was more painful than even I'd prepared for. It brought home the foreboding of the similar admissions we were going to have to make to everyone else in the coming weeks.

Social Services didn't ring, so at five minutes to five, Rob rang Mr Landers. I was pacing the floor beside him.

'No — I don't think you were listening yesterday,' Rob said. 'We do *not* want another all-parties meeting ... No, I don't care what CAMHS think ... No, they do *not* know what's best for Alex ... No, it's too late, I'm afraid. We want Alex accommodated elsewhere until she's well enough to come back ... I don't know, there must be a foster home that can take her ... Well, I'm sorry it's short notice, but you had plenty of warning ...' Suddenly Rob's face turned deep scarlet. 'Kindly take that back,' he said in barely suppressed fury. 'No! — if anyone *abandoned* Alex, it was you lot, months ago. We fought tooth and nail for that girl ... Right. Apology accepted. Now what are you going to do about Alex? She knows she's going and prolonging it is not fair ... Right, tomorrow morning. Speak to you then. Goodbye.'

Rob slammed the phone down. 'Bastard!'

By twelve o'clock the following day we'd heard nothing, so we rang again. This time it appeared Mr Landers was unavailable. We were put through to his assistant, who sounded confused.

'I spoke to Mr Landers an hour ago,' she said. 'As far as I'm aware the plans to accommodate Alex have been postponed. The all-parties meeting has been brought forward to next week.'

Rob had to fight to keep his voice calm. 'Could you tell your Mr Landers that, unless we hear to the contrary, we will be delivering Alex personally to your offices on Friday morning.'

Mr Landers rang back an hour later. They'd found a foster home that could accommodate Alex. They were expecting her at five o'clock this afternoon.

We thanked him and put down the phone. Rob didn't utter a word, but slid open the patio doors and walked into the garden. I didn't follow. There was nothing either of us could say to make this moment any easier. Besides, I had some packing to do.

A dull mist had settled over my emotions by the time I'd zipped up her blue suitcase. Rob wanted to collect Alex from school with me. I said no, I wanted her last day to be as simple and unceremonious as possible, not seem unusual. So I was standing alone in the playground for the last time, still a nameless face to most, when Mrs Coley delivered Alex to me.

'I'm sorry it didn't work out,' she said, sympathy and sadness etched on her face.

I led her upstairs and asked her to gather together all the things she wanted to bring with her. A few minutes later she held out a handful of photos and cards.

'Is that all?' I asked wide-eyed.

'Yes,' she declared, as breezily as if she were leaving for a day's outing to the coast.

Rob was putting her suitcase in the back of our car when Alex and Daniel said their goodbyes. Alex looked nonplussed, Daniel looked at the floor. Then they exchanged an awkward embrace.

'I'll wait in the car,' I said, as Rob came in to say his own goodbye.

When they emerged a few minutes later, Rob's face was pained: Alex's was unreadable.

Alex climbed in the back and with a final wave we turned out of Mallard Close.

My stomach was in knots when we pulled up outside the home of Janet Brindle, the foster carer. I switched off the engine and looked into my rear-view mirror. Alex was staring at the imposing three-storey town house, her face as pale as a ghost.

'Right!' I exclaimed, performing a brave smile for both of us. 'Are we ready?'

We climbed out of the car, opened the tiny wrought-iron gate and pulled on the enormous doorbell.

When it was over, I scrambled back into the car with just one tangible thought – drive! But fifty metres later, I was crying so hard I couldn't see the road ahead of me. I pulled in to the side and switched off the engine. Then I buried my head in my arms and cried until I thought I might break.

Memories of the handover were vague. I remembered Alex disappearing into the garden with two of the other foster children; I remembered tissues being handed to me by the sympathetic carer; I remembered someone introducing me to a social worker who made me sign a form, and I remembered Janet beaming reassuringly as she said that Alex would be 'fine'.

'Look,' she'd said, pointing through the kitchen window to where Alex was tearing around with the other children, 'she's settled in already.'

The peace that descended over our house that evening was the saddest I'd ever known.

Chapter Thirty

*T*he following day, we rang and told all those who needed to know that Alex had left. We'd formulated a short spiel, which we delivered like automatons to each of them, and promised we'd ring again when 'things had settled down'.

Then we went to ground. We closed the curtains, shut the door to all but Daniel's comings and goings, and switched on the answer machine. Rob made it clear he was through with talking about the situation and retreated to his garage. I sat on the sofa and stared at an oil-mark on the wall.

One day Rob found me sobbing until I couldn't breathe and suggested we get away for a while. I didn't care one way or the other but he said it would be good for Daniel, so we booked a last-minute summer holiday to France. Rather symbolically, we were allocated a caravan stuck out on its own on the very outskirts of the camp site, but this had its advantages – in the main, shielding us from the throngs of perfect families having the time of their lives. I had never felt more detached and desolate in my life. I recall little of what we did for the week, but Daniel and Rob made the most of it – enjoying each other's company unspoiled for the first time in years.

Alone in my caravan bunk, an unopened book beside me, I wondered how Alex was doing; how she was coping with rejection for a second time. My heart twisted and I groaned with the ache of it.

At the end of the week, I heaved my lifeless spirit out of the caravan bunk and home to Mallard Close, where I crawled back into bed with my crushing thoughts of Alex and her suffering.

'She's doing amazingly well,' Greg announced two weeks later at an all-parties meeting. I felt a crash of conflicting emotions inside me. 'She loves her new room,' he continued somewhat proudly, 'she's getting on well with the other children and she can't wait to start her new school.'

Sheila grinned. 'You must be so relieved,' she said.

I managed a nod. But Rob wasn't feeling as charitable. '*If* you'd read the files, you'd know that Alex settled equally well with us. And you'd also know that any normal child couldn't settle that quickly, however unpleasant their previous home might have been,' he said.

Flickers of weary impatience crossed their faces, and as the minutes passed I could feel a swift homecoming for Alex slip further from us.

This meeting had originally been fixed with the purpose of finding a satisfactory route to getting Alex home to us as quickly as possible. Or, in other words, to agree an urgent psychological assessment of Alex and the treatment she needed.

With only a quarter of an hour to go, however, the discussion was not unfolding as planned and I could feel a sense of panic lathering up inside me. Sheila had already emphatically declared Fountains attachment centre as unsuitable, firstly, because it had 'limited psychiatric oversight' – a suitably vague argument that Rob and I had disagreed with but which had secured Greg and Mr Landers' support; and secondly, because the other children admitted there were 'far more disturbed than Alex', a point we hadn't even attempted to argue.

Nor had she been willing to commit to an alternative assessment.

Suddenly Rob sat bolt upright. 'It's the money, isn't?' he asked.

Mr Landers flushed and the other two shifted uncomfortably in their seats. The ensuing silence gave Rob his answer.

'How much will an alternative assessment cost?' Rob asked. 'Five thousand pounds? Ten thousand pounds? Twenty even?'

'Something like that,' Mr Landers squeezed through his teeth.

'Surely that's a fraction of the cost of keeping Alex in care for the next ten years?'

It was the truth and the room fell quiet. The looks they now exchanged were more sober and reflective and I sensed a shift in the proceedings. My tension eased as they agreed to an assessment.

As we left the room, Rob squeezed my hand. I liked how it made me feel – we'd not done enough hand-holding recently.

'Daniel! Slow down! You'll—' Too late. My hands flew to my face, Daniel shrieked. Grimacing, I opened one eye to see my son partially folded, head first, inside the linen basket, the wheels of his roller skates still spinning on his flailing feet.

Something tight inside me snapped, propelling a laugh from deep within a place that had lain dormant for so long.

'Mum!' Daniel cried indignantly through a mouthful of laundry.

'Sorry,' I spluttered, and laughed even harder, each convulsion growing more manic with the outpouring of relief as the mass of dark sludgy emotions I'd carried for so long began to dissolve.

Daniel, unable to extricate himself from the basket, was not amused. Which made me laugh even harder. With tears pouring down my face, I clasped my son's waist and gave his body a yank. However, his shoulders were firmly wedged inside and the action only served to send me toppling backwards onto the floor, bringing Daniel and the basket on top of me. His indignation was no match for the hilarity of the situation, and he began to laugh too. For the next few minutes the house resounded with the welcome noise of happiness.

And as the laughter finally wound itself down, I knew we'd turned a corner. It was time to start moving on.

I decided to launch the new start with a spring-clean of the house, beginning with Alex's room. It had remained untouched and closed off since the day she'd left almost three months ago.

Two hours and a few tears later, her room had been aired, dusted and vacuumed, her books stacked with perfect sloping precision, and the remains of her belongings bagged, boxed or folded neatly behind cupboard doors. Dotty the Dalmatian was carefully placed between the crease of her freshly laundered pillow and duvet. The room was now ready for her return after the assessment – or that's what I told myself.

The following day, with the house glossy and twinkling from the vigorous clean-up, I decided to tackle the mountain of accumulated filing. I began by sorting the papers into relevant piles, at the end of which exercise Alex's pile was the deepest – a year's worth of letters from Social Services and CAMHS, school reports, internet research print-outs, etc. After working through everything else, I took the 'Alex' bundle into the study where we kept all her other paperwork. As I was lifting one of the box files off the top shelf, a dusty sheaf of papers landed on the floor beside me. I picked them up and, on quick inspection, saw that they appeared to be duplicate copies of various reports we'd already had, dating from before Alex came to us. I frowned. I couldn't remember making the copies, so where had they come from? Then it came to me. The copies had been given to us by Mary, our social worker, who'd been unaware that we'd already received the originals from Alex's social worker. I'd shoved these copies on the top shelf and forgotten about them.

I was about to throw the bundle in the bin but noticed they were in much better condition than the torn, tatty, coffee-stained originals. I located these in another box file and, before making the switch, decided to check that the copies were exact duplicates and I wasn't about to throw away anything I should keep. Halfway through the bundles, I noticed an extra document in the pile of copies that Mary had given us. It was made up of several sheets of notes handwritten by Carol Franklyn, the Family Support Worker who had been assigned to Michelle and Alex at the time.

I felt a fluttering in my stomach: I was filled with a strong premonition that this document would offer a much greater insight into Alex's years with Michelle than anything we'd had before and I cursed myself for not having noticed it until now. I began to read.

For the next fifteen minutes the silence of the room was punctuated with small gasps of shock and sighs of lamentation as I absorbed the shocking and appalling day-to-day reality of Alex's existence in that house. What a truly terrible start in life she had been given. And, indeed, how terrible the wretchedness of life for Michelle who, reading between the lines, was a warm and well-meaning young woman who'd never stood a chance at motherhood.

Then a statement jumped out at me and brought my reading to a grinding halt.

My eyes widened and my heart did a double-beat as I read the sentence again: Michelle told me she knew the moment Alex was conceived because from that point onwards she was unable to touch any alcohol, as she suffered terrible sickness throughout her pregnancy.

I read on feverishly, but that was it. By the time I'd read to the end, I'd seen no more mention of Michelle's lack of alcohol intake during pregnancy.

I tried to grasp what I'd just read. Could this be true? Suddenly I was on my knees, pulling out files and reports from every box. An hour later, I'd found no other mention of Michelle's abstention from alcohol. But neither had I read anywhere that she *did* drink during her pregnancy.

So I dug out Alex's file of medical reports and found the relevant paediatric report. The paediatrician stated that, given Michelle's alcoholism, it was highly likely that the learning difficulties Alex presented with were the result of foetal alcohol exposure. And suddenly, it all made sense. He'd *made the assumption* that Michelle drank during pregnancy, based on information passed down to him like Chinese Whispers – information which the system had had neither the time nor the funding to verify one way or the other.

I knew it! I just *knew* it!

Before leaving the study, I took a copy of the family support worker's report, highlighted the relevant sentence, and put it in an envelope to Greg together with a short letter asking him to notify everyone who needed to know that Alex could not have Alcohol Related Neurodevelopmental Disorder.

'Do we have to go?' Daniel pleaded with me a month later.

'Yes. We do. And it will be fine,' I replied, with an air of reassurance that didn't match the nerves pulling and twisting at my guts. In a couple of hours, we would be visiting Alex for the first time and all three of us were filled with apprehension at the idea of it. And no one, I suspected, was more anxious than Daniel. Being a child, he'd adapted quickly and happily to life without Alex. Now, suddenly, his old life was about to come crashing into his new one.

We drove in silence during a journey not dissimilar to the one we'd made almost four years ago – except we'd been different people then, happy and excited. Today I just felt sick and sad.

Alex was waiting by the front door of her new home with a crooked smile on her face.

'Hello,' she said sweetly, but equally managing a wounded look upwards at Janet, who was standing protectively behind her, hands on her shoulders.

I wanted to flee. 'Hello, love,' I said instead. 'Wow! I like your funky top!'

We all tittered uncomfortably and stepped inside.

Janet was a legend in the world of fostering for her success with so many damaged children, and she couldn't have been nicer. Not just with Alex but with us too. Within minutes she had us relaxed and laughing with a tale of a particularly wayward foster child, a can of blue spray paint and a neighbour's immaculate rose garden.

'I'd have ten of your Alexes any day!' She concluded the story, bathing our daughter with an affectionate look.

My smile wilted. That comment dashed any hope we'd harboured that she might already have begun to have concerns about Alex. I was tempted to caution Janet – warn her not to get too excited – but Rob and I had agreed that we wouldn't voice our concerns to her. When the day came that Janet was knocking on CAMHS' doors, it was vital there should be no suggestion we might have influenced her.

So when, later that day and out of Alex's earshot, Janet talked with poignant regret of having to withdraw Alex from swimming classes as she was terrified of water, Rob and I said nothing. That Alex loved water and had a certificate for swimming was something Janet would have to discover for herself.

An hour into the visit, it was clear we posed no immediate threat to Alex's well-being and we were given the implicit go-ahead to take her out for an ice-cream.

Alex's demeanour, having so far presented as shy and a little nervous with us, changed as soon as we got into the car and out of Janet's sight. Before we'd turned the corner, she'd whipped Daniel into a hilarious frenzy, the two of them tickling each other and squealing with laughter.

Rob and I exchanged a wry but grateful smile. The tension had dissolved.

Once inside the cafe, I made a half-hearted attempt to calm them down but it dawned on me that I didn't care any more. Even when Alex started to blow bubbles into her Coca-Cola and Daniel responded with an even louder raspberry from his armpits, I didn't care. Our bizarre set-up was way too fragile to worry about the other patrons.

Over the next half an hour, Rob and I made several attempts to ascertain how things were going for Alex in her new home and at her new school, but she was as adept as ever at deflecting our questions and we knew not to probe. We left the café in high spirits and spent the remainder of our allotted time chasing each other around a nearby park. It was a bitter-sweet interlude.

When it came to saying goodbye, I thought I detected a momentary look of wistfulness in Alex's eyes but it disappeared as quickly as her sugary sweet voice (now back in force) could say 'Thank you for a nice time.'

Casting aside my cynicism, I embraced her and whispered into her ear, 'Thank *you* for a nice time. Look after yourself. We'll see you again soon.'

She flinched and I immediately let go.

We didn't know it then, but this visit had set the tone for all our future visits: entirely led by Alex, chaotic, fluffy . . . but in the main comfortable.

By December, almost six months after Alex had left, we wrote to Mr Landers asking why there had still been no new assessment – particularly in light of Alex's ARND misdiagnosis. Two weeks later we received our reply: the local authority did not share the nature of our concerns for Alex. She was happy and settled in her new home and plans were for her to remain with Janet. However, he explained, the local authority took very seriously their responsibility for meeting Alex's needs and plans had been made for a psychological assessment to be undertaken without delay. Lastly, he hoped we would support the professionals in everything they did for Alex.

In spite of his words, I reacted with little more than indifference. Mr Landers and Social Services were still grasping at the wrong end of the stick, and any long-term plans they might have had for

Alex were about as stable as Alex herself. There remained every chance she would come home to us: that this wasn't imminent was not unwelcome news. In truth, we had some healing of our own to do before then.

Alex was now officially a 'Looked-After Child' and, as such, she had quarterly review meetings attended by everyone involved with her care and education. These meetings offered the opportunity to share information and to discuss any issues or concerns. As Alex's legal parents, we were invited to attend these meetings. We could have declined the invitation, but as we would be visiting Alex every twelve weeks, it was vital we were kept abreast of her new life.

Just before Christmas, Greg informed us that he would be handing over his role to a new social worker, Tracey Bryant, and that our first opportunity to meet Tracey would be at the next review meeting. After weeks without any progress, this news of fresh blood gave me renewed hope.

With only ten minutes remaining of the review meeting, which had so far offered little more than the usual gushing praise for Alex, Tracey Bryant had not yet made her appearance. Greg cast another glance at his watch. I suppressed a sigh.

'I suggest we reschedule—'

But he broke off at the sound of heels hurrying along the corridor towards us. The door burst open with welcome relief. 'I'm so sorry I'm late,' Tracey said. 'The traffic was a nightmare!' The tiny, bird-like lady then took a few moments to catch her breath, sit down, stretch a perfect smile onto her face and introduce herself.

Despite her stature, she appeared the antithesis of Greg. She took to the floor with an air of supreme confidence and conviction.

She was, Tracey said, familiar with Alex's history. She would be helping Alex to adjust to her new life and, most importantly, she said: 'I'll be helping Alex make sense of the many traumas she's experienced in her short life.' She said this with her eyes squarely averted from ours and I flinched. It was a pointed reference to our abandonment of Alex, and a sense of foreboding and uneasy disappointment descended on me.

This foreboding grew when it became evident that Tracey was

newly qualified and had no experience of working with adopted children.

We'd arrived at the meeting with open minds, determined to get off on the right foot with this lady. However, when she announced she'd done some research on ARND to help her understand Alex, Rob finally spoke.

'But she doesn't have the condition,' he said, keeping his tone even.

Tracey frowned, said nothing, but began hastily thumbing through her files. In the meantime, I sought Greg out with my eyes. I'd assumed he would have informed Alex's new social worker of the misdiagnosis. I pulled out our copy of the family support worker's report and showed her the relevant comment.

'Has this been verified?' Tracey asked, the question seemingly directed at everyone but ourselves.

There followed a moment of bemused shaking of heads.

'No,' I said on their behalf, 'but nor is there any proof that she did drink during her pregnancy.'

Tracey barely met my steely gaze.

'I'll look into it,' she mumbled stiffly, her smile gone.

This was not a good start.

Keen to introduce ourselves to Tracey less formally and, if possible, to show her we weren't the appalling parents she clearly thought we were, we stayed behind after the meeting. But it wasn't to be.

'I'm sorry, Mr and Mrs Allen, but I'm in a hurry,' she said, gathering up her papers without a trace of regret. 'I have a family in crisis I have to go to now, but I'll ring to arrange a convenient time to visit you in the next few weeks.' Then she stretched an unnecessary smile onto her face, turned on her heel and left.

We didn't know it then, but we'd just met the person who was about to put a bomb under our lives.

Chapter Thirty-One

Rob and I were very different people when it came to dealing with adversity and our emotions. I'd been born into an emotionally expressive family, as volatile as we were loving. In my house, arguments had been as commonplace as exuberance or laughter, and we'd certainly never had the restraint to let any tension simmer unvoiced. Rob, on the other hand, had been born into a smaller and prouder family, who were uncomfortable with emotional outpourings, positive or negative. Fortunately, they were also a kind, secure and close-knit family whose lives, until now, had been relatively uncomplicated.

In short, Rob wanted to put a lid on difficulties; I wanted to be able to slam a kitchen door or scream into a pillow.

While our lives had been relatively stress-free, this difference between us had been positive – indeed, it was one of the things that first attracted us to each other. Rob had a lovely, calm, clear way of seeing things which I envied. And for him, my energy, and my ability to talk about anything and everything was refreshing and brought him out of his shell. However, faced with our deepening problems, this discrepancy in our temperaments began to breed tension between us and gave an uneasy edge to Christmas that year.

The first hint that Janet was starting to struggle with Alex arrived on our doormat at the end of January. It was a copy of her quarterly report on our daughter. As a PS to an otherwise positive report she had written, 'I just want to add that, although Alex is a lovely girl, she functions way, way below her chronological age in all areas of her development – emotionally, socially and academically.'

Since Janet still understood Alex to have ARND, wasn't she just stating the obvious?

No. And we understood, only too well, why she'd felt compelled to note the developmental problem.

'Ahh, let me just sit down,' Rob said with a little twinkle in his eyes. It was now February of 2002, and we were tucked away in a corner of a restaurant during our second visit to Alex.

Alex and Daniel were mischievously gleeful, their anticipation of Rob's looming fall to the floor at fever pitch. He duly enacted the process of seating himself on a stool and falling instead in an exaggerated heap on the floor. 'Aaagh!'

The two children roared with laughter. Their surreptitious removal of his stool had, of course, worked.

'Can you do that to mine?' Alex pleaded, her voice high with excitement.

'And mine!' Daniel added.

Rob and I complied, and for the next five minutes the two of them amused themselves with the falling-down game amidst much hilarity and laughter.

I sat back contentedly, relieved that once again our visits with Alex were proving to be so easy and upbeat.

At the end of February Social Services rang to cancel the home visit Tracey had scheduled at the first review meeting – she was off sick. A month later, Tracey would cancel a second time. In fact, neither she, nor anyone else from Social Services, would ever make that visit.

Fifty miles away, the tide was beginning to turn.

'Alex! Put that down!'

The order seemed to scream at her from nowhere, freezing her to the core.

'Now!'

Alex dropped the rock and sprinted red-faced to her bedroom, leaving Janet to check the dog was still breathing.*

'Mel, I'm going home for a few weeks.'

---

* This, and subsequently narrated incidents and events that occurred with Janet and Alex, are based on information supplied by Janet Brindle.

'Home?' I asked, turning around and looking at Rob in confusion. The expression on his face, at once sombre and nervous, turned my world inside out.

'To Australia.'

Very slowly, I put down the whisk, fumbled for a chair and sat down. Why? The question remained unsaid because, as an ice-cold chill ran through me, I knew the answer.

Somewhere along the line our relationship had changed and cracked under the constant strain of Alex. There had been no arguments, just more and more time apart and little more than polite talk to fill the gaps when we should have been talking about our pain.

'When will you be back?' I managed to squeeze out the words. *Oh, God. Please say you're coming back.*

'I'm not sure yet – work has given me a three-month sabbatical.'

'Three months!' I dropped my head into the crook of my arm and everything went dark. How had we let it get to this? When we looked at each other, we both had tears in our eyes. 'We'll work this out,' I said.

'I know.'

'What do we tell Daniel?'

'That I've taken some time off work to see my family.'

He was right. The thought of telling Daniel we needed time apart was too awful to contemplate. He'd endured enough upset and upheaval as it was.

Rob's announcement had an unexpected effect on our relationship. Sure, it had taken a battering, but during the week leading to his departure, our conversation was lighter and altogether more connected than it had been in months. We even found ourselves making each other laugh again.

Love is indeed a strange thing.

As the next review meeting in April got under way, I found myself unexpectedly open-mouthed. The school began their contribution by reporting some unusual and disturbing behaviour that even I hadn't seen coming as soon as this. Not only was the behaviour unsettling for the other children, her teacher explained, but Alex had been observed deliberately provoking children she'd previously accused of bullying her.

At this news, I almost leapt in the air and shouted 'Told you! Told you!' Instead, I confined myself to asking whether Alex could now be referred for a psychiatric assessment.

But any hope I had of this was premature. Although the professionals agreed that Alex was acting strangely, they felt her behaviour was almost entirely symptomatic of her learning difficulties.

Somehow I kept my composure as, once again, I took a back seat in the proceedings while the rest shared their thoughts on my daughter.

It appeared Alex was giving each of them conflicting information. To one, her favourite subject was science, to another it was art and to yet another it was reading; she told one that she loved PE, but to another she said she didn't because she found it too hard; to one she talked with sad fondness of the different family members whom she missed, while to another she claimed not to remember them. Janet reported that Alex never mentioned them.

I watched with a small, albeit joyless, sense of glee as these disparate accounts hung awkwardly in the room. However, Tracey was quick to excuse these inconsistencies as symptomatic of Alex's frequent and traumatic life changes and, of course, her muddled thoughts.

I suppressed another sigh.

At the end of the meeting, I confronted Tracey about Alex's ARND misdiagnosis. It was evident Janet, and Alex's school teachers, were still under the impression that Alex had the condition. Tracey, without lifting her eyes from her paperwork, informed me that Alex had been referred to a specialist hospital for tests to try and ascertain the cause of her developmental delay.

Finally.

The following week, despite the recent revelations from Janet and Alex's school, CAMHS decided that Alex did not warrant a clinical psychological assessment. They considered her now settled, and functioning well within her capabilities.

*

'Have you met my new helper?' Alex asked me during another visit. There was a glint in her eye that suggested this was a significant question.

'No. Who's that?' I asked, twinkling back at her. With Rob away and Daniel on a school trip I was visiting Alex alone. It was turning out to be an unusually intimate meeting, with the two of us sparking off each other with affectionate teasing.

'Um . . . um . . . Tracey.'

Alarm bells. 'Yes. I have. Why?'

'Mmm . . . er . . .'

'Go on. Why?' I asked, intrigued.

'Um . . . she's angry with you.'

The sparkle in my eyes dimmed a fraction. 'Why's that?'

'Um, I don't know.'

I didn't believe her ignorance for a moment and it took me a while to banish the little knot of anxiety in my stomach.

'Careful love,' I said grabbing the back of Daniel's coat before he could topple over the railings in his eagerness to see his dad emerge through the double doors. We were in the arrivals hall at Heathrow and I was wishing I could share his enthusiasm. My stomach was churning and my thoughts were in turmoil. Did Rob and I still have a marriage? Had the break reinforced what a mess his life was here, in England, or had he missed us enough to convince him the mess was worth it? I had no idea. Although we'd spoken on the phone many times in the past few weeks, the conversations had been kept deliberately brief and light.

Just before I thought I might dissolve in my own nerves, Rob walked through the doors. My heart quickened. I managed to lift my arm in a wave, managed a smile. But with every step Rob took towards us, I was desperately trying to read his face for answers. He looked tanned and healthy; he looked relaxed; he was smiling . . .

And then I was in his arms, Daniel somewhere between us, the rest of the world forgotten. We stood like that until our arms ached from the embrace. When we pulled apart our eyes were wet with relief.

'Dad,' Daniel broke through our grins, tugging on Rob's arm, 'can I push the trolley? I've got a surprise for you when you get home. I made it in DT.'

As we battled our way through the throngs of people, my hand firmly inside Rob's, I offered a silent prayer of thanks.

But then the bomb went off.

'Rob!' I screamed.

He found me by the front door, the blood drained from my face, grasping the banister with one hand and holding a letter in the other.

'What?'

I was shaking so hard he had to fumble to get a hold on the paper. The house went silent.

A minute later, Rob and I looked at each other, mute with shock and bewilderment. In the letter, Tracey had accused us of having significantly harmed Alex. Consequently, the local authority would be initiating proceedings in order that Alex never be allowed to return to our care. Furthermore, to protect Alex from any further harm, all our future visits with her were to be supervised by a social worker. She concluded her letter with an invitation to a meeting to discuss the matter further, and suggested we seek legal advice.

'Mel, this isn't funny any more,' Rob said.

And deep inside me, a fear like no other began to seep into my bones. For the first time in my life, I felt the handle on my life slipping right out of my grasp, taking with it the confidence and faith I'd so taken for granted until now.

Two days later Tracey called to arrange the meeting for the following week. There was not a trace of sensitivity in her voice – her tone was bright, airy and far too sweet. I found myself wondering whether she was enjoying this.

Over the next eighteen months, I would come to learn how easily and quickly a mind can go mad. In my case, the process started around this point, with conversations in my head – conversations that arose from a searing sense of injustice, which real life was not redressing. Inside my mind, I would spend endless waking hours reasoning with

Tracey and her colleagues, giving elaborate speeches vindicating us from the monstrous allegations of abuse and pleading with them to do the right thing.

And as the injustices continued to mount, so these conversations would become more desperate and feverish and angry until my head would eventually feel like a pressure cooker about to explode.

Chapter Thirty-Two

When the day of the meeting with Tracey and her team dawned, I had rehearsed my speech a hundred times.

However, the proceedings opened with a surreal bang, voiding my speech in an instant.

'Why did you make Alex fall on the floor?' was Tracey's opening gambit.

'Sorry?'

'Why did you make Alex fall on the floor?'

I wondered whether she'd momentarily lost the plot. But as I frowned hard, it came to me.

'You mean why did we take Alex's stool away?'

'Yes.'

'Oh that!' I gave a small chuckle of relief before recounting the incident at the restaurant table during our Christmas visit two months ago.

Tracey, however, did not share my relief. Her expression remained resolutely cold and grave. 'That's not the way Alex recalls it,' she said.

Rob and I traded a look of bemusement. 'And how *did* she recall it?' Rob asked.

'Well, for starters, it scared her.'

'Oh, that's rubbish!'

'Actually it's not,' Tracey said, icily. 'She was in tears after you'd left.'

'No, she wasn't!' I spluttered instinctively before realising I'd just accused Tracey of lying and then quickly fell silent. Now what? As silence hung in the room, the reality of what was unfolding began to dawn. Alex, for reasons I didn't yet understand, had just moved things to another level. But what frightened me more was that her acting had been good enough to convince both Janet and Tracey that the game *she herself had instigated* had in fact not been a game but a deliberate act of cruelty on our part.

And so the meeting began. Unable to resolve the fall-down game incident, Tracey calmly moved on to the other concerns prompting her decision to initiate proceedings.

She talked of the significant harm Alex had suffered as a result of our misguided belief that she had Reactive Attachment Disorder and a voice in her head, citing numerous examples of our supposed mistreatment of Alex. As the blows rained on we made urgent attempts to defend ourselves, several times looking to Tracey's supervisor and manager, willing them to understand even if Tracey didn't. But other than a few unhelpful comments like 'We understand this must be very difficult for you, Mr and Mrs Allen,' they remained largely detached – they themselves little more than a formality at meetings as significant as this.

Half an hour into the meeting I'd taken all I could and I broke into a sob.

Rob sprang to his feet.

'Mr Allen. Please—'

'No! Don't "please" *me*. You've known us for what? Five minutes? You've never been to our house. You've never met our son. You're not interested in our side of the story. You, by your own admission, know virtually nothing about RAD. I can tell for a fact you know even less about the voice. So how do you get to do this to us?'

Tracey was prepared. 'I'm doing it for Alex,' she said, her voice icily calm.

Rob and I were beaten.

The remainder of the meeting was taken up by Tracey's line manager explaining the technicalities of a Care Order. From the little I registered, it appeared that, until now, Alex had been accommodated by the local authority on a voluntary basis – a situation in which the minor day-to-day decision making had been left to Janet and the larger, more significant decisions had been shared between ourselves and Tracey. About one third of the nation's looked-after children fell into this category of care. The other two thirds were subject to a Care Order made by the courts under Section 31 of the

Children Act 1989. These were the children whom the local authority considered to have been seriously harmed, or were at risk of
being seriously harmed, by their parents. These were children who
needed protecting from their parents. Parents, as we were now
being told, like us.

It was only as we were driving home that Rob remembered we'd
taken a video of the falling-down game. As soon as we returned
home we burned a copy onto DVD and sent it to Tracey.

A week later we received an apology of sorts and notification that
supervision during our visits with Alex was no longer necessary.
However, there was no suggestion of the care proceedings being
dropped. In fact, Tracey would continue to use this incident against
us, suggesting some months later, that the only reason Alex had
been laughing during the incident was because she'd felt she had no
other option. In other words, she'd been forced into laughing.

We now felt as if we were under siege, and surviving the ongoing attack from Social Services while putting on a brave face for
Daniel was all-consuming. Our troubled relationship was put on the
back burner, where once again it simmered.

In June Alex underwent a series of tests to determine the cause
of her developmental delay, all of which came back negative. In addition, she underwent a brain scan which revealed no abnormalities,
nor any evidence of brain damage.

I approached the July review meeting with dread. With Rob away
on business I was going alone and would be seeing Tracey for the
first time since she'd made her allegations.

However, any anxieties I might have carried into the room were
eclipsed by Janet's opening announcement.

'I think Alex might have a mental disorder,' she began. 'She's
begun muttering to herself. And she's got this strange little walk,'
she explained, distaste skirting the edges of her frown. 'She's even
started twitching which, of course, the kids rib her about. I've tried
talking to Alex but she doesn't seem to have any idea she's doing it.'

The revelations didn't end there. The school was supporting
Janet's beliefs. They reported that Alex's 'odd' behaviour was also
causing them serious concern. Although quiet and well-behaved, she

was a loner and behaved in such a manner as to bring unwelcome attention to herself. She was becoming less and less amenable to instructions, and one teacher reported she often *chose* to forget what she had learnt or been told. Although they could cater for some of Alex's needs, they said, they did not know what made her tick.

Although unfortunate for Alex, this news made my heart soar. We had read an article by a consultant which informed us that, although children like Alex were extremely adept at maintaining a façade of normalcy in their behaviour, once the hormones 'kicked in' the real person began to show through, or 'leak'. Maybe Alex wasn't unique after all.

However, once again, Tracey had her own agenda and her own explanation. Although the tests had come back negative, she felt Alex was displaying symptoms typical of a child with autistic tendencies – a condition Alex had never been diagnosed with but which conveniently appeared in several places in her files as a possible explanation for her difficulties. In fact, Alex's files were littered with medical conditions recorded without a specialist in sight, all indelibly printed there for anyone to misuse.

My protestations fell on deaf ears. I watched in disbelief and despair as the others intellectually worked their way to a reassuring link between autism and Alex's current behaviour.

Later that summer, the country became engulfed in a heat wave – as oppressive and stifling as the air that now hung between Rob and me.

'I won't be back until late tonight,' Rob called out airily, as he made his escape to work one late August morning.

Ordinarily I would have responded with an equally airy 'OK, love. Have a good day,' reluctant to rock an already unstable boat. But this morning, after less than an hour's sleep in last night's oppressive heat, I was feeling prickly and sensitive. I ran down the stairs to the front door, the palm of my hand connecting with the door as Rob attempted to shut it behind him.

'We need to talk,' I said.

'Not now.'

'Yes, now.'

'I've got to go to work.'

'Then go in late.'

'Mel, please. I'm not in the mood.'

'You're never in the mood to talk.'

'That's not fair.'

'Isn't it?'

Rob turned away. I watched his shoulders lift and then slump in a sigh. 'OK,' he surrendered. 'But not now. I'll cancel the meeting and come home early. We can talk then.'

However, at three o'clock that afternoon he rang home, full of apologies. He'd been unable to rearrange the meeting and wouldn't be able to come home early after all.

We did not talk that night.

At the beginning of September, we received Tracey's completed Core Assessment of Alex's needs.* Unsurprisingly, it did not concur with our views and beliefs. Nor did we recognise ourselves in the picture of the parents she was portraying. But most importantly, I felt, nowhere did it report the serious and escalating concerns held by Janet and by Alex's teachers.

As part of the proceedings, the Post-Adoption Centre was appointed to undertake an official assessment of Alex's long-term placement needs. A consultant at the Post-Adoption Centre completed that assessment in October. Once again, their findings did not tally with our own, and it was decided that Alex should remain long-term with Janet.

I should have been hardened to these reports by now, but I'd be stewing on these for days.

Fifty miles away, Alex sat cross-legged on her bed, rigid with fury. Because of Eloise's tale-telling, Alex had not been allowed to watch her TV programme and the insides of her head were now raw and swollen with the battle raging within her. She squeezed her palms

---

* When a child becomes officially looked after, a core assessment record is required. This is carried out by Social Services and is intended to provide a structured, in-depth assessment of the child's needs. It forms the foundation for any future decision making and planning and is essential when a Care Order is being sought. All parties and professionals involved with the looked-after child contribute to the Core Assessment.

against her ears but nothing could silence the din. 'Don't! Don't! Don't!' she muttered, slapping at her temples. But it had been a bad week and the effort needed to stay in control was suddenly too great.

Launching herself off her bed and into Janet's bedroom, her wild eyes searched the room for something sharp. The knitting needle! Grabbing the needle, she scurried out of the room, across the landing and into Eloise's bedroom. Breathing heavily, she scanned the room until she found what she was looking for – Susie, Eloise's favourite doll and comforter. Slamming Susie onto Eloise's desk, she raised her other hand high into the air before skewering the needle into one of Susie's eyes. She repeated the action again and again, her arm working faster and faster, spearing, slashing and ripping until there was nothing left of the doll's face.

She paused. Silence. Then the horrible noise of Eloise's screams from the doorway.

Chapter Thirty-Three

The completion of the core assessment and the Post-Adoption Centre assessment gave Tracey the green light to make the formal application to the courts and we were advised to seek legal representation immediately.

After an anxious morning on the phone trying to find a solicitor who offered legal aid representation, we found Ms Sarah Valence of Mealey Dunn Solicitors. We were keen to meet with her as soon as possible but she advised us a consultation was not necessary until we'd received the application documents and notification of the first hearing.

The day before our next visit with Alex, I rang Janet to establish whether or not Alex knew about the impending court proceedings.

'Oh, gosh, no,' Janet replied. 'Alex is not particularly settled at the moment and we felt it might unsettle her even more. No, I won't tell her anything until Tracey has the care order in her hand.'

'Whoa, careful with that!' Rob said.

Too late. The armful of Christmas presents I was carrying up the stairs toppled from my grasp, taking with it Rob's new digital camera. We watched in horror as it bounced down the stairs landing with a final *thwack* at the bottom.

'Mel!' he bellowed.

'Oh God, Rob. I'm so sorry. If it's broken, I'll buy you a new one,' I said, and sprinted down the stairs to evaluate the damage.

'Leave it alone!' Rob shoved me aside to pick up the camera for himself.

'There's no need to push,' I shrieked, rubbing my shoulder where it had bounced off the banister.

He was oblivious. 'Oh bloody hell. The battery compartment

won't shut,' he said. 'Why do you have to be so careless, it was obvious you were carrying too much.'

   'I said I was sorry.'

   'You're *always* sorry.'

   'What do you mean by that?'

   'Nothing.'

   'Yes you do. What do you mean—'

   'Nothing! OK?'

   'Jeez. No need to shout.'

   'I'm not shouting. You are.'

   'No, you are!'

   'No. Actually, you are.' Then he barged past me, yelling, 'Oh, for
Christ's sake, grow up.'

   'No, *you* grow up!' I screamed after him.

   The back door slammed shut and the house was plunged into
shocked silence. The lid on our simmering relationship had finally
blown.

A February morning in 2003 – another year somehow survived –
and I'd just shoved the last breakfast plate in the dishwasher. I was
rushing to get to work when the doorbell rang. Thinking it was the
postman, I hastily opened the door to find Tracey's supervisor,
Lesley, standing there holding a large, fat brown envelope.

   'Can I come in?'

   'Sure,' I managed in a small voice and led her inside. 'Would you
like a cup of tea?'

   'No, thank you. I can't stay long, I just want to give you this –'
she handed me the envelope '– and to make sure you understand
what will be happening over the next few months.'

   She looked almost apologetic, which only served to unsettle me
more. How bad could it be?

   I pulled out the wad of documents. The first was headed 'Notice of
Proceedings Hearing.' My stomach did a somersault. The first hearing was in five days' time. Then I flicked through the documents
which followed – far too detailed and numerous for me to read with
Lesley hovering over me, so I lied and told her our solicitor had
explained the process. With a parting look of sympathy, she left.

Then I rang to say I'd be late for work, made myself a cup of tea, and sat down with the documents.

I, Tracey Bryant make the following statement, which I believe to be true . . .

With a feeling of dread, I began to read, slowly at first. On page three I gasped with shock and then outrage. Then I gasped again and again. My reading was growing quicker with each line. Like sprinting over searing hot sand, the words were too painful to linger over. Soon I was skimming the words until I was no longer reading them and I let the document fall to my lap. 'No! No! No!' I clutched at my stomach, and then I began to rock. In the distance, the phone started ringing, and went on ringing and ringing until, unanswered, it stopped. I was now struggling to understand what was happening, struggling to comprehend what I had read.

Why? What had we ever done to Tracey to deserve this? She had taken the truths and facts of one story, manipulated them, taken them out of one context and then put them into another. Then she shaped every sentence, the tone and the colour of her statement, loading everything to her bias until she'd created a completely new story. A story of two dangerous and harmful parents who had, over a period of years, systematically abused and harmed an innocent child who must never again be allowed to return to the hands of her abusers.

I was crushed under the weight of pain and grief, and battered by a betrayal that was inconceivable. I had never felt more betrayed, and I was frightened. Very frightened. How was this going to affect Daniel? Could we lose him too? Oh my God! Panic began to envelop me, making my heart pound and leaving me gasping for air. I forced myself to breathe deeply, pull myself together, and then pick up the next document. I dropped it instantly. This was way beyond anything I could deal with alone. I needed Rob. I'd read the rest when he came home.

I was tempted to stay at home, but to be alone with my thoughts was not an option. I needed distracting and I could think of no more comforting a place to escape to than my work.

As I gathered up my bag and keys, the image of Rob bracing himself to read the chronology made me wince further. This was the last thing we needed.

By the time he came home that evening, the documents and a large gin were waiting for him by his armchair. However, without saying a word, he gathered up the papers in one hand, the drink in the other and disappeared upstairs.

Ten minutes later, Daniel appeared looking worried. 'Is Dad not feeling well?'

'He's fine,' I smiled reassuringly, though inside I was breaking. 'He just needs some quiet time while he reads some important papers.'

'Are they about Alex?'

'Yes.'

'Oh,' he said, his face clouding over.

I pulled him into my arms. 'It'll be OK,' I said, fighting back tears I couldn't allow him to see. 'It's nothing to worry about.'

But five minutes later, with Daniel shielded behind the clamour of an all-action PlayStation game, I stumbled into the kitchen, turned the radio up loud and slid to the floor. Hugging my knees, my desolation ruptured into a violent sob. Waves of despair sent streams of tears bleeding into my jeans and turning them black.

My life – our life – was in pieces, our family irreparably splintered. And we still had a court case to survive. Another painful wave of anguish heaved in my chest. How would we survive this? Rob and I were barely together; Daniel had begun chewing his nails and was frequently woken by nightmares. And I, well . . . I was going mad. How was I to hold it all together? God, what a mess!

Right then, I could have willingly died – the idea of nothingness seeming almost blissful. But then I felt a small nudge on the side of my leg. I raised my tear-streaked face to find Scooter purring around me. I threw him a weak smile and thoughts of death vanished. Slowly, my sobs subsided. For Daniel's sake, we had no choice but to get through this court case in one piece.

The following day we rang Sarah Valence, our solicitor. Unfortunately she was out of the office and would not be returning until Sunday.

'But the hearing is on Monday,' I said with rising panic in my voice.

'Don't worry, Mrs Allen,' the lady on the phone said, 'the initial hearing is just a formality. There's nothing Ms Valence needs from you at this stage.'

I put the phone down, only marginally reassured.

Then I spent the rest of the week busying myself with tidying up our files and learning about Care Proceedings.

In order to obtain their Care Order, the local authority (Tracey and her team) would have to convince the court of two things: Firstly, that we had seriously harmed, or were at risk of seriously harming, Alex. And secondly, that the local authority could adequately care for Alex.

Their evidence for the former would be presented in a document outlining the details of the harm we'd inflicted on Alex. These details would have to meet the criteria for harm as laid out in the Children's Act of 1989. It would be known as the Threshold Criteria document.

Their case for the latter would be presented in a document known as the Care Plan. Essentially, this plan would provide a description of what the local authority would do if it was given overall responsibility for Alex or, in other words, how they proposed to care for her, including where she would live, which school(s) she would attend, etc. This care plan would have to convince the judge that it was in Alex's best interests to be cared for by the local authority.

I was relieved to learn that a care order did not fall under the criminal jurisdiction; we could not be prosecuted for the alleged 'harm' we'd inflicted upon our daughter; and as far as we could ascertain, Daniel would play no part in the proceedings.

Chapter Thirty-Four

The dynamics between Alex and Janet were changing. Janet, once a short-term foster carer, had now become Alex's legal long-term carer. In effect, Alex now had a new mum. And as Alex still had RAD, relinquishing control to Janet was no more likely than it had been to relinquish it to us.

'I'm going to slice myself – put a knife across my arms and slice myself,' Alex sang aloud from under her bed. 'Then everyone will see how horrible you are to me.'

'Alex! Stop that silly nonsense,' Janet yelled from downstairs.

Alex complied for a second before resuming in a whisper, 'I hate you. I want to go home.'

Then she froze. Why on earth had she sung that?

February 2003 and the day of the initial hearing dawned, bringing with it nerves that twisted inside my stomach long before I'd even left my bed. The day ahead yawned like a terrifying and cavernous black hole. I sensed it would be unpleasant but could do nothing to prepare myself for what lay in store.

I took a bite of toast but it stuck in my throat. A small bowl of cereal fared no better. I pushed both aside and sipped on my coffee. Rob and I sat in silence.

Later, as I cleared away the breakfast dishes, Rob accidentally knocked the bowl of uneaten cereal onto the floor.

'Jeez Rob! Be careful will you!' I snapped.

'OK, calm down,' Rob said and began slamming doors as he searched for the dustpan and brush.

As I dodged the broken china I offered a silent thanks to the kind friend who'd offered to have Daniel for a sleepover last night.

'Where are the keys?' Rob called out irritably, as we prepared to leave.

'I don't know. Somewhere. Try the kitchen table,' I called back.

'Mel, I'm not stupid! They're not there!'

He stomped into the bedroom and proceeded to fling the contents of my handbag onto our bed.

'Rob!' I beseeched as I watched my perfume canister roll off the bed and crash to the floor.

Suddenly Rob went limp and dropped his head. For a moment, the only sound in the air was of our ragged breathing.

He stood up, came over and folded me into his arms. 'Sorry, let's not do this. Not today.'

I curled tighter into his chest.

There was nothing grand or imposing about the law courts building. From the outside it looked like any ordinary council premises – the tax office maybe, or a library. On entering, we were met by a cheerful security guard who ran an electronic scanner down our clothes and checked the contents of our bags. Before directing us to the check-in desk, he warned us to avoid the coffee from the vending machine – Rob and I smiled for the first time that morning.

We were guided into a large room which resembled an airport departure lounge. In one corner sat an official behind a reception desk. We gave her our names, which she duly ticked off a sheet. We would be in Court Three today, she informed us, and then suggested we wait in the reception until our solicitor had arrived.

For the next ten minutes I watched as people arrived in small streams, a few looking as nervous as us, but the rest looking as though today – this place – was as familiar to them as their own front room.

Rob had just begun pacing the floor when a bright-faced young lady approached. Her arm was outstretched in greeting and her smile was wide and relaxed.

'Mr and Mrs Allen?'

We nodded.

'Hi, I'm Sarah. Have you been waiting long?'

I felt some of the tension leave my body.

We followed the slim, dark-suited solicitor out of the reception area, down a carpeted corridor and into one of a series of small side rooms – private consultation rooms in which each party waited to be summoned by the judge. However, we'd barely introduced ourselves when there was a knock on the door from the barrister representing Tracey and the Social Services.

'Can I have a word?' the barrister asked Sarah. The two of them left the room.

Sarah returned ten minutes later. 'It looks as though we may have a wait. Alex's social worker and her manager have arrived at the wrong court. It's going to take them at least forty-five minutes to get here.'

It was too much and I scoffed. They weren't even competent enough to find the way to their own party.

'Why aren't we surprised?' Rob quipped and Sarah appeared to swallow a sardonic smile.

We used the waiting time to outline for Sarah our story and the events that had led to the care proceedings. As always, there were too many strands to our story for Sarah to grasp fully, but by the time we'd been notified that the hearing would be in five minutes, she'd got the gist of it.

'I'm nervous,' I said, pacing the floor and drawing in deep breaths of air.

'Don't be,' Sarah said. 'Nothing much will happen today. The proceedings won't start in earnest until the next hearing.'

Sarah was right. This hearing turned out to be nothing more than a formality, before three magistrates, to decide in which type of court and before which judge the care proceedings would be held. In our case it would be held in a county court before Judge Kerrick, with the next hearing in ten days' time.

It had taken less than fifteen minutes and we'd emerged relieved it was over, but feeling a little foolish for having expended so much nervous energy anticipating something far worse.

'You have a choice,' Sarah said. 'Either you contest the order, or you don't.'

With a week to go before the first hearing, Rob, Sarah and I were sitting in her office, discussing our options.

'We're going to contest it, of course,' Rob said.

But Sarah winced and I sensed then it wasn't that simple.

'Before we go on, I just want you to know that I'll represent you in whatever choice you make,' Sarah said. 'But I think you need to consider contesting the order very carefully.'

'Why?'

'For starters, the chances of your being successful are remote. In fact, I've never come across anyone who has successfully contested a care order like this,' she said. 'Secondly, it will mean putting the rest of your life on hold for the next however many months. There will be experts to find, witnesses to summon, and mountains of paperwork and reports to deal with. Not to mention the stress.'

'We don't care,' I said.

'Are you sure?' she asked with raised eyebrows. 'Contesting it will have a huge impact on Alex. Once we start bringing in our own experts, she'll be under even more scrutiny – subjected to even more assessments.'

I landed with a bump. I hadn't considered that.

'But Tracey hasn't told the truth,' I said, my voice rising with desperation. 'And we believe she's twisted everything. We don't want that on our records.'

Sarah's expression did not inspire much hope.

'Can't we compromise?' Rob asked. 'Make a deal with them: we won't contest, if they take out all the abuse stuff.'

'It doesn't work like that,' Sarah said. 'A judge will only grant a care order if he thinks you pose a threat to Alex.'

'So let's prove we don't.'

'That means contesting their care order.'

My head slumped to the table. We were in a perfect catch-22.

'Is there nothing we can do?' Rob asked.

Sarah shook her head regretfully. 'No. But remember, there's always the chance the judge may not like or agree with their care plan for Alex and may rule against it.'

I doubted it.

Sarah proved herself a force to reckon with from day one. Before we'd even entered the courtroom, she had persuaded the barrister for the local authority to withdraw their application for an interim care order – a temporary order preventing us from taking and harming Alex between now and the end of the proceedings. Apparently, Tracey had argued fiercely in favour of this interim order but had been overruled by her manager, who did not believe we posed any immediate threat to Alex.

We thanked Sarah.

'My pleasure,' she grinned. 'I don't think Tracey's taken the news too well though.'

'Good!'

A few minutes later, our hearing was announced.

'Here goes,' Rob said, taking my hand and giving it a squeeze. I squeezed back. *Yup – here goes.*

Whether by coincidence or design, we were led into the same room where our adoption hearing had taken place – a bright and contemporary courtroom, large enough to seat about seventy-five people, the court clerks and, of course, the judge, who sat on an imposing raised bench facing his court. When everyone had settled down, the clerk asked us all to be upstanding for Judge Kerrick, who made his formal entrance from a side door.

'Please sit,' the grey-haired judge said.

The proceedings had begun.

The purpose of these hearings is, firstly, to acquaint the judge with the child's case as presented by the local authority, secondly to formally appoint an independent guardian to represent the child during the proceedings, and lastly, for the judge to make directions with regard to the filing of all necessary statements and records prior to the final hearing when he will make his judgement.

We discovered very quickly that the only people with a voice during these hearings would be the solicitors and barristers. Since we would not be contesting, there would be no taking to a witness box, no impassioned pleas and certainly no interruptions. Anything we had to say would have to be typed up in a statement prior to the next hearing. Until then, we could do little but sit on our hands and bite our tongues.

Watching helplessly as the barrister presented the local authority's case was tantamount to torture. And when it was over and we'd put as much distance between ourselves and the hearings as possible, I discovered a rack of painful red welts where I'd been clawing at my arm with my nails.

There are many players involved in care proceedings. In Alex's case, in addition to the main players (ourselves and our solicitor, Social Services and their legal team, Alex's appointed guardian and her solicitor), there were the secondary players who wouldn't enter the courtroom. They would be required to make assessments and file reports necessary to inform the judge before he could grant a Care Order. These players included Alex's teacher, her special needs co-ordinator, a health worker and the educational psychologist. And then, later into the proceedings, a clinical psychologist, a psychotherapist and an attachment therapist.

It didn't take long for Alex to deduce that something significant was happening to her life, and when Tracey began asking her questions like 'Do you like living here with Janet?' and 'Would you like to live with Janet for ever?' Alex knew her life with us was over. Her fear that she might one day have to return to resume the role of the dutiful daughter she could never be was over. She relaxed her guard.

'Hello Alex,' little Lara chirped as she and her mum passed Alex in the playground.

'Fuck off, you bitch,' she spat, from under the hood of her rain mac.

Lara flinched in shock and began to cry.

'Stop it! Stop shouting at each other!' Daniel screamed at us before fleeing into the garden.

Rob and I, oblivious until now of our son's presence, reacted like fire to a bucket of water. Leaving behind another of our volcanic rows, we sprinted after him.

'Leave me alone!' Daniel cried out from where he was cowering behind a bush.

'It's OK,' we tried to soothe him.

'No it's not!' and then he exploded into tears.

The sound tore at my heart.

'Oh God. Daniel, we're so sorry. Come here. It's going to be all right.'

'Go away,' he said, but his tone was weakening.

So Rob and I crawled on our knees to where he crouched and enfolded him in our arms. While we rubbed his back and made soothing noises, Rob and I locked grave eyes. *This has to stop*, the exchange said.

We spent the remainder of the weekend resolutely playing happy families, but Rob and I were not connected. On Sunday evening I poured out our troubles to Sophie.

'I think I might have a temporary solution,' she offered. The following day, I put it to Rob.

'A friend of Sophie's has a flat to rent. It's in the next road along so Daniel can come and go as he pleases. What do you think?'

Rob didn't speak. Not because he was taken aback, but because he needed time to digest the idea.

'It's only temporary,' I said, 'at least until this is all over. Then maybe the three of us can go away for a while. Put ourselves back together again. Yeah?'

Tears were now rolling down my cheeks.

My husband looked at me bleakly. He nodded. Then the two of us slumped to the floor, our backs against opposing cupboard doors, broken but resigned.

It was only temporary, I reaffirmed silently to myself. But all I could think was how clichéd that sounded.

As soon as we'd composed ourselves, we sat down with Daniel and broke it to him that Rob was moving out for a while. Initially Daniel panicked, tried to persuade us otherwise in a torrent of questions and pleading – *Why? Please don't! Don't worry, I won't mind if you argue. Can't you go to Australia like you did last time?* But we held firm. *It's better for all of us this way. It won't be for ever, and Dad won't be far away. You can come and go as much as you want.*

'In fact, it will be so close, we can walkie-talkie each other,' Rob said. 'And if you're really lucky, I'll do you both barbies at the weekend.'

I watched as the panic subsided to deliberation, then a small smile and then acceptance. By the time we'd bribed him with the promise of an all-singing, all-dancing cabin bed for his second bedroom and a summer holiday for the three of us to Spain, I knew Daniel was going to be OK.

After he'd disappeared to design the layout of his new room, Rob and I reaffirmed our vow of friendship – not just for our son's sake but for our own. We needed each other more than ever now.

Chapter Thirty-Five

*T*he judge had given us just three weeks to prepare and file our first statement. While we waited for our first consultation with Sarah, I set about making our story as easy as possible for her to access and grasp. I began by weeding out any irrelevant documents from our files, but winced at the mountain that remained – Sarah was an overworked legal aid solicitor with a limited budget. Why should she make us an exceptional case? She'd met us twice and had no reason yet to question the validity of Tracey's statement.

But it was vital our solicitor read the files, for no one so far ever had. And though we'd pleaded with many a professional to do so, they'd never had the time. Added to which, Alex's flawless act – sweet, innocent, slightly wounded but bumbling – was the only 'truth' they'd seemed to care about.

So the question now was how to convince Sarah. I thought about the past assessments and reports. To the keen and experienced eye, these files blazoned the truth. But to the careless or blinkered, the truth was not as obvious. So I took a copy of all the documents and, working through five years' worth of records, I began painstakingly highlighting the evidence to support our beliefs – evidence manifested largely through the gaping discrepancies and contradictions in facts recorded in the many different reports and assessments.

Five days later, with all the highlighted copies indexed and bound neatly together, I was ready. If this didn't convince the judge, nothing would.

As we waited to be called into Sarah's office, I was raring to get on with it. After months of pleading our case in exchanges that existed only inside my head, we would now finally have our say. In fact, better than that. We would have our testament printed in black and white in a document copied to all. And this time what we had to say could not be ignored, dismissed or lost.

We spent the next two hours carefully taking Sarah through our story and our 'evidence', beginning from the moment we applied to become adopters up to the present day. Mostly she took notes and only occasionally asked questions. When we were finished, our throats were dry from talking.

'I'll email you the first draft by Friday,' she said.

After a round of firm handshakes, we left. I felt a ton lighter.

As promised, Sarah emailed us the first draft of our statement. However, as I worked my way through the document my earlier optimism began to shrivel with every word. By the time I'd reached the end, I was feeling more than just bemused: the document was ten pages long, but it offered nothing more than a plodding and simplistic account of the past five years – nothing that everyone didn't already know – and nowhere had she incorporated our evidence. Why?

Later that evening, Rob reacted with equal dissatisfaction. 'If anything, she's made us look worse.'

I agreed, but we had to tread carefully nevertheless. We could not afford to alienate Sarah, so when we called her the following Monday, Rob's tone was light and affable.

'Thanks for the draft . . . yes, it's great . . . there are just a few things we'd like to change, if possible.' There was a pause. 'Thursday? . . .' He looked to me for confirmation. I nodded. 'Good. We'll see you at four o'clock on Thursday, then.'

Rob and I moved a step forward in our separation on Wednesday of that week when he signed the tenancy agreement on the flat. He would be moving out of Mallard Close at the weekend.

'Are you OK?' he asked on delivering the news.

'Yeah. You?'

He nodded. 'Is it OK if I keep my stuff in the garage?'

'Oh God, of *course* it is!' I cried, suddenly not fine at all.

Later that evening, as Rob began to pack, I drowned my sadness in a bottle of wine and back-to-back soaps.

*

As we would learn some months later during a routine review meeting, it was at this time that Janet made a phone call to Social Services. She was growing increasingly concerned about Alex, whose 'episodes' were increasing in frequency. She was acting more and more disturbed, muttering to herself and twitching a lot. She had begun using expletives, words and phrases that Janet had been unaware she even understood. She was spending more and more time in her bedroom. And she was threatening to run away, saying she wanted to live with us instead.

So Tracey made an appointment for Alex to see her GP. But no referral was made to CAMHS – Alex was able to convince the doctor that she behaved this way solely to wind people up.

There was an awkward edge to the first half of our meeting with Sarah. We couldn't admit we didn't like the tone or content of our statement without offending her, but she was too astute not to sense our dissatisfaction. After half an hour of treading around the issue, Sarah got straight to the point: if we made the tone of our statement too highbrow, it would grate with the judge and, as we were not contesting the care order, the 'evidence' we wanted to include had no place in the proceedings.

'Great,' I quipped miserably. We were once again caught in catch-22.

Daniel and I helped Rob move into his flat over the weekend and, as promised, he cooked for us at the end of it. The atmosphere was unexpectedly light and cheerful. And not just for the benefit of Daniel, who'd fallen in love with his kooky-shaped bedroom and the prospect of the dens he could build in it.

But on Sunday night I didn't sleep – 'our' bed felt lopsided and cold.

Later that week I took a phone call from a lady called Mandy Knox from CAFCASS (Children and Family Court Advisory and Support Services). She had been appointed as Alex's guardian and, she explained, part of her role was to meet with us and to learn more about our situation and thoughts regarding Alex. We agreed to meet with her the following week.

*

'How are you feeling?' Sophie asked me, her face creased with concern. Daniel was spending his first night at his dad's and we were tucked away in our usual spot in Soprano's.

'Fine,' I said, emphatically.

'Are you sure?'

'Absolutely. To be honest it's a relief. And we're great friends,' I added heartily, 'better than we've been in ages.'

'OK,' Sophie accepted reluctantly, 'but you know where I am if you need me.'

'Absolutely! Now, are we going to get another drink? Or shall we sit here all night, getting maudlin?'

Mandy Knox was a large lady with feet that spilled over her sandals. And she loved to talk. Within minutes of meeting her, the house was filled with the reverberations of her chatter. 'Alex is such a sweet little thing,' she said now. 'You must be sad. She misses you, you know. She told me. It's such a shame things didn't work out, but don't blame yourself. Children like Alex are not easy to look after. They've been through so much that it takes them a long time to learn how to trust. It's such a shame. She wants to know if she can have a picture of your cat for her treasure box. Scooter?' *Yes.* 'She loved that cat, she told me . . .' And so on, and on.

Rob and I sat like nodding dogs, smiling as stiffly. Halfway through the proceedings, Rob and I traded a look – an implicit decision not to challenge her perception of Alex. We didn't know Mandy and couldn't judge how she might react to having her views challenged. We didn't dare risk falling out with her too.

As the days ticked on towards the next hearing, my fight for justice continued to rage inside my head.

Meanwhile, in Alex's world, another shift had taken place. With the introduction of the sappy and unsuspecting guardian, Alex didn't need Tracey on her side any more. Which was fortunate, as Alex could sense a change in Tracey's manner towards her.

During their next session, and with nothing left to lose, Alex erupted. In a moment of fury she hurled a glass jar of pens at Tracey, who was forced to dive behind the desk to protect herself.

Weeks later, when I read the account of this, I imagined Tracey's heart beating triple time as she considered her next move – and the little girl she'd once thought she understood.

By the end of April, even Tracey was running out of plausible excuses for Alex's increasingly erratic behaviour, and Janet was growing ever more desperate with the situation at home. Following a visit to Alex's GP, CAMHS were once more appointed. Without delay, Alex was referred for a psychiatric assessment.

The sense of vindication we felt on hearing this news was huge. We'd been right. Alex needed help, and I couldn't wait to tell family and friends. A welcome blanket of calm began to settle over my mind.

However, any hope that this assessment would reveal the true extent of Alex's problems was dashed when we met with the consultant psychiatrist. He did not share the gravity of our concerns for Alex and, like everyone else, felt a nurturing environment would eventually ease her out of her troubles.

The calm inside my head shattered once more.

I stumbled through the next few days, but the war inside my head was picking up momentum, tumbling round and round as the mounting things I needed to say beat against my skull. Mentally, I was in trouble. I tried to breathe the terrifying sensation away, but though, with sheer willpower, I could turn off my mind, I couldn't turn off the injustice. And within minutes my mind would be clamouring for justice again.

I used to think the phrase 'I thought my head would explode' was a cliché. I now knew it wasn't. Furthermore, I was terrified of the consequences. I had an image of a slow spin getting faster and faster until it had spun itself into a violent detonation, leaving my head a mushy mess. And of seeing out my days humming and rocking in the corner of a padded room.

One morning as I reached under the sofa for the remote control, I pulled out Rob's Snow Patrol CD. Like an unstable tower of bricks, my strength collapsed beneath me. I managed to stumble to the phone, find my doctor's number, and make the call.

An hour later, I was on medication. And two days later I slipped, with indescribable relief, into its sedative haze. A haze which would see me through to the other side of the hearings.

Chapter Thirty-Six

'Finance Office,' I announced cheerily down the office phone. At the end of the week, I would be stopping work for the summer holidays.

'Could I speak to Mrs Allen?'

'Speaking.'

The man cleared his voice. 'Oh, hello, Mrs Allen, this is Mr Landers. I'm afraid I have some unfortunate news. Yesterday, Alex ran away. She's all right now,' he reassured me quickly, 'but she was very distressed and . . . er . . . we're wondering whether it might be advisable not to visit on Sunday.'

My heart was beating fast. 'What happened?' I asked and Mr Landers proceeded to recount the episode.

Alex had been acting strangely all morning, agitated and unsettled. Then, just before lunch, she'd locked herself in the bathroom with a knife. Janet had tried to coax her out but Alex had been hysterical.

'You fucking bitch!' she had screamed at Janet over and over again. Social Services had been called, but they too had been unable to coax Alex out. Tracey had made an emergency call to Dr Howarth, but nothing he'd suggested over the phone had had any calming effect on Alex. Eventually, they'd been forced to break down the door and she'd bolted past them and dived behind the sofa.

As Janet and the others tried to calm her down, Alex kept muttering as though to another entity, 'don't listen to them, don't listen to them'. The stand-off had continued for two hours, and it was only when Janet had begun babying Alex in her speech that she eventually emerged from her hiding place, red-faced and emotionally exhausted.

However, only minutes later and despite almost four hours of trauma, Alex completely regained her composure and displayed no signs of the terrifying ordeal she'd just lived through.

Overnight, everything changed. What had gone before was now virtually obsolete. As soon as possible, Alex was to start an intensive course of Theraplay® – a structured play therapy for children and their parents.*

Over the next few weeks, Alex's disturbed behavioural episodes grew in frequency, and as quickly as Tracey and the guardian amended their reports, they were having to re-amend them.

Two weeks before the final hearing, Alex 'dissociated' in class and was taken to the medical room where, for an hour and a half, she lay curled up, sweating, and unable to communicate.

Until now, Tracey had managed to find excuses for all Alex's episodes: the pressures of a school test; a school play; an impending birthday; a recent visit; a forthcoming visit – to mention a few. But this episode could not be excused.

Dissociation occurs when an individual splits with their primary personality and develops a secondary personality in their subconscious. Dissociation, or 'split personality', is evidence of a serious mental health problem, and Alex needed help urgently.

Unfortunately, it was not possible to begin the one-to-one Theraplay® as Janet's training course in the method was not scheduled for another couple of months. So, once again, CAMHS was approached. However, with cavalier disregard for the escalating symptoms of severe disturbance, they held that Alex's unsettled behaviour could be put down to her sense of uncertainty – she didn't yet know where she would be living long-term and she was due to start a new school in a year's time. They felt that intensive therapy would only unsettle Alex further and recommended deferring it.

Rob and I were flabbergasted and incredulous. But, then again, we weren't really surprised. The truth was that nobody knew where to begin in regard to treating Alex. So far, she'd managed to convince every psychologist, psychiatrist and therapist she'd encountered into thinking there was little wrong with her apart from some learning

* The goal of Theraplay® is to enhance attachment, self-esteem, trust in others and joyful engagement. The method is fun, physical, personal and interactive, and replicates the natural, healthy interaction between parents and young children.

difficulties. Even if Tracey could find a therapist astute enough to see through the act, any subsequent therapy would require genuine co-operation from Alex. And, from all we'd read, the only therapy capable of producing that sort of cooperation was attachment therapy.

So, for now, we all crossed our fingers – Janet, in the hope that Alex's behaviour would settle once she knew where she would be living long-term; and ourselves in the hope she'd still be in one piece by the time the attachment therapy – the Theraplay® – could commence.

'Based on Alex's recent behaviour you now have good grounds for contesting the care order,' Sarah began. It was a week before the final hearing and Sarah had asked to meet with us.

'What would that entail?' Rob asked.

'Effectively, starting again. A hearing date would be set—'

'No! No more,' I broke in and looked at Rob. He agreed. Emotionally, we were exhausted, and would gain nothing. We were not fighting for custody. We'd seen their final care plan, and there was nothing in there that we actually disagreed with. Moreover, we no longer needed a judge to acquit us of Tracey Bryant's poisonous allegations – Alex had done that already.

'No. Let them have their care order, and let's move on with our lives.'

'I think you've made the right decision,' Sarah said. 'And,' she added, 'remember, there's always the option of discharging – or ending – the care order later down the line if you're not happy with the way she's being cared for.'

'And if circumstances change and it's right for her and for us to have her back?'

'Then, again, you apply for a discharge.'

'OK.'

A week later, the care order was granted. Emerging hand in hand from the courtroom, emotionally drained but soothed by relief, we stumbled past Tracey and her team, who stood in a muted and sober knot, through the foyer and out into the sunshine. The twenty-ninth of September, 2003, and it was over.

For Alex, however, things were just about to get even worse. The granting of the care order did nothing to stabilise her deteriorating

behaviour, and three weeks into her 'new life' Alex had another —
and major — episode. Grabbing a packet of painkillers and some
matches, she locked herself once more in the bathroom and began
screaming threats of suicide and burning the house down. Janet, her
ear to the door, was pleading with Alex to come out when she heard
what sounded like spray from an aerosol can igniting.

'Alex! Stop!' she yelled, and made a desperate lunge for the door.
It wouldn't budge. She dialled 999 and within minutes the police,
the fire brigade, and an ambulance had arrived. The police broke
down the door to find Alex cowering under the sink, surrounded by
burned-out rolls of toilet paper.

'The pills! Alex, did you take any pills?' Janet asked urgently, but
Alex had shut down and wasn't speaking. As a paramedic gathered
Alex into his arms, Janet grabbed the pack of painkillers from
the floor and did a quick count. Only four appeared to have been
swallowed, but Alex was nevertheless rushed to hospital where,
after a thorough check-up, she was declared fit enough to come
home.

'What do you mean, come home?' a distraught Janet questioned
down the phone to the staff nurse. 'She's just tried to kill herself and
very nearly the rest of us in the house!'

The nurse didn't seem to have taken this in. 'She's fine now,' she
said. 'She's laughing and joking with the nurses.'

'I'm sure she is,' Janet said, unamused. 'But she's not coming back
until I'm sure she won't try this again.' She slammed down the
phone and called Tracey.

The following day Alex was home, on the promise to Janet that if
she had one more of her 'turns', *that was it.* Finished. The local
authority would have to find somewhere else for her.

'It's not just Alex I have to consider,' Janet explained. 'There are
the other children too.'

Alex lay like a fist beneath her duvet, her head clamouring with
noises of rage prompted by the giggling coming from the bathroom.

'Shut up! Shut up!' Alex muttered under her breath. 'You stupid,
fat girl with piggy stupid eyes. *Shut up!*

A phone downstairs started to ring. 'I'll be back in a minute, Maisie,' Janet's voice called out to the new girl.

'I'll be back in a minute, Maisie,' Alex mimicked in an ugly tone from under her duvet. 'Maisie, oh Maisie. I love you, Maisie,' she chanted, her expression twisted with hate.

In the bathroom, Maisie started to sing. 'The wipers on the bus go splish, splash, splosh. Splish, splash, splosh . . .'

Alex writhed in her bed, and kicked at the wall. She slapped at her ears, and clawed at her hair and scalp. No! No! No! But control was slipping from her grasp like a fat eel through tiny hands. The din inside her head was swelling, stabbing, crowding out reason.

'The wipers on the bus go splish, splash, splosh.' Maisie giggled again. Suddenly Alex could take no more. On legs no longer hers, she ran out of her room, along the corridor and into the bathroom, shutting the door behind her.

'If you don't *shut up*, I'll . . .' Alex's words trailed away. Maisie was holding her nose and her breath and had fully submerged herself under the bath water. Alex stomped over to the bath, braced to pull Maisie out of the water by her hair and issue one of her menacing threats. But Maisie moved first. Emerging like a rocket out of the water, she gulped back an exaggerated lungful of air and plunged beneath the water again. Oblivious to Alex. The bathroom fell silent.

Alex's mind faltered. Her heart began to thump violently in her chest and her insides grew hot. She cast a furtive look behind her. They were alone. She reached out a hand above the bath water, and hesitated there for a second. But only for a second. Reaching into the water, Alex pushed one hand down over Maisie's face, the other on the girl's stomach. Maisie jerked in shock and pushed upwards. Alex pressed down harder. Maisie's eyes sprung open and she began to writhe, her arms and legs slapping against the bath and the water. Alex lost her grip for a moment and Maisie shot to the surface, grabbing some air. Alex pushed her under again, this time pinning her to the base of the bath. Maisie continued to flail violently but all Alex could hear was the rush of blood roaring through her own blackened mind. The seconds ticked by. Then . . .

'Alex!' a voice screamed from the door. 'Oh my God!'

A hand grabbed Alex from behind and yanked her backwards. Alex slammed onto the wet floor, curled into a ball and switched off.

Maisie struggled for breath.

Within hours, Alex had been moved into emergency care. Following a series of crisis meetings, she was placed in a small residential unit for disturbed children, where she remains today. Tracey resigned. We would learn months later that we were not the only family she'd put through the mill. We toyed briefly with the idea of legal action but quickly dismissed it. The idea of embroiling ourselves for another five or ten years in an ugly legal battle with Social Services was as unthinkable as leaping into a snake pit.

We decided, instead, to settle for an apology. However, for various reasons, Raymond Landers and his team did not feel 'able' to offer us an apology. During a humiliating meeting, the memory of which still makes me cringe, he did declare himself sorry 'for the way things had turned out for us'.

And Alex, we reminded him.

Epilogue

Two years have passed and life is enjoyable again. We remain Alex's legal parents and continue to visit her – and though she grows older and more mature, the essence of the visits remains jovial and frothy.

Although far from ideal, the unit serves her well, there are no expectations on her to bond, and no expectations on her to love. Due to the nature of the home – a residential unit for damaged and volatile children – there is a high proportion of adults to children. This suits the entertainer in Alex, who continues to captivate the unsuspecting with her doe-eyed looks, her skittishness and her wit.

She also attends a special needs school where, again, she is not short of the attention her difficulties demand.

But I fear for her future. As incredible as it might appear, Alex remains untreated. No one from the original team remains actively involved with her, and Theraplay® requires a full-time one-on-one carer, which the unit doesn't provide. Medication will not be an option until a complete and secure diagnosis is made. It seems that, once again, Alex has been 'lost in the system'. She has not seen a psychiatrist since the care proceedings.

Alex has an ever-changing rota of carers, none of whom, we suspect, have any understanding of what lies behind the smile and the impression of bumbling ineptitude. We have learned that Alex requires careful handling, and my guess is that her carers are reluctant to rock an unsteady boat.

Unless Alex has another breakdown or becomes unmanageable, or a danger to herself or others, she will be left alone to scrape through adolescence relatively intact. If this turns out to be the case, our best hope is that she will charm her way through a half-decent life: detached but otherwise OK.

Ultimately my hope remains that one day she *will* get the treatment she needs. She is innately a people-lover who under different circumstances would have so much more to give. I cannot stress enough just how acutely witty and entertaining she can be. Maybe, with some luck (long overdue) and a prevailing wind, she might yet be given the chance to love and to feel loved.

For ourselves, though shaken by the experience and still somewhat fragile, we have at last begun to move on. Life is beginning to feel normal again.

People ask whether or not we regret the decision to adopt a child like Alex. Aside from the strain those years put on Daniel's life, the answer is no. Alex taught us so much. She gave us a unique insight into the complex makings of a human being, and changed my perception of humankind for ever.

Despite the difficulties, Daniel has emerged a stronger, wiser and more tolerant person. He, more than most, understands that people are shaped by their experiences and we are proud of his tolerance towards others.

Unhappily, Rob and I are still separated. However, he continues to live a few doors away from me and Daniel, and we holiday together. United by respect and friendship, Rob and I remain exceptionally close. I hope we always will.

Useful Reading and Websites

Further Reading on Reactive Attachment Disorder

Thomas, Nancy, (1997), *When Love Is Not Enough*, Colorado, Families By Design

Hughes, Daniel, (1999), *Building The Bonds Of Attachment*, USA, Rowman & Littlefield Publishers

Gerhard, Sue, (2004), *Why Love Matters*, London, Routledge

Verrier, Nancy, (1993), *The Primal Wound*, Lafayette, Nancy Verrier

Bowlby, John, (1997), *Attachment & Loss*, London, Pimlico

Keck, Gregory & Kupecky, Regina, (1998), *Adopting The Hurt Child*, Colorado Springs, NavPress

Welch, Martha, (1989), *Holding Time*, London, Ebury Press

Levy, Terry & Orlans, Michael, (1998), *Attachment, Trauma and Healing*, New York, AEI Press, USA

Magid, Ken & McKelvey, Carole, (1988), *High Risk: Children Without a Conscience*, New York, Bantum Dell Pub Group (Trd)

Jernberg, Ann & Booth, Phyllis, (1998), *Theraplay*, New York, Josey Bass

Websites

www.attach.org – Association for Treatment and Training in the Attachment of Children (ATTACh) – promoting awareness about the development of relationships between children and their parents

www.attachmentdisorder.net – offers support and information

www.radkid.org – offers information about Reactive Attachment Disorder, also known as Detachment Disorder or Attachment Disorder, as well as resources for its treatment

www.healtheheart.org – provides resources, support information and more, related to reactive attachment disorder therapy www.thelittleprince.org – offers information and personal stories for parents of children with Reactive Attachment Disorder

http://adsg.syix.com – Attachment Disorder Support Group

http://forums.about.com – search for Reactive Attachment Disorder – discussion forum for parents and care providers caring for children diagnosed with RAD

http://members.tripod.com/~radclass – self-guided primer for the understanding and treatment of RAD

http://c.webring.com/hub?ring=theattachmentdis – includes sites that have information and/or support for people dealing with Attachment Disorder